New Perspectives on th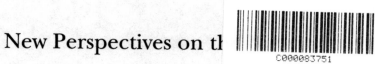

New Perspectives on
the Nativity

Edited by Jeremy Corley

t&t clark

Published by T&T Clark International
A Continuum Imprint
The Tower Building   80 Maiden Lane
11 York Road   Suite 704
London SE1 7NX   New York NY 10038

www.continuumbooks.com

Many Scripture quotations contained herein are from the New Revised Standard Version Bible copyright © 1989 by the Division of Christian Education of the National Council of the Churches of Christ in the U.S.A. Used by permission. All rights reserved.

Permissions to quote from copyright poems in Chapter 10 are listed on the Acknowledgments pages (pp. vii–viii), which constitute a continuation of the Copyright page.

British Library Cataloguing-in-Publication Data
A catalogue record for this book is available from the British Library

ISBN-10: 0-5673-1200-9 (Hardback)
         0-5676-2904-X (Paperback)
ISBN-13: 978-0-5673-1200-6 (Hardback)
         978-0-5676-2904-3 (Paperback)

Typeset by Newgen Imaging Systems Pvt Ltd, Chennai, India
Printed on acid-free paper in Great Britain by Athenaeum Press Ltd., Gateshead, Tyne & Wear

Contents

Acknowledgments

This page constitutes a continuation of the copyright page. Grateful acknowledgment for permission to quote from copyright poems in Chapter 10 is hereby noted:

To Richard Hendin and Peterloo Poets, Calstock, Cornwall, for quotations from U. A. Fanthorpe's poem, "The Sheepdog," published in U. A. Fanthorpe, *Christmas Poems* (Calstock: Peterloo/London: Enitharmon, 2002).

To Ben Kennedy, Mary Bergin-Cartwright, and Oxford University Press for a quotation from David Gascoyne's poem, "Birth of a Prince," published in David Gascoyne, *Collected Poems* (Oxford: Oxford University Press, 1965).

Also to Ben Kennedy, Mary Bergin-Cartwright, and Oxford University Press for a quotation from Andrew Hudgins' poem, "The Cestello Annunciation," published in *Upholding Mystery: An Anthology of Contemporary Christian Poetry*, edited by David Impastato (New York: Oxford University Press, 1997).

To Bruce Hunter of David Higham Associates and Carcanet Press for quotations from Elizabeth Jennings' poems, "The Annunciation," "Meditation on the Nativity," and "Christmas Suite in Five Movements," published in Elizabeth Jennings, *Collected Poems* (Manchester: Carcanet, 1986), now reprinted in Elizabeth Jennings, *New Collected Poems*, edited by Michael Schmidt (Manchester: Carcanet, 2002).

To Quinn Marshall and New Directions Publishing Corporation, and to Alice Roser and Bloodaxe Books, Newcastle upon Tyne, for quotations from Denise Levertov's poems, "Mass for the Day of St Thomas Didymus," "The Avowal," and "Annunciation," all from Denise Levertov, *Selected Poems* (New York: New Directions Publishing Corporation, 2002), published in the U.K. as *New Selected Poems*, edited by Paul A. Lacey (Newcastle upon Tyne: Bloodaxe, 2003); also for quotations from Denise Levertov's poems "On the Mystery of the Incarnation" and "Nativity: an Altarpiece" from Denise Levertov, *A Door in the Hive* (New York: New Directions Publishing Corporation, 1989) and "Letter to a Friend" from Denise Levertov, *Evening Train* (New York: New Directions Publishing Corporation, 1993); all three poems published in the U.K. in *A Door in the Hive/ Evening Train* (Newcastle upon Tyne: Bloodaxe, 1993).

To Paul Stark and the Orion Publishing Group, for quotations from R. S. Thomas' poems "Covenanters" and "Mother and Child," published in R. S. Thomas, *Collected Poems* (London: Dent, 1993).

To Prof. Geza Vermes and Foxcombe Press, Oxford, for a quotation from Pamela Vermes' poem "Think," published in Pamela Vermes, *The Riddle of the Sparks* (Oxford: Foxcombe, 1993).

Every effort has been made to trace poetry copyright holders, and if any material remains unacknowledged the editor wishes to apologize and will supply full acknowledgment in any future editions of the book.

Abbreviations

For the reader's convenience, all journal titles are given unabbreviated. This list covers book series.

BETL: Bibliotheca Ephemeridum Theologicarum Lovaniensium
BZNW: Beihefte zur Zeitschrift für die neutestamentliche Wissenschaft
FCNTEC: Feminist Companion to the New Testament and Early Christianity
ICC: International Critical Commentary
JSJ Supplement: Supplement to the Journal for the Study of Judaism
JSNT Supplement: Supplement to the Journal for the Study of
   the New Testament
JSP Supplement: Supplement to the Journal for the Study of
   the Pseudepigrapha
NICNT: New International Commentary on the New Testament
NIGTC: New International Greek Text Commentary
OBO: Orbis biblicus et orientalis
SBLDS: Society of Biblical Literature Dissertation Series
WBC: Word Biblical Commentary
WMANT: Wissenschaftliche Monographien zum Alten und Neuen Testament
WUNT: Wissenschaftliche Untersuchungen zum Neuen Testament

Contributors

Ian Boxall teaches New Testament at St Stephen's House, University of Oxford, UK. His publications include *The Books of the New Testament: SCM Studyguide* (SCM, 2007) and *New Testament Interpretation: SCM Studyguide* (SCM, 2007).

Warren Carter is professor of New Testament at Brite Divinity School, Texas Christian University, Fort Worth, USA. His books include *Matthew and Empire: Initial Explorations* (Trinity Press International, 2001) and *John and Empire: Initial Explorations* (New York: T&T Clark, 2008).

Jeremy Corley teaches biblical studies at Ushaw College, Durham, UK. His publications include *Ben Sira's Teaching on Friendship* (Brown University, 2002) and a booklet, *Unlocking the Gospels: Five Keys for Biblical Interpretation* (Liturgical Press, 2004).

Christopher Fuller is assistant professor of Theology at Carroll College, Helena, Montana, USA. In 2002 he earned his PhD from Graduate Theological Union, Berkeley, with his dissertation on "Pasolini as Interpreter of the Gospel of Matthew."

John Kaltner is Virginia Ballou McGehee Professor of Muslim–Christian Relations at Rhodes College, Memphis, Tennessee, USA. His books include *Ishmael Instructs Isaac: An Introduction to the Qur'an for Bible Readers* (Liturgical Press, 1999) and *Inquiring of Joseph: Getting to Know a Biblical Character Through the Qur'an* (Liturgical Press, 2003).

Nicholas King, S.J., is tutor in New Testament at Campion Hall, University of Oxford, UK. His publications include *What is a Gospel?* (Kevin Mayhew, 1982) and *The New Testament, Freshly Translated* (Kevin Mayhew, 2004).

Ann Loades is Professor Emerita of Divinity at the University of Durham, UK. Her publications include *Searching for Lost Coins: Explorations in Christianity and Feminism* (SPCK, 1987) and *Feminist Theology: Voices from the Past* (Polity Press, 2001).

Leonard J. Maluf teaches philosophy and New Testament at Blessed John XXIII National Seminary, Weston, Massachusetts, USA. He has published *The Prophecy of Zechariah: A Study of the Benedictus in the Context of Luke-Acts* (Pontifical Gregorian University, 2000) and has translated many books and articles.

Patricia M. McDonald, S.H.C.J., teaches biblical studies at Ushaw College, Durham, UK. She is author of *God and Violence: Biblical Resources for Living in a Small World* (Herald Press, 2004), as well as numerous articles.

Thomas O'Loughlin is professor of historical theology at the University of Nottingham, UK. He is author of *Liturgical Resources for Advent and Christmastide* (Columba, 2006) and *Adomnán and the Holy Places: The Perceptions of an Insular Monk on the Location of the Biblical Drama* (T&T Clark, 2007).

Barbara E. Reid, O.P., is professor of New Testament Studies at Catholic Theological Union, Chicago, USA. Her books include *Choosing the Better Part? Women in the Gospel of Luke* (Liturgical Press, 1996) and *Taking Up the Cross: New Testament Interpretations Through Latina and Feminist Eyes* (Fortress, 2007).

Bernard P. Robinson formerly taught biblical studies at Ushaw College, Durham, UK. He is author of *Israel's Mysterious God: An Analysis of Some Old Testament Narratives* (Grevatt & Grevatt, 1986), as well as many articles on biblical subjects.

Benedict T. Viviano, O.P., is Professor Emeritus of New Testament at the University of Fribourg, Switzerland. His publications include *The Kingdom of God in History* (Glazier, 1988) and *Matthew and His World: The Gospel of the Open Jewish Christians: Studies in Biblical Theology* (Academic Press Fribourg, 2007).

Henry Wansbrough, O.S.B., formerly master of St Benet's Hall, University of Oxford, UK, was general editor of *The New Jerusalem Bible* (Doubleday/Darton, Longman & Todd, 1985). His books include *The Lion and the Bull: The Gospels of Mark and Luke* (Darton, Longman & Todd, 1996) and *The Passion and Death of Jesus* (Darton, Longman & Todd, 2003), and he is a former member of the Pontifical Biblical Commission.

Introduction

Jeremy Corley

The nativity stories hold a fascination for Christians, as well as for many in our society who do not regularly attend church. Preachers and teachers looking for fresh approaches to the Christmas stories will find here an in-depth look at many aspects of popular devotion. In fact, this volume offers new perspectives on the nativity for any reader wanting to go deeper into the Christmas message.

Although "there is nothing new under the sun" (Eccl 1:9), this volume boldly claims to offer "new perspectives" on the stories of Jesus' birth. While nothing is entirely new, these essays develop earlier approaches in novel ways, offering a wide variety of perspectives—literary, political, feminist, theological, poetic, Islamic, and liturgical—on the familiar Christmas story.

It is a decade and a half since Raymond Brown produced the revised version of his landmark work *The Birth of the Messiah* (1993). Hence the new volume opens with Henry Wansbrough's survey of the last fifteen years of scholarship on the infancy narratives. His survey notes that various new approaches have been taken further (especially literary and feminist studies), whereas use of the narratives to establish historicity has receded in scholarly discussion.

Thereafter, four chapters deal with Luke's infancy story. Ian Boxall observes that narrative studies are now uncovering its foreshadowings of the passion and resurrection, but that painters such as Ghirlandaio had already made these artistic connections long ago. Barbara Reid surveys Luke's portrayal of three female prophets (Elizabeth, Mary, and Anna), who prepare the way for the presentation of Jesus as a prophet in the rest of the Gospel, and who offer role models for female preachers today. Leonard Maluf offers a new understanding of Zechariah's prophetic utterance (the Benedictus), by situating this text more firmly in its Jewish background. Finally, Nicholas King reflects on the significance of the Greek term *katalyma* ("inn," or perhaps "guest room") in Luke's second chapter. Preferring the traditional rendering ("inn"), he indicates how this understanding prefigures the later journeys of Jesus and the gospel message in Luke and Acts.

The next four articles are concerned with Matthew's narrative. Warren Carter reads Matthew 1–2 against the background of Roman power in first-century

Palestine, showing how Rome's empire is not the setting for a nice religious tale that is separate from politics. Rather, the conflict between the infant Jesus and the ruling powers will be repeated more dramatically in the life and death of the adult Christ. Benedict Viviano explores Matthew's genealogy of Jesus, often disregarded as obscure. Viviano proposes that the genealogy implies a theology of history, where the three ages listed (Abraham to David; David to the Exile; the Exile to Jesus) form part of a grand scheme of seven ages of salvation history. Bernard Robinson investigates possible sources for Matthew's nativity story within the context of biblical and Greco-Roman history writing. He explains that Matthew's frequent use of Old Testament quotations and perhaps his male-centered approach betray his likely background as a Jewish scribe. Christopher Fuller, by contrast, focuses on the Magi story as presented in Pier Paolo Pasolini's classic Italian film *The Gospel According to St Matthew* (1964). Fuller notes that in accordance with Mikhail Bakhtin's literary theories, the movie adopts a carnivalesque approach to this episode.

The last three essays consider more specifically the religious value of the infancy stories. Ann Loades reflects on presentations of the nativity in British poetry from the latter part of the twentieth century, where new questions are posed that were not asked in previous generations. John Kaltner explores the references to Jesus' birth found in the Qur'an and in later Islamic tradition. According to Kaltner, Christians and Muslims share many traditional beliefs about Mary as a sinless virgin mother and as a model of faith and submission to God, and such shared beliefs can help present-day Muslim–Christian dialogue. Finally, Thomas O'Loughlin addresses the perennial Christian challenge of recalling the nativity. In his view, our contemporary preoccupation with history ("But what actually happened?") can blind us to the mystery presented in the nativity stories and remembered in the liturgy and Christian tradition. The appendix presents a list, compiled by Patricia McDonald, of more than twenty resemblances between Matthew 1–2 and Luke 1–2.

Among the diverse approaches and viewpoints of the articles in this volume, some common themes emerge. Perhaps the strongest theme is the inadequacy of critical historical study to do justice to the message of the nativity stories. Indeed, because these stories include miraculous elements such as the angels and the moving star, historical investigation can only produce limited results. Hence other approaches can be more fruitful—literary, theological, feminist, socio-political, and liturgical.

The difficulties in the nativity stories, found by critical historical study, lead some contributors to consider Nazareth as the likely historical birthplace of Jesus, so that the stories of the birth at Bethlehem are viewed as a later theological construct to support Jesus' identity as Davidic Messiah. Personally, however, I am less skeptical than some contributors about Bethlehem as Jesus' birthplace. My own view is that the tradition of Jesus as "son of David" is well rooted, appearing in some of our earliest New Testament texts (Rom 1:3; Mark

10:47). Moreover, the tradition of the nativity occurring in Bethlehem appears independently in Matthew and Luke, and despite the prophecy of Micah (5:2) there was no strong expectation of a Messiah coming from Bethlehem within Second Temple Jewish literature.

The essays also offer various cultural and literary insights. For instance, a theme running through several articles is the way that events in the nativity stories (whether in the Gospel of Matthew or Luke) foreshadow what happens later in Jesus' life. Another interesting theme is the importance of a neglected second-century text, the *Protevangelium of James,* in the developing Christian tradition about the nativity. This text has not only often formed the Christian imagination (e.g., the birth of Jesus in a cave, and the role of Mary's parents Joachim and Anne), but also has parallels with Islamic tradition about Mary and Jesus.

My thanks are due to the executive committee of the Catholic Biblical Association of Great Britain for suggesting the project and contributing several of the articles. Thanks are also due to the other contributors, including several members of the Catholic Biblical Association of America. Here at Ushaw College I am grateful to Patricia McDonald and to John Marsland for help with this project, especially with proofreading.

Chapter 1

The Infancy Stories of the Gospels since Raymond E. Brown

Henry Wansbrough, O.S.B.

One of the greatest scholars of the gospel infancy stories was Raymond E. Brown (1928–1998),[1] and Joseph Fitzmyer concludes his 2008 book with a short reminiscence of his lifelong friend.[2] Fitzmyer's penultimate section is devoted to "The Unjust Criticism and Persecution of Raymond Brown," in which he stresses Brown's patience and courtesy, and his refusal to reply in kind to the campaign of abuse to which he was often subjected. In the 160-page supplement added in the second edition of *The Birth of the Messiah* (1993), Brown does indeed reply to critics, shooting from the hip with objectivity and deadly accuracy, but always with courtesy.[3] At the same time, he accepts correction, and indeed welcomes it, with unstinted generosity. Valued and experienced an ecumenist as he was, he reserves his fiercest fire for those who accuse him of disloyalty to the Church. Thus René Laurentin had widely and intemperately criticized his fidelity to a Catholic position and receives volley after volley of well-aimed gunfire, whereas Michael Goulder, who was "gentlemanly" in his debate with the first edition (1977), earns polished silver bullets.[4]

Much of the criticism Brown received, particularly from within the Catholic Church (one Catholic periodical announced his death with the brutal headline, "Fr Raymond Brown, Modernist Scripture Scholar, Dead at 70"), was drawn by his refusal to limit discussion to sterile issues of historicity and his concentration on the meaning and theological presentation of scriptural stories.[5] For him the Word of God was alive and active, forming the Church and its members, rather than merely informing them about the past. His importance

---

[1] See Raymond E. Brown, *The Birth of the Messiah* (New York: Doubleday, 1977; second expanded edn; New York: Doubleday, 1993).
[2] Joseph A. Fitzmyer, *The Interpretation of Scripture* (New York: Paulist, 2008), 110–13.
[3] Brown, *Birth*, 573–732.
[4] For Brown's comments on René Laurentin, see ibid., 575 n. 8; on Michael Goulder, see ibid., 619.
[5] See also Raymond E. Brown, *The Death of the Messiah: From Gethsemane to the Grave* (2 vols; New York: Doubleday, 1994). Not long before his death he remarked to me that he had often been asked to complete a trilogy on the Birth (1977 and 1993), Death (1994), *and Resurrection* of the Messiah, which he had absolutely no intention of doing (hoping instead

lay precisely in the impetus that he gave to such a method of study, finally liberating Catholics from the shadows of the Modernist controversies. The number
and quality of the contributions of Catholic scholars to the debates that follow
are testimony to his salutary influence.

It can never be doubted that Christianity is a historical religion, founded on
what actually happened—the ministry, death, and resurrection of Jesus Christ.
If these did not happen, "then our faith is vain" (1 Cor 15:17). In the case of the
gospel infancy narratives, as in all accounts of the birth and infancy of men
and women who have made an indelible mark on the world, exact historicity is
not the main interest. The importance of the infancy narratives lies not in the
precise historicity of the events but in what these narratives show about Jesus,
or rather, about Christian belief in Jesus.[6]

One instructive controversy appeared in the pages of *Bible Review* for
2000 between Steven Mason and Jerome Murphy-O'Connor.[7] That Jesus was
born at Bethlehem is one of the few facts of the infancy stories on which
Matthew and Luke agree.[8] Against Murphy-O'Connor, Mason maintains
that historically the holy family lived in Nazareth and that the placing of
Jesus' birth at Bethlehem is simply a statement that he was (in some sense)
son of David. Similarly, François Bovon declares, "The birth probably took
place in Nazareth. By Luke's time, however, only Bethlehem could be considered as the birthplace of the Messiah."[9] Etienne Nodet also points out
that John consistently (John 1:46; 7:52; cf. 4:43–45) says that Jesus was from
Nazareth, without a word about Bethlehem, even when it would have been
appropriate.[10]

That Jesus was son of David is a principal message of Matthew's first chapter,
with its great drum-roll of Israelite history and its story of the divinely inspired
adoption of Jesus into the House of David. In this case theology will have
shaped quasi-history, or (to put the matter more clearly) the theological truth
that Jesus was the fulfillment of the promises to David and his lineage was
expressed by the placing of Jesus' birth at Bethlehem. Each of the two evangelists will have used this location and decorated it in his own way, expressing in
a picturesque narrative form some aspects of the theological truth about Jesus
that seemed to him important.

---

to experience the Resurrection personally). As the Birth filled one volume and the Death
two, perhaps the Resurrection would have earned three volumes.

[6] Brown, *Birth*, 576.

[7] Steven Mason and Jerome Murphy-O'Connor, "Where was Jesus Born? O Little Town of
Nazareth or Bethlehem?" *Bible Review* 16 (2000) 31–46.

[8] More than twenty parallels between the infancy narratives of Matthew and Luke are,
in fact, noted by Patricia McDonald, "Resemblances Between Matthew 1–2 and Luke 1–2,"
in the appendix of the present volume.

[9] François Bovon, *A Commentary on the Gospel of Luke 1:1–9:50* (Hermeneia, Minneapolis:
Fortress, 2002), 82.

[10] Etienne Nodet, *The Historical Jesus?* (London/New York: T&T Clark, 2008), 106.

Is there another side to the matter? Murphy-O'Connor, resident in Jerusalem for over forty years and the author of a standard guidebook to the Holy Land,[11] appeals to the evidence of Justin Martyr (who came from Nablus, a mere three-day walk from Bethlehem), and to the *Protoevangelium of James*, that already in the second century a particular cave at Bethlehem was venerated as the birth-place of Jesus. So old a tradition deserves serious consideration, and may very well accord with the historical facts. In this case, then, theological interpreta-tion is important, but it is founded on a factual outline.

The theological emphasis that Jesus is son of David is the principal message of the teaching that Jesus was born at Bethlehem. Even were it to be proved that he was born at Nazareth, this message of Davidic sonship would still stand, but in this case it seems that we have a reading of the actual facts. It is, fair enough, the theological and christological truth that matters, but in this case it is a reading of actual, historical events. Such controversies over the "bare facts" continue to be waged,[12] but it is largely thanks to Raymond Brown that they no longer fill the whole frame.

It is suitable that this book, partly sponsored by the Catholic Biblical Association of Great Britain, should begin with a survey of work to date since the revised edition of Raymond Brown's great work (1993). Brown's reading was encyclopedic, and his judgment both so careful and so trustworthy that it forms a fitting starting-point for any further investigation. Scholars con-tinue, however, to search the Scriptures and to have new insights. This essay attempts to pinpoint some of the advances made between the revised edition of Raymond Brown's work and the present day, focusing on some of the new insights that have been published. It cannot claim to be comprehensive. Two obvious limitations (besides the author's incomplete competence and the restrictions of space) should be indicated here. It is based only on works that were available to me in Oxford and Jerusalem, and it concentrates chiefly on articles in books and periodicals, leaving aside verse-by-verse commentaries, of which a number of excellent examples have been published since 1993.

A basic preliminary is a neat article by Jack Dean Kingsbury on the sec-ond Greek word (*genesis*) in Matthew's Gospel. Should the opening phrase

[11] Jerome Murphy-O'Connor, *The Holy Land: An Oxford Archaeological Guide* (fifth edn; Oxford: Oxford University Press, 2008).

[12] For instance, Gerd Lüdemann (who generally doubts the historicity of the gospels) thinks the accounts historically worthless: "The assumption that Mary was raped almost forces itself upon us"; see his *Virgin Birth? The Real Story of Mary and Her Son Jesus* (Harrisburg: Trinity Press International, 1998), 78—cf. my section below on "Feminist Issues" (pp. 19–22). On the other hand, a concern to defend the literal historicity of the accounts appears in the work of the distinguished veteran Peter Stuhlmacher, *Die Geburt des Immanuel: die Weihnachtsgeschichten aus dem Lukas-und Matthäusevangelium* (Göttingen: Vandenhoeck & Ruprecht, 2005). Gregory W. Dawes also criticizes what he considers Brown's indifference to historicity: "Why Historicity Still Matters: Raymond Brown and the Infancy Narratives," *Pacifica* 19 (2006) 156–76.

in Matt 1:1 be translated "Book of the *birth* of Jesus Christ" or "of the *origin*..."?[13] The former implies cradle stories, whereas the latter is wider and more relational. Despite Brown's brusque rejection of the latter translation,[14] choice of the latter throws a flood of light on Matthew's first chapter. The birth itself occurs only in a subordinate temporal clause in the final verse of the chapter (1:25). The genealogy outlines the relationship of Jesus to the great figures of Israel's past, including especially Abraham and David.[15] "Son of David" (1:1) will be a crucial title of Jesus for Matthew.

In an excellent use of narrative theology Kingsbury also shows that the latter part of Matthew's first chapter further clarifies Jesus' origin and functions. Jesus' ultimate origin is in God, for the conception is by the Holy Spirit (1:18, 20), is promised in the Word of God (1:23), and occurs without the normal human means (1:25). More telling still is the concentration on the names of Jesus in each section: first, that the child will be the Messiah (1:18a, Matthew's comment); second, that he will be Jesus the Savior (1:18b–21, narrative); third, that he is "God-with-us" (1:22–23, Matthew's comment); and fourth, that he is Jesus (1:24–25, narrative). "The purpose of 1:18–25 is to hold up names of Jesus to theological reflection," concludes Kingsbury.[16]

Matthew's Use of Scripture

Some interesting work has been done on Matthew's use of Scripture as the background to his infancy narrative. First, we may ask: is the shadowy figure of Joseph in the birth stories so named because this accords with history or for the sake of an Old Testament model (Genesis 37–50)? The name of the New Testament Joseph has often been seen as chosen for the guardian of the holy family after the model of the patriarchal Joseph, who also went down to Egypt and looked after the members of his family. It is also relevant that Joseph of the New Testament was, like the Joseph of the Old Testament, a man of dreams.[17]

Andries van Aarde applies the figure of Joseph rather differently. In a preliminary article in 2000, followed by a book in 2001, he suggests that the Joseph of the infancy stories is no more than an ethical paradigm: "To me it seems Joseph was a legend."[18] It is, rather, Joseph of the Old Testament who

---

[13] Jack Dean Kingsbury, "The Birth Narrative of Matthew," in *The Gospel of Matthew in Current Study*, ed. David E. Aune (Grand Rapids: Eerdmans, 2001), 154–65.

[14] Brown, *Birth*, 49.

[15] On the genealogy in Matt 1:1–17, see Benedict T. Viviano's chapter in the present volume.

[16] Kingsbury, "Birth Narrative," 160.

[17] Brown, *Birth*, 599.

[18] Andries van Aarde, "The Carpenter's Son (Mt 13:55): Joseph and Jesus in the Gospel of Matthew and other texts," *Neotestamentica* 34 (2000) 173–90, here 188. See also his book *Fatherless in Galilee: Jesus as Child of God* (Harrisburg: Trinity Press International, 2001).

is the model for Jesus himself. Van Aarde picks up an old article by Aubrey W. Argyle on the patristic tradition about Joseph as foreshadowing Jesus: the patriarchal Joseph was "righteous, afflicted and sold by his brethren, steadfast in resisting temptation, unjustly accused, arrested, imprisoned, humiliated, but afterwards exalted, the benefactor of others, tender-hearted, forgiving his brethren who had wronged him."[19]

This connection becomes all the more likely from the prominence enjoyed by Joseph in Jewish literature of the time, both canonical and extra-canonical, whether he is alluded to by name (Sir 49:15; 1 Macc 2:53; *Jubilees* 39–43) or is left unnamed (Wis 10:13–14; 1 *Enoch* 89:13). Argyle points out the close similarity in the wording of Joseph's escape from Potiphar's wife (Gen 39:12) and that of the young man in the Garden of Gethsemane (Mark 14:52). Joseph is especially prominent in the *Testaments of the Twelve Patriarchs*, dated by van Aarde to the late second century BCE, but by others well into the Christian era. This attractive theory becomes slightly difficult in van Aarde's application. He uses it to explain elements in Jesus' behavior, maintaining that Jesus was abandoned by this paradigm (or even paragon), Joseph. This would explain Jesus' tension with his own family, his defense of the fatherless, his calling God his father, and his unyielding judgment on divorce.

Of greater significance, but not unrelated, is work done on the fulfillment of Scripture in Matthew's infancy stories. This is particularly important for Matthean formula quotations. Matthew employs Scripture not to show that the future has been foretold, but in the sense of typological fulfillment: the Scripture establishes a significant pattern repeated but surpassed by New Testament events. Most clearly, in Matt 2:5–6 he introduces the quotation by the unusual formula "for so it has been written." In all other formula quotations in the infancy narrative he uses the word "fulfill" (1:22; 2:15, 17, 23). This does not mean that the Old Testament text predicted what was to happen, that it "really" referred to the New Testament event, but that the New Testament event provides "the fullest expression of a significant pattern of events,"[20] a divinely intended pattern of events, established at the time of the scriptural text.

So the Immanuel prophecy (Isa 7:14) was not spoken with Isaiah's tongue in his cheek because his hearers could not understand the full meaning of his words. Rather this established a pattern: the king was faithless, the nation was under threat from an imperial power, and the birth of Immanuel was a sign of God's guarantee of protection in the face of that power. Just so, in the New Testament context (Matt 1:23), Herod was faithless and the temptation

---

[19] Aubrey W. Argyle, "Joseph the Patriarch in Patristic Teaching," *Expository Times* 67 (1956) 199–201, here 199.

[20] James M. Hamilton, Jr., " 'The Virgin Will Conceive': Typological Fulfillment in Matthew 1:18–23," in *Built upon the Rock: Studies in the Gospel of Matthew*, ed. Daniel M. Gurtner and John Nolland (Grand Rapids: Eerdmans, 2008), 228–47, here 233.

was to submit to the imperial power (Augustus in Jesus' time, or Domitian in Matthew's). There is also an escalation in Matthew's case over Isaiah's: unlike the girl of Isaiah's Hebrew prophecy, Mary remains a virgin in her motherhood; the deliverance is not from hostile powers but from sin; and what is promised is not divine protection, but divine presence—the theme that runs through Matthew (1:23; 18:19; 28:20).

Other Matthean formula quotations reflect this principle of patterning. Thus, Matt 2:15 exhibits an escalation over the Old Testament situation (Hos 11:1), in that God's son, summoned from Egypt into the desert, will in this instance remain faithful, unlike historical Israel of the exodus. Similarly for the puzzling quotation about Rachel (Jer 31:15) at Matt 2:18: as every well-informed reader of the story would know, in the following verses of Jer 31:16–17 Rachel's sorrow is swallowed up in joy at the salvation of the nation, in a way appropriate to Jesus' deliverance from Herod.

This is the way Matthew regularly uses typology,[21] as we can see from Matt 12. David provides the pattern for setting aside the Law, and a greater one than David is here (Matt 12:3–4). The Sabbath can be broken for the sake of the Temple, and "a greater one than the Temple is here" (12:5–6). Similarly, in the case of the sign of Jonah, the prophet's release from the sea beast after three days will be the pattern for the one greater than Jonah (12:40). Finally, the pattern set by the judgment of Solomon will be repeated on a higher plane, because "a greater one than Solomon is here" (12:42).

This brings us to the final puzzling fulfillment quotation of the infancy narrative (Matt 2:23). It is unique in several ways. First, the quotation is attributed to "the prophets" in the plural, not a singular prophet, and second, it is introduced in the Greek by *hoti recitativum*. There may be a third unique feature, in that it may consist in one Greek word, "he will be called," drawn from Isa 7:14. In his 2001 article Maarten Menken discusses at length the solutions proposed about *Nazōraios* ("Nazorean").[22] Is the word derived from the Hebrew *nēṣer* (the "shoot of Jesse" in Isa 11:1)? But the Hebrew letter ṣ (*tsade*) is normally transliterated into Greek as *s* (*sigma*). Is Jesus said to be a *nāzîr* (nazirite), after the model of Samson, who liberated his people (Judg 13:5, 7; 16:17)? But first, *nāzîr* is a strictly defined legal term (Num 6:1–21), and Jesus was not a holy man after this model, and second, the Greek word would in this case be spelt *naziraios*, as in the Greek manuscripts of Judg 13:5. A third solution, using the normal meaning of the word, would be that Jesus was so called because he was to be an inhabitant of Nazareth (as Matt 26:71).

---

[21] Here I am indebted to lectures delivered in Wales by Richard (Dick) France in March 2008; see also Richard T. France, *Jesus and the Old Testament* (London: Tyndale Press, 1971).

[22] Maarten J. J. Menken, "The Sources of the Old Testament Quotation in Matthew 2:23," *Journal of Biblical Literature* 120 (2001) 451–68.

While Menken prefers the interpretation using *nāzîr*, he does mention that the great scholar Marie-Joseph Lagrange already in 1923 opted for the third solution.[23] Nazareth was a contemptible little place (cf. John 1:46), not mentioned in the Old Testament, nor Josephus, nor any secular source until the fourth century CE. If this third solution is correct, Matthew is referring not to any specific passage in one of the prophets, but to all the passages in the prophets (hence the plural) in which the Messiah is said to be humble and despised and suffering for his people. Here again the explanation is typological: the Old Testament provides a context into which Jesus fits and which he surpasses.

The Story of the Magi

When we come to Matthew's second chapter, some discussion has centered on the story of the journey and visit of the magi. It seems to be generally accepted that this story is somewhat muddled, and that the best solution is to assume that Matthew combined two sources. The first of these sources accords with his midrashic treatment of Jesus' birth and infancy based on the birth and infancy and miraculous escape of Moses. It is this that yields Herod's plan to kill the newborn leader and the holy family's escape into Egypt until the angelic message of Matt 2:20 (mirroring Exod 4:19) bids them return. By way of contrast, the story of the magi and the star is entirely different, based on the story of Balaam, the Gentile who honors Israel.[24]

The combination of the two stories poses difficulties: as Brown notes, Herod's frustration "becomes ludicrous when the way to the house has been pointed out by a star which came to rest over it, and when the path to the door of the house in a small village has been blazed by exotic foreigners."[25] Why did the star that had guided the magi from the east suddenly disappear, only to reappear again at the critical moment?[26] Was it really worth reintroducing the star when Herod has already directed them to Bethlehem? Did Herod complacently sit back and wait for the answer of the magi, omitting to

[23] Marie-Joseph Lagrange, *L'évangile selon S. Matthieu* (Paris: Lecoffre, 1923).

[24] Brown, *Birth*, 113–16 (Moses) and 190–96 (Balaam). For some enlightening background on the Balaam traditions from the *Targum of Pseudo-Jonathan*, see David Instone-Brewer, "Balaam-Laban as the Key to the Old Testament Quotations in Matthew 2," in *Built upon the Rock*, ed. Gurtner and Nolland, 207–27, esp. 214–21.

[25] Brown, *Birth*, 191.

[26] Dale Allison's charming essay on the moving star as a guiding angel ("The Magi's Angel," in his *Studies in Matthew: Interpretation Past and Present* [Grand Rapids: Baker Academic, 2005], 17–35) can hardly be used to contradict this. He points out that in the ancient world stars were regarded as living beings, and therefore suitable as guides. On the vexed astronomical question, he wittily concludes, "We cannot look for an angel that has come and gone."

send his highly developed secret service to accompany these well-informed strangers?

Brown proposes an outline of the original magi-story before it was combined with the Herod-story.[27] John Nolland replies by taking seriously Ulrich Luz's criticism that the magi-story can never have existed independently, but "is designed with a view toward the Herod episode. The Magi are Gentiles; that required some form of confrontation with Israel."[28] This forms the basis of his article, and he gives a list of references (of variable probative value) to passages in the New Testament where there is a correlation or even parallelism between Jewish and Gentile responses to Jesus,[29] maintaining that throughout the New Testament honor done to Jesus from Gentiles must always be confronted by rejection from Israel. This does not, to my mind, settle the question. It would be possible to argue by the same logic that there should have been a story in Luke where the infant Jesus, acknowledged by the poor and destitute shepherds, was also rejected by the rich.

A case can be made that this contrast between two personalities (or groups) is typically Matthean.[30] In Matthew's own long parables he repeatedly, or even invariably, contrasts good and bad characters. Furthermore, the contrast in this story at the beginning of the Gospel between hostility from the representatives of Israel (Herod and his court) and support from Gentiles is echoed emphatically at the end of Matthew's Gospel by the contrast between condemnation by Israel (Caiaphas and his court) and Pilate's insistence on Jesus' innocence. The only real difficulty about Brown's reconstruction of an originally independent magi-story is his inclusion in it of the magi's stop-off in Jerusalem and their question.[31] In this reconstruction these are left in the air. They are clearly designed to elicit the response from Herod and his court, and have no sense apart from this.

Luke's Language

The language of the Lukan infancy narrative is most painstakingly examined by Chang-Wook Jung, principally to establish whether Luke is imitating the Old Testament or translating from a Semitic source, but also to discern his exact relationship to the Septuagint (LXX). Is he using the LXX or simply copying a Semitic style? Early in the book he criticizes Brown for not sufficiently

---

[27] Brown, *Birth*, 192.
[28] John Nolland, "The Sources for Matthew 2:1–12," *Catholic Biblical Quarterly* 60 (1998) 283–300.
[29] Ibid., 289 n. 19.
[30] Michael Goulder, *Midrash and Lection in Matthew* (London: SPCK, 1974), 55.
[31] Goulder's demonstration (ibid., 238) of the pervasiveness of Matthean style makes it extremely perilous to attempt an exact reconstruction of any underlying oral sources.

distinguishing Semitisms and Septuagintalisms, and finally for abandoning the attempt to distinguish Semitisms from instances of precisely Septuagintal influence, relying too heavily on his close friend Fitzmyer's acknowledged skills as one of the foremost Aramaic scholars in the world.[32]

Jung himself begins with the essential task of making a series of important definitions, distinguishing "hard core Septuagintalisms" from "secondary Septuagintalisms."[33] The former expressions, couched in slightly abnormal Greek, can be explained *only* as dependent on the LXX. He distinguishes also "unsuccessful Septuagintalisms," a number of which do occur in Luke 1–2, either because the author does not wholly succeed in imitating the LXX or because he deliberately adapts it (an example is the phrase "*conceive* in your womb" in 1:31, where Luke prefers the word he regularly uses for "conceive" to the normal Septuagintal idiom "*have* in your womb"). Jung also distinguishes "hard core Lukanisms" from "secondary Lukanisms." The former are expressions frequent in Luke outside the infancy narratives, but occurring elsewhere in the New Testament only twice or less, while the latter occur more frequently outside the Lukan writings.

Throughout the book the argumentation is careful and exact, though admittedly there are many instances where other scholars may evaluate the conflicting evidence differently. After minutely discussing three quotations from the Old Testament and three allusions to it and four other frequent phrases, Jung concludes that there are no "hard core Semitisms" in Luke 1–2, but that all Semitisms are in fact Septuagintalisms.[34] So the influence of the Old Testament on Luke 1–2 is uniquely through the LXX. However, since non-Lukanisms (phrases that are distinctly different from Lukan usage elsewhere) do occur, Jung concludes that Luke is using a written source, itself imitating the LXX, though he insists, quoting Mark Coleridge, that Luke was "master" of his source(s).[35]

Three criticisms of this painstaking and enlightening analysis might be made. First, the database for the conclusions is persuasive but somewhat narrow. Second, it is unfortunate that no specific attention, other than passing remarks, is given to the Lukan Canticles. It would have been enriching to apply to them the careful techniques of analysis in order to see whether any advance might be made on their authorship. Did Luke compose them himself? Are they Maccabean hymns? Have they been adapted to their context? Why do

---

[32] Chang-Wook Jung, *The Original Language of the Lukan Infancy Narrative* (JSNT Supplement 267; New York: T&T Clark, 2004), 34–36; cf. Brown, *Birth*, 623.

[33] For the phrase "hard core Septuagintalisms" (as for the phrase "hard core Lukanisms") it would have been helpful to indicate that the picturesque slang means that no other explanation is adequate.

[34] Jung, *Language*, 210.

[35] Ibid., 214; cf. Mark Coleridge, *The Birth of the Lukan Narrative* (JSNT Supplement 88; Sheffield: JSOT Press, 1993), 17.

they range so widely, away from the dominant Christology of the narrative? It is remarkable, as Ulrike Mittmann-Richert observes, that in neither Magnificat nor Benedictus is there mention of or allusion to Christ.[36] Coleridge in fact succinctly shows that the emphasis of the Magnificat is on God, of the Benedictus on the Baptist, and only of the Nunc Dimittis on Jesus.[37]

A third criticism may be made. Even in such a specifically linguistic study there might have been room for more discussion of the theological reasons why Luke employed a Septuagintal style of Greek in the infancy narrative more than in Luke chapters 3–24 and Acts. Jung generally follows the scholarly consensus here: "Luke intentionally imitated LXX style in order to show a close connection between the OT and the first part of the Gospel."[38] Why did Luke wish to show this close connection, and here alone? If Luke wished to present these two chapters almost as part of the Old Testament, perhaps even as its conclusion, is he concerned with the problem of God's justice, demonstrating that the inclusion of the Gentiles does not imply the exclusion of Israel, or is he showing the continuity of Old Testament values and piety, particularly the option for the poor of the LORD, into the period of fulfillment? Fascinating, therefore, but certainly beyond the scope of this study, would be a detailed investigation into the nature, extent, and purpose of Luke's source(s) here.

Analysis of Luke's Sources

A sharp divergence of approach to Luke's sources for the infancy narrative[39] becomes visible between two veteran exegetes, François Bovon and Marie-Emile Boismard. Bovon has long been a major player in the Lukan field, his commented bibliographies of the last thirty-three, then the last fifty-five years of Lukan studies being especially significant.[40] This lends special authority to his 2002 commentary on Luke 1:1–9:50 in the Hermeneia series, where he does not pronounce exactly on Luke's sources, but persistently refers to "the legends available to him" or "the form-critically late legends in Matthew 1–2

---

[36] Ulrike Mittmann-Richert, *Magnifikat und Benediktus* (WUNT 2/90; Tübingen: Mohr Siebeck, 1996), 7.

[37] Coleridge, *Birth*.

[38] Jung, *Language*, 213.

[39] A constant theme has been that despite his claims to reliability as a historian in 1:1–4, Luke's grasp of the past is less reliable than of the later history. It seems to me that the vexed question of the date of the census is firmly settled by Nodet's demonstration that Quirinius' census was part of the reorganization after the removal of Archelaus. Luke's purpose in including the census was to show Joseph's peaceful obedience to the law, in contrast to the rebellious Zealot movement that was initiated at this time (Nodet, *Historical*, 109, 123). It was also, to be sure, a literary device to get the holy family to Bethlehem.

[40] François Bovon, *Luke the Theologian: Thirty-Three Years of Research, 1950–1983* (Allison Park, PA: Pickwick, 1987); idem, *Luke the Theologian: Fifty-Five Years of Research, 1950–2005* (Waco: Baylor University Press, 2006).

and Luke 1–2."[41] An interesting argument for Luke's part in the composition of the whole is Bovon's insistence that the whole thrust of Luke 1:5–80 must be compared to the story of Cornelius in the Acts of the Apostles, which was clearly composed by Luke:[42]

1. A "pre-Christian" righteous person (Zechariah/Cornelius) receives a divine message.
2. At almost the same time a "Christian" figure (Mary/Peter) receives a divine message.
3. Then the two figures meet.
4. Finally the events already announced occur.

One difficulty about this structure is that Zechariah and Mary are not actually recorded as meeting in Luke 1:39–56 (though Mary meets Zechariah's wife Elizabeth)! An advantage, however, of Bovon's approach is that it places all the stress on the role played by the stories in the development of Christology. Historicity plays no part in his approach. Whatever the origin of the stories of the Baptist and of Jesus, the step parallel between them is Luke's work.

The 1997 work of Boismard offers a strong contrast.[43] After so many writings in which he seems to attribute the authorship of more and more of the New Testament to Luke, it is surprising to see a reversal of this tendency. For many decades this doyen of the French Biblical School in Jerusalem continued to give great authority to the *Harmony of Pepys*, a manuscript of around 1400 CE, once owned by the Carolingian diarist Samuel Pepys, and now housed in the Pepys Library at Magdalene College, Cambridge. It was given its first scholarly edition in 1922.[44] Boismard is aware that it may seem surprising to set about reconstructing the Gospel of Luke from a medieval document, probably translated into English from a French text that was itself dependent on the Latin translation. For this reason his exposition is ordered psychologically rather than logically.

Boismard's thesis is that Proto-Luke (an earlier version of the Gospel) here developed a document produced by the disciples of John the Baptist. This Baptist document was not a Christian text. It described the annunciation to Zechariah, the birth, circumcision and naming of John, presenting John as the unique savior. There are some interesting variations from the familiar story. Zechariah is now the high priest, alone behind the curtain of the Holy of Holies on Yom Kippur (the Day of Reconciliation), which is why he is praying

---

[41] Bovon, *Commentary*, 44 (with an appeal to Rudolf Bultmann).
[42] Ibid., 29.
[43] Marie-Emile Boismard, *L'évangile de l'enfance (Luc 1–2) selon le proto-Luc* (Paris: Gabalda, 1997).
[44] Margery Goates, ed., *The Pepysian Gospel Harmony* (Early English Text Society 157; London: Oxford University Press, 1922).

for the people, and the people are waiting outside. The angel announces, "Your prayer will be heard, and you and many will rejoice, for he [John] will save the people." Elizabeth is not sure of her pregnancy until the infant leaps in her womb (why?), at which she, not Mary, pronounces the Magnificat, giving thanks for the release from her sterility.[45]

According to Boismard's theory, the evangelist Luke took this Baptist document, expurgated it of the attribution of salvation to the Baptist, and used the incidents as a basis for comparison with Jesus by means of a similar set of scenes, in each of which, to be sure, Jesus has the advantage. As Boismard feared, this outline of the development of Luke 1–2 does seem far-fetched, but the details are not without some insights. For instance, why is Zechariah struck dumb for his question, while Mary is praised for hers? Because at Luke 1:34 Mary merely asks for an explanation, "How this *is* to be," whereas Zechariah at 1:18 had truculently asked, "How *can* this happen?" The local census is exaggeratedly spread to "all the world" in order to ensure that these events involve the whole world, which is to be saved.[46] The historical difficulty is cheekily solved by the surmise that Quirinius' name was added later.[47]

A similar thrust in the same direction, though vastly different, is provided by Richard Dillon's article on the Benedictus.[48] There the suggestion appears that the Benedictus (without Luke 1:69–70) was originally the climax of a Baptist story, written up after the destruction of the Temple in 70 CE. This story was complete in itself, celebrating the Baptist's preparation for the coming of the LORD God. The Jesus-part of Luke 1–2 was modeled on this; the intrusive verses 69–70 were added (Jesus as the son of David becomes an important theme in Acts 2:26–35; 13:23, 32–37, and the verb employed in Luke 1:69 for the horn of David, "raised up," is most surprisingly the verb technically used for the resurrection of Jesus); and the Baptist's task of preparation was now to be understood of the Lord Jesus, who would also achieve the "forgiveness of sins." A further interesting detail is that the Benedictus and the Magnificat are compared in structure: the former falls into two strophes (or poetic sections), the first celebrating God's mercy to Israel, the second God's task for the child. By contrast, in the Magnificat the order of the two strophes is reversed, the first strophe dwelling on God's choice of the individual, the second on God's mercy to Israel. Dillon admits that other structures may also be envisaged.

---

[45] The three canticles are mentioned, but in the *Pepysian Harmony* their text is not given; however, the Magnificat is attributed to Elizabeth in three late manuscripts of the Gospel.

[46] Boismard, *L'évangile*, 88 ; but Luke makes a habit of exaggeration, and easily slips in "all."

[47] Ibid., 88 n. 1.

[48] Richard J. Dillon, "The Benedictus in Micro- and Macro-Context," *Catholic Biblical Quarterly* 68 (2006) 457–80. For a new interpretation of the Benedictus, see Leonard J. Maluf's chapter in this volume.

Bovon has some fascinating observations on the two main canticles. In his view, the Magnificat originated in Pharisaic circles, for almost every line has a parallel in the *Psalms of Solomon*, which reflects this background. It was adapted only slightly by Luke, for it surprisingly has no mention of a child or of giving birth.[49] The Benedictus, on the other hand, is a poem of the Baptist movement, lightly re-touched by Luke.[50] Bovon also effectively relates Simeon's canticle to the welcome given to their returning sons by the aged Joseph (Gen 46:30) and Tobit (Tob 11:9–15), as well as to similar motifs in Greek literature (the two old servants of Odysseus).[51]

Step Parallelism and Christology in Luke

Several authors go beyond Raymond Brown's presentation of the step parallelism in Luke 1–2 between the Baptist and Jesus.[52] Brown presented Luke's comparison of the two harmonious figures as at least partly intended "to persuade unconverted disciples of JBap [i.e., John the Baptist]. Yet, as time went on and some of these unconverted disciples seemingly turned hostile to the Christian movement, the motif of subordinating JBap became stronger in Christian writing"—notably in the Fourth Gospel.

Karl A. Kuhn asserts that both the Baptist and Jesus are presented as exalted figures, since Luke "is clearly not interested in glorifying Jesus at John's expense."[53] The principal purpose of the step parallelism is christological.[54] Part of the message of the step parallelism, and especially such Lukan incidents as the Visitation, is that there is no trace of rivalry but only partnership between the two figures. A further notable difference in the presentation is that John the Baptist is introduced as preparing the way, not for "Jesus" (as in Mark 1:2–3 and Matt 3:3) but rather for "the LORD" (Luke 1:17, 76). For Luke the coming of Jesus is this coming of the LORD: Jesus is described by adjectives that not only contrast with John—who will be "great before the Lord" and "filled with the holy Spirit" (1:15)—but that apply in Jewish tradition only to God, such as the absolute use of "great" (1:32) and "holy" (1:35). This reflects

---

[49] Bovon, *Commentary*, 56–57.

[50] Ibid., 68.

[51] Ibid., 97. Brown (*Birth*, 457) mentioned only the messenger speech in Aeschylus' play *Agamemnon* (1–30).

[52] Brown, *Birth*, 250–52. The following quotation is from p. 284.

[53] Karl A. Kuhn, "The Point of the Step-Parallelism in Luke 1–2," *New Testament Studies* 17 (2001) 38–49, here 42.

[54] An interesting sidelight is cast by Steven Harmon's article, "Zechariah's Unbelief and Early Jewish-Christian Relations," *Biblical Theology Bulletin* 31 (2001) 10–16. He sees Zechariah's move from disbelief to belief (admirably presented in a neat Lukan fifteen-step chiastic structure, a typical example of Luke's literary patterning) as being intended as a model for a similar move on the part of God-fearers.

what Larry Hurtado describes as the "early Christian mutation" of ancient Jewish monotheism and the divine agent tradition, seen in the merging of devotion to God with devotion to Christ.[55]

Similarly, John J. Kilgallen points out that in the annunciation to Mary the message that "he will rule for ever and his reign will have no end" (1:33) goes beyond the normal bounds of expectation of the Messiah.[56] The promise that "the power of the Most High will cover you with its shadow" (1:35) is tantamount to saying that the sacred *shekinah* (the glorious divine presence) will descend upon Mary, and according to ancient male-oriented embryology, "God is given a role by which he defines the reality to be called Jesus."

A fascinating suggestion of a source—or at least a connection—for the words of the angel to Mary is put forward by George Brooke from his extensive knowledge of the Qumran Scrolls.[57] An Aramaic fragment from the first century BCE (4Q246) has close parallels to Luke 1:32–35. It presents an interpreter (perhaps Daniel) explaining a vision of the king of Egypt, the king of Assyria, and a third king who will be "called great" and "will be called the Son of God and the Son of the Most High" in a time of great turmoil, followed by an eternal kingdom of great peace. Are Luke and 4Q246 dependent on the same source? Brooke declares, "When the same four items occur in a few lines in one text and in as many verses in another, some kind of explanation is called for."[58] In fact, James Dunn plausibly maintains that this text uses all these titles corporately of the people rather than of an individual.[59] Moreover, there is no transfer of power from the One of Great Age to the Son of Man. This leaves Luke's usage as still an advance on the Qumran text.

Brooke also refers to the much-discussed 1QSa 2.11–12, part of a Qumran text known as the *Rule of the Congregation*.[60] The phrase in the Qumran text, "when God engenders [*or* brings to birth] the Messiah," does seem to suggest divine parentage, or at least a close link to 2 Sam 7:14. The Hebrew verb seems to have been finally established as *yôlîd*, which normally means "engender," used only of parentage. This would suggest properly divine parentage. Can it be used poetically in a weaker sense to mean "cause to be born"? Brooke does not suggest what the exact relationship between the Qumran texts and Luke may be, simply ending with the enigmatic observation, "Thus the manuscripts

---

[55] On the resultant devotional "binitarianism," see Larry Hurtado, *One Lord, One God: Early Christian Devotion and Ancient Jewish Monotheism* (Philadelphia: Fortress, 1988), 93–124.

[56] John J. Kilgallen, "The Conception of Jesus," *Biblica* 78 (1997) 225–46, here 225. The following quotation (explaining Luke 1:35) is from p. 238.

[57] George J. Brooke, "Qumran: The Cradle of the Christ?" in *The Birth of Jesus*, ed. George J. Brooke (Edinburgh: T&T Clark, 2000), 23–34.

[58] Ibid., 26.

[59] James D. G. Dunn, "'Son of God' and 'Son of Man' in the Dead Sea Scrolls," in *The Scrolls and the Scriptures*, ed. Stanley E. Porter and Craig A. Evans (JSP Supplement 26; Sheffield: Sheffield Academic Press, 1997), 198–210.

[60] Brooke, "Qumran," 29–30.

from Qumran provide us with several of the planks that make up the cradle
of Christ. But much of its overall structure and the baby it cradles are strictly
speaking from another carpenter's shop altogether."[61]

If, as Kilgallen suggests, it is the role of God to define the reality to be called
Jesus, we may perhaps here insert mention of a scintillating little essay in the
same collection by the eminent scientist and theologian Arthur Peacocke, enti-
tled "DNA of our DNA."[62] He first establishes by quotations from the then-
Cardinal Joseph Ratzinger and Raymond Brown that a human father would
not be considered in Roman Catholic doctrinal terms to exclude absolutely the
possibility of Jesus' divinity.[63] Jesus could have been divine even if hypotheti-
cally he had had a human father. In consequence, Peacocke poses the problem
that without human paternity either Jesus would lack the Y-chromosomes necessary for maleness (parthenogenesis in insects always produces a female, with
XX-chromosomes) or God would have to compensate by directly supplying the
Y-chromosomes. Would the latter result in a Docetic Jesus, who only appeared
to be human? What becomes of the patristic theological principle, "What is
not assumed is not redeemed"?

A further dimension of the christological orientation of the infancy narrative (so strongly and repeatedly insisted on by Raymond Brown[64]) is provided by Mark Coleridge. He shows how Luke 1–2 "set in motion and lay
the ground for all that follows by articulating in narrative form a vision
of the divine visitation and human recognition of it," thus "preparing for
the birth of a distinctively Lukan christology."[65] By contrast to Brown, who
characterizes the incident of the appearance of the twelve-year-old Jesus
in the temple (Luke 2:41–52) as "an episode of another origin and subject
matter that cannot be fitted into a diptych structure,"[66] which "has the air of
an awkward appendage and spoils the symmetry of the diptychs," Coleridge
regards this final episode as the deliberate climax of these chapters. It must,
however, be admitted that Brown, in both these exegeses of this incident, by
no means sidelines it as unimportant: even if it does not fit into the pattern
of parallels in the infancy story, this does not diminish its importance or
significance.[67]

---

[61] Ibid., 33.

[62] Arthur Peacocke, "DNA of our DNA," in *The Birth of Jesus*, ed. Brooke, 59–67.

[63] Joseph Ratzinger, *Introduction to Christianity* (New York: Herder & Herder, 1969), 208;
Raymond E. Brown, *The Virginal Conception and Bodily Resurrection of Jesus* (New York:
Paulist, 1973), 42.

[64] Brown, *Birth*, 481.

[65] Coleridge, *Birth*, 22–23.

[66] Brown, *Birth*, 252. The next quotation is from his earlier work, *An Adult Christ at Christmas*
(Collegeville: Liturgical Press, 1977), 38.

[67] The solution of Bovon (*Commentary*, 29) is that the incident (after the two births) pairs
with the Visitation (after the two annunciations). In content, however, these form an awkward pair.

Skilfully using the techniques of narrative criticism, Coleridge shows how this incident is no mere cameo-appearance of Jesus as a youth, a bridge between childhood and the adult state. Instead of explanations and interpretations given by angelic intervention, as in earlier episodes, Jesus, speaking for the first time in Luke, himself moves to center-stage and reveals himself as Son of God—as the angel had already identified him in 1:32, 35. He is his own interpreter, not only confirming the earlier angelic message but introducing the first mention of the peculiarly Lukan term *dei* = "it is necessary" (2:49), stressing the divine necessity of the fulfillment of God's plan of salvation. Finally comes also the implied human recognition—a gradual and puzzled recognition, but all the more numinous for that—in the statement that Mary stored up all these things in her heart (2:51). Bovon has some apposite comments on Jesus' adolescent behavior,[68] though he might also have commented on Mary's maternal self-restraint! It is not, however, necessary to go as far as Anselm Grün, who sees here adolescent rebellion, "the first family conflict...Jesus is not a loving and dutiful child."[69]

Feminist Issues

An issue that has certainly developed considerably since Brown's *Birth of the Messiah* is that of feminist interpretations of the biblical data on the birth of Jesus, especially in the Matthean account. The virgin birth (or more precisely, virginal conception) is another of the very few facts shared by both evangelists. Of those who dispute it, almost all (some exceptions will be mentioned later) reckon that it was not invented by Matthew or Luke, but that the two evangelists believed it, and set about giving it an explanation.

One of the first significant modern publications on this issue was Jane Schaberg's *The Illegitimacy of Jesus.*[70] John Meier took issue with this in the first volume of *A Marginal Jew*, in such a way that it was some time before she could bring herself to read his book without sweating. Her rebuttal of Brown's "misrepresentation" of her position is less violent: principally protesting that she did not hold that Mary was raped, but left it an open question "whether the pregnancy of Mary was the result of the seduction or rape of Mary or the result of her free choice to have sex with someone other than Joseph."[71] In any case there was, in Schaberg's view, nothing virginal or miraculous about the birth of Jesus.

---

[68] Bovon, *Commentary*, 113.
[69] Anselm Grün, *Jesus: The Image of Humanity* (New York: Continuum, 2003), 33.
[70] Jane Schaberg, *The Illegitimacy of Jesus* (San Francisco: Harper & Row, 1987). For a critical response, see John P. Meier, *A Marginal Jew, vol. 1* (New York: Doubleday, 1991), 222, 246.
[71] Jane Schaberg, "Feminist Interpretations of the Infancy Narrative of Matthew," in *A Feminist Companion to Mariology*, ed. Amy-Jill Levine with Maria Mayo Robbins (Cleveland: Pilgrim, 2005), 15–26, here 24. For Brown's position, see *Birth*, 601, 635–37, 707–708.

Schaberg does, however, suggest that it was more probable that Mary was raped, and that God, "siding with the wronged woman," made her son his own. This would account for her "frightened haste" (Luke 1:39) in the Visitation story, and the mention of "humiliation" (Luke 1:48) in the Magnificat. The conception by the Holy Spirit was never meant to imply that there was no human father, for Paul equally states that Isaac was "born through the Spirit" (Gal 4:29), and Philo mentions that Rebecca conceived "through the power of God" (*On the Cherubim* 13.47). According to Schaberg, the notion of virginal conception is a second-century invention, to cover up the scandal of the tradition of illegitimacy.

This is far from the only position held by prominent feminist scholars, laid out by Schaberg in *A Feminist Companion to Mariology*.[72] Three male interpreters have different solutions. Bruce Chilton presents Jesus as a *mamzēr*, that is, not an illegitimate child, but a child born of a positively illegitimate union (such as incest).[73] In first-century Judaism, a *mamzēr* was always regarded as an outcast. Throughout his life, therefore, Jesus was negotiating the treacherous terrain between belonging to the people of God and ostracism in his own community. This would account for his efforts to set up a new family structure (Mark 3:35). John Dominic Crossan regards the story of the miraculous birth of Jesus not as apologetic, but as a positive rival, a challenge to and confrontation with the story (told by Suetonius, *Augustus* 94.4, and Dio Cassius, *Histories* 45.1–2) that the mother of the Roman emperor Octavian Augustus was impregnated in a dream by a god in the form of a snake in a temple.[74]

More closely argued is the contention of Roger Aus, who considers that Matthew's account of the virgin birth is entirely unhistorical.[75] He shows that almost every detail of Matthew's infancy story is paralleled in the Judaic tradition of the story of Moses, though his sources vary in their cogency. The chief witness is Josephus (*Antiquities* 2.9), who is surely a valid witness to the Jewish tradition about Moses' youth current at the time of Matthew. Whereas Pseudo-Philo is another strong witness,[76] the difficulty of dating the rabbinic tradition makes it a less secure basis for the tradition behind Matthew. Aus argues, however, that Matthew's account is purely midrashic, and that the creators of midrash did not even intend their readers to believe that their accounts were historical. "The question itself would have seemed strange to them"—and then a final cheeky quip, "Brown himself simply does not appreciate the nature of

---

72 Schaberg, "Feminist," 25.
73 Bruce Chilton, *Rabbi Jesus: An Intimate Biography* (New York: Doubleday, 2000).
74 John Dominic Crossan, "Virgin Mother or Bastard Child?" in *A Feminist Companion to Mariology*, ed. Levine with Robbins, 37–55.
75 Roger David Aus, *Matthew 1–2 and the Virginal Conception* (Lanham, MD: University Press of America, 2004).
76 The unrivalled authority of Pierre-Maurice Bogaert lends weight to the increasing tendency to date this work before 70 CE; see his article, "Luc et les Ecritures dans l'Evangile de l'enfance à la lumière des 'Antiquités bibliques,'" in *The Scriptures in the Gospels*, ed. Christopher M. Tuckett (BETL 131; Leuven : Peeters, 1997), 243–70, here 244.

Judaic haggadah."[77] This is strong language! The question is whether so many of the details in Matthew's account are derived from the Jewish tradition earlier than Matthew, or whether Matthew simply relates the historical details in such a way as to bring out the parallel with Moses.

Also of considerable concern to feminist interpreters are the five women mentioned in Matthew's genealogy. To find a common factor between the earlier four and Mary has long been a problem for interpreters. A typical male approach is to leave the problem unsolved: the women are all "fraught with *or thought to be fraught with* sexual impropriety."[78] Is this really the full reason for inclusion of these predecessors of Mary? A typical feminist interpretation is that of Elaine Wainwright, who sees in them a critique of patriarchy, paradigms representing courage, initiative, and countercultural values.[79] Similar is the view of Irene Nowell: "These women are courageous, hospitable, and creative, and they have risked life and reputation to ensure our future."[80]

Amy-Jill Levine sees all of these five women as examples of "higher righteousness."[81] It is, however, difficult to fit Bathsheba into this structure. Wim Weren's suggestion is helpful here: the five women all represent positive and energetic action from which the history of God's people advances, Bathsheba by her "important role in the turbulent period of the succession."[82] Another useful suggestion is that all except Bathsheba come into the story from outside.[83] The new factor in Weren's suggestion is the naming of Uriah rather than Bathsheba. Since Bathsheba is a Jew, she is not named, but instead her husband Uriah is the more prominent, for his loyalty and determination contrast nobly with David's shabby behavior.

---

[77] Aus, *Matthew*, 80 and 82 n. 177.

[78] Brendan Byrne, *Lifting the Burden* (Slough, UK: St Paul's, 2004), 21–22 (his italics).

[79] Elaine Wainwright, "The Gospel of Matthew," in *Searching the Scriptures, vol. 2: A Feminist Commentary*, ed. Elisabeth Schüssler Fiorenza (New York: Crossroad, 1994), 633–77, here 642–43.

[80] Irene Nowell, "Jesus' Great-Grandmothers: Matthew's Four and More," *Catholic Biblical Quarterly* 70 (2008) 1–15, here 15.

[81] Amy-Jill Levine, "Matthew," in *The Women's Bible Commentary*, ed. Carol A. Newsom and Sharon H. Ringe (Louisville: Westminster John Knox, 1992), 252–62, here 253.

[82] Wim J. C. Weren, "The Five Women in Matthew's Genealogy," *Catholic Biblical Quarterly* 59 (1997) 288–305, here 301.

[83] Worth recording is a further suggestion from Edwin D. Freed, *The Stories of Jesus' Birth: A Critical Introduction* (Sheffield: Sheffield Academic Press, 2001). He uses contemporary Jewish sources and legends to show that it was considered that God or the Spirit made a special intervention in the lives of all four of the women in the genealogy. This is the factor they share with Mary. He also regards this as a defense of Mary against Jewish accusations of immorality (p. 46). Brown concluded his witty and sparkling discussion (*Birth*, 595–96) by pointing out that in the case of three of the named women the man has been at fault in some way ("the unworthies named in the genealogy"). This does not, however, apply to Ruth, so will not do as the common factor that the Old Testament women of the genealogy share with Mary. Nodet (*Historical*, 118) simplifies the situation by saying that all the women are outside the Law, and they "redirect and reshape the posterity of Abraham and of David."

In contrast to the usual male contention that Luke is favorable to women, Schaberg is emphatic about Luke's negativity toward women in most of the Gospel, complaining that he makes the chief function of women to be nurturing.[84] Only in the infancy story are they more powerful. Elizabeth makes the only christological confession by a woman in this gospel, calling Jesus "Lord" (Luke 1:43). Mary is "the only woman to whom Luke has given a full speech of proclamation, the Magnificat," in which her proclamation is "precious to women and other oppressed people for its vision of their concrete freedom from systemic injustice."

Conclusion

While Brown addressed most of the pertinent issues to a greater or lesser extent, more recent studies have considered questions (both broader and more specific) within Matthew 1–2 and Luke 1–2. There is a developing appreciation of the literary skill of Matthew and Luke, while use of the narratives to establish historicity has diminished in scholarly discussion. Various new approaches have been taken further (especially literary and feminist studies), but no new paradigm has yet totally superseded the work of Raymond Brown.[85]

---

[84] Jane Schaberg, "Luke," in *The Women's Bible Commentary*, ed. Newsom and Ringe, 275–92, here 281. The following quotations are from pp. 283–84. On Luke's portrayal of women see also Barbara E. Reid's essay in the present volume.

[85] As a final tribute to the author of *The Birth of the Messiah* it is worth stating that few indeed are the articles and books here discussed that do not take as their starting-point (or at least engage earnestly with) the opinions there expressed with such clarity and courtesy by Raymond Brown. A bibliography of publications on the infancy narratives from 1990 till 2009 appears at the end of this volume.

Chapter 2

Luke's Nativity Story: A Narrative Reading

Ian Boxall

Luke's vivid portrayal of the nativity of Jesus provides a rich tapestry of setting, action, and characterization that has fed the Christian imagination down the centuries. The dramatic appeal of the worldwide census under the Emperor Augustus; the moving sight of a baby lying in a manger; the rustic appeal of a band of shepherds, interwoven with heavenly intervention through a choir of angels: all this has given Luke's birth story pride of place in the popular memory. Though the magi may have played a more significant role in artistic representations of the nativity up to the Late Middle Ages, it is Luke's shepherds who have taken center stage in Western art from the Renaissance onward. Furthermore, no doubt aided by St Francis' crib or crèche at Greccio, the Christ child in a manger remains at the heart of Christmas devotion and piety. Here as elsewhere in his Gospel, through his skillful use of words and his capacity to create powerful images, Luke reveals himself to be the consummate literary artist. The evangelist Matthew, by contrast, devotes no more than half a verse to the event of the birth ("In the time of King Herod, after Jesus was born in Bethlehem of Judea"—Matt 2:1a), before moving on to his tale of the magi.

Picturing the Nativity

It is perhaps no wonder, therefore, that among the traditions about St Luke are those that view him as an artist, and the patron saint of artists. Already in the fourth century, the church historian Eusebius describes Luke as having left us examples of "the art of curing souls" (Eusebius *Hist. eccl.* 3.4). By at least the sixth century, appreciation of this artistry had developed into a tradition that saw Luke as literally an artist, the painter of icons of Our Lady.[1] Numerous examples survive claiming to be Luke's handiwork, from the portrait of the

---

[1] On Luke as artist, see Heidi J. Hornik and Mikeal C. Parsons, *Illuminating Luke: The Infancy Narrative in Italian Renaissance Painting* (Harrisburg: Trinity Press International, 2003), 14–23.

Virgin in Rome's Basilica of Santa Maria Maggiore to an icon housed in the little Syrian Orthodox church of St Mark in Jerusalem.

Inspired by this tradition, painters throughout the ages have often placed themselves in the position of Luke. Several artists have depicted the scene of Luke painting Mary, offering a self-portrait in their depiction of the evangelist. Rogier van der Weyden (*St Luke Drawing the Virgin and Child*, ca. 1435) and Giorgio Vasari (*St Luke Painting the Virgin*, ca. 1565) are good examples. But it is the vivid scenes of Luke's Gospel—notably from his infancy narrative—that have been especially inspirational for artists, who have been among Luke's most illuminating interpreters. It is the contention of this essay that interesting parallels can be drawn between this visual commentary on Luke by the artists and the kind of readings offered by recent literary approaches to the gospels. Hence it will attempt to sketch out some contours of a holistic reading of Luke's birth narrative, using some of the insights of narrative criticism.

To set the scene for what is to follow, one particular artistic interpretation of Luke's nativity story is worthy of mention, to be picked up again at a later stage. This is the altarpiece of *The Nativity and Adoration of the Shepherds* (1483–1485) by Domenico Ghirlandaio, commissioned for the Sassetti Chapel of the church of Santa Trinità in Florence. It seems to combine the scenes of the birth (or the immediate aftermath) and the visit of the shepherds after their angelic encounter. At the center of the panel is the Christ child, newly born and not yet wrapped in swaddling clothes, being adored by his mother and by a group of recently arrived shepherds. I mention it here for a particular detail that Ghirlandaio and other artists have noted, but which is hardly detected by commentators on this passage working with a historical–critical approach. Yet it is a detail that a more holistic reading of Luke's birth story typical of a narrative-critical approach might allow more space for.

In Ghirlandaio's representation, there stands in between the child and the ox and donkey, not a manger or feeding trough, but a stone sarcophagus, albeit filled with hay.[2] Worshippers contemplating Ghirlandaio's altarpiece at Mass would be presented in this depiction of Christ's birth with a stark anticipation of his death. The one laid in a manger at his nativity is destined to be laid in a tomb at the culmination of Luke's first volume (Luke 23:53), a tomb that will become the gateway to life. Other details in Ghirlandaio's painting underscore this foreshadowing of the story of Christ's passion. One of the shepherds, standing behind his contemporaries, carries a lamb in his arms, a reminder that the child is the Lamb of God who takes away the sins of the world (John 1:29). In front of the baby is a goldfinch, a well-established symbol of the passion of Christ.[3] The viewer of this altarpiece would be left in no doubt: in Christ's beginning lies his end.

---

[2] Ibid., 92–121.
[3] Ibid., 110.

Trends in Lukan Scholarship

Trends in gospel study over recent decades have encouraged critical biblical scholars to revisit the ancient tradition of Luke the artist, as well as opening up fresh possibilities for rereading Luke's narrative with the eyes of our artistic predecessors. The shift in historical–critical approaches (from source- and form- to redaction- and composition-criticism) in the second half of the twentieth century laid the foundations for a greater appreciation of Luke's skill as a writer and creative adapter of his traditions. Titles such as Howard Marshall's *Luke: Historian and Theologian* (1970) and Eric Franklin's *Christ the Lord: A Study in the Purpose and Theology of Luke-Acts* (1975) highlight this regard for the evangelist's distinctive message.[4]

Ironically, the classic work of redaction criticism on Luke's Gospel, Hans Conzelmann's *Die Mitte der Zeit* (translated into English as *The Theology of St Luke* [1960]), disregarded the infancy narratives in its account of Luke's theology.[5] For Conzelmann, Luke's first two chapters, including the nativity story, are lacking in distinctive Lukan features and therefore irrelevant to Luke's purpose: "The introductory chapters of the Gospel present a special problem. It is strange that the characteristic features they contain do not occur again either in the Gospel or in Acts."[6] Among these "characteristic features," Conzelmann notes the analogy between John the Baptist and Jesus, the special role played by Mary and the virginal conception, Jesus' descent from David and the place of Bethlehem. Yet a wider perspective might suggest that some of these features are not quite as distinctly "characteristic" of only the first two chapters as Conzelmann suggests. A particular example is the special role played by Mary. Her role among the eleven, the brothers, and the other women in Acts 1:14 is problematic for Conzelmann's case. This he dismisses in a footnote: "It is difficult to avoid the suspicion that Acts i, 14 is an interpolation."[7]

Nevertheless, the majority of redaction-critical commentators have plowed a rather different furrow with respect to Luke 1 and 2.[8] Eric Franklin comments on the function of Luke's first two chapters: "They serve, not as the first chapter of an unfolding narrative extending to the end of Acts, but as the prologue to the two volumes. They are the statement which the work as a whole explains

---

[4] I. Howard Marshall, *Luke: Historian and Theologian* (Exeter: Paternoster, 1970); Eric Franklin, *Christ the Lord: A Study in the Purpose and Theology of Luke-Acts* (Philadelphia: Westminster, 1975).

[5] Hans Conzelmann, *The Theology of St Luke* (ET, London: Faber and Faber, 1960).

[6] Ibid., 172.

[7] Ibid., 172 n. 1.

[8] For example, Paul S. Minear, "Luke's Use of the Birth Stories," in *Studies in Luke-Acts*, ed. Leander E. Keck and J. Louis Martyn (Philadelphia: Fortress, 1966; London: SPCK, 1968), 111–30; Eric Franklin, *Luke: Interpreter of Paul, Critic of Matthew* (JSNT Supplement 92; Sheffield: JSOT Press, 1994), 356–57.

and justifies…"[9] For Franklin, then, the infancy narrative is integral to understanding Luke's overarching purpose, introducing themes that will be played
out and developed further in the remainder of Luke-Acts.

   More recently, narrative-critical and other literary approaches have sought
to read Luke's book (or in most cases, what is believed to be his two-volume
work of Luke and Acts) in a thoroughly holistic way. A pioneer here has been
Robert Tannehill's *The Narrative Unity of Luke-Acts*.[10] Taking a wider perspective, Tannehill offers a reading in which the infancy narratives play a far more
integral role in the unified narrative of Luke-Acts than Conzelmann allowed.
A similar approach has been adopted in this essay, on the presupposition that
a narrative reading can be expected to show particular appreciation of the
literary artistry of Luke's narrative, akin, if not identical, to that of artists such
as Ghirlandaio.

Luke's Birth Story as Narrative

As we turn to Luke's birth story (Luke 2:1–20), it is worth reminding ourselves
of some of the features of a narrative-critical approach.[11] Such a reading will
attend to the final form of the story, rather than any hypothetical sources
underlying it or supposed motives behind its composition. This final form will
presume a particular "symbolic world," which the reader is invited to enter into,
embracing—at least temporarily—its assumptions and being moved by its perspective. A narrative reading will approach the passage holistically—both in
terms of its internal structure and as an integral part of a larger narrative (in
this case Luke-Acts).[12] Thus it will be especially attentive to literary parallels
connecting one passage with others elsewhere in the text. It will be less interested in the real historical author (whose identity may be lost to us) than in the
"implied author," that is, the picture gleaned from the text as to the kind of
author implied. Similarly, attention will be on the "implied reader," sometimes
called the "ideal reader"—the kind of reader who will always respond to the
text in the way it suggests an attentive reader should. A narrative approach will
have an artist's eye for what we might call "narrative threads," such as repetition of phrases and recurrence or development of themes. It will be interested

---

[9] Franklin, *Luke: Interpreter of Paul*, 357.
[10] Robert C. Tannehill, *The Narrative Unity of Luke-Acts: A Literary Interpretation* (2 vols;
     Philadelphia: Fortress, 1986, 1990).
[11] For a brief survey of narrative criticism and other literary readings, see Ian Boxall, *SCM
     Studyguide to New Testament Interpretation* (London: SCM, 2007), 112–25. For a more detailed
     introduction, see Mark Allan Powell, *What is Narrative Criticism?* (Minneapolis: Fortress,
     1990; London: SPCK, 1993).
[12] Though some recent scholars have proposed a "loosening of the hyphen" linking Luke
     and Acts, so as to treat them as separate texts, I will presume a unity of author and pur-
     pose between them.

in the characters within the narrative, their capacity to evoke sympathy, empathy, or antipathy, and how they develop within the unfolding story. In what follows, particular attention will be paid to the final form, symbolic world, literary patterns, and characterization.

Before progressing further, however, I wish to make two brief qualifications. First, although some narrative critics claim to "bracket off" questions of history, this seems to me short-sighted. In the case of the birth story, for example, the implied readers are surely expected to have some awareness of Roman history and Jewish traditions, for example, concerning Roman imperial propaganda about the Augustan age or Bethlehem's connection with messianic prophecy. Any narrative approach, in other words, should be regarded as complementing rather than replacing historical critical methods.

Second, the reading I am offering here is not one that a first reader of Luke 2:1–20 might detect—even an ideal first reader. It presumes several readings of Luke (and also of Acts), not least because it understands the birth story in light of events later in the Gospel. I find justification for this in Luke's prologue (Luke 1:1–4), which states that Theophilus—whom I take to be Luke's patron who paid for his work to be published—has been "instructed" (Greek *katēchēthēs*), a verb closely related to our word "catechesis." Theophilus would then be a Christian convert, and Luke's work is intended for all those who, like him, need "assurance" about their adoption of the faith. Such readers could be expected both to have background knowledge of the story of Jesus, and to read (or more likely hear) Luke's version of that story on more than one occasion.

Establishing the Final Form of the Story

Among the interests of historical critics have been the question of Luke's sources for the infancy narrative, and the evangelist's motives in writing as he does. Narrative critics, however, study the narrative as it has come down to us. For them, questions of the prehistory of the text as we have it are irrelevant. Decisions still need to be made about what is the "final form," owing to variant readings in the ancient Greek manuscripts, but fortunately, there are few of these in Luke's birth narrative.

The most significant variants are in relation to the angelic message to the shepherds. In Luke 2:11, although the vast majority of manuscripts read "Christ the Lord" (the preferred reading in English translations), there are several alternative readings: "the Lord Christ," "the Lord's Christ," "Christ Jesus," "Christ Jesus the Lord," "Christ a Savior," and simply "Christ." These variants hardly make a great difference to the overall meaning.

A more significant variant is found in Luke 2:14: do the heavenly host proclaim "peace and favor/good will" (Greek *eudokia*) to all humans? The King James Version opts for this reading: "Glory to God in the highest, and on earth peace, good will toward men." Or should we opt for the more limited reading: "peace to humans of favor/good will" (Greek *eudokias*)? If we accept this second reading, then a further interpretative difficulty raises its head. Whose favor or goodwill is being spoken of? Is it a reference to a human attitude, offering heavenly peace to those minded to receive it? The Douai Bible, following the Vulgate's *bonae voluntatis*, translates literally: "Glory to God in the highest: and on earth peace to men of good will." An alternative interpretation of *eudokias* has God as the source of this "good favor," meaning that peace will be received by those on whom he chooses to bestow it. This is the interpretation followed by the New Jerusalem Bible: "Glory to God in the highest heaven, and on earth peace for those he favors." In a holistic reading, any solution must attend to Luke's two other uses of the *eudok-* word-complex (Luke 3:22; 10:21). Both point to "good favor" being God's, and thus suggest the second reading *eudokias* as the original.[13] The angelic choir thus sings of peace for those who follow the pattern of Jesus, the beloved Son with whom the Father is well pleased (*eudokēsa*, 3:22). If we follow this reading, then those working in English rather than Greek will find both the NRSV and the New Jerusalem Bible reliable guides for the final form of the birth story.

As it stands, then, the nativity story falls fairly neatly into three sections, each of which has a different set of main characters:

2:1–7: The *birth of Jesus*, set against the backdrop of Augustus' census (Mary and Joseph are the key players);

2:8–14: The *angelic annunciation* to the shepherds (the angel of the Lord and the heavenly host are active, while the shepherds are passive observers);

2:15–20: The confirmatory *visit of the shepherds* to Bethlehem, and their return (the shepherds now take on the active role, though matched by Mary in verse 19).

We shall return to some of these characters at a later stage.

Luke's Symbolic World

Underlying this three-part story is a particular "symbolic world" (or "narrative world") that the reader must reconstruct from the various signals provided. The term "symbolic world" describes the system of shared meanings, assumptions, and values held in common by a particular group through which that group is able to make sense of the world they inhabit. Luke Timothy Johnson

---

[13] Joseph A. Fitzmyer, *The Gospel according to Luke I–IX* (Anchor Bible 28; New York: Doubleday, 1980), 410–12.

puts it thus: "A symbolic world is not an alternative ideal world removed from everyday life. To the contrary, it is the system of meanings that anchors the activities of individuals and communities in the real world. Nothing is more down to earth and ordinary than a symbolic world."[14]

Narrative criticism presumes that the ideal reader will enter into the symbolic world presupposed by the text. This might involve temporarily suspending one's own judgments as to what the world is really like. Thus a "hermeneutic of generosity" is called for, open (though not uncritically so) to the perspective envisaged by the text, rather than a "hermeneutic of suspicion" targeting unacknowledged assumptions and motives embedded in the text.[15] Even this is not a straightforward move, however. Robert Tannehill reminds us that reconstructing a symbolic or narrative world from the text involves a certain element of imaginative "free play," working as it does with suggested as well as explicit connections.[16] The interpreter plays a key role in deciding which details should take priority in reconstructing a symbolic world, and how they should be linked.

Nevertheless, what is offered here is a tentative sketch of the symbolic world painted by Luke's story, giving priority to narrative signals in the birth narrative that seem to be "foregrounded" by their prominent place in its structure, or by regular repetition throughout the wider narrative. First of all, it is a world organized and interpreted according to both Roman and Jewish religio-political realities. Luke's explicit opening statement sets these events within the reign of Emperor Augustus (Luke 2:1; cf. 3:1), acclaimed by his people as savior and establisher of peace. Leaving aside the historical difficulties with the worldwide census (Luke 2:2),[17] Luke portrays a world—essentially the Mediterranean basin—in which crucial events are determined by the imperial court in Rome. This focus on Rome's influence, and a certain degree of benevolence among its functionaries, will continue into the Acts of the Apostles, which breathes the air of the (essentially urban) Roman Mediterranean world.

However, although Rome is apparently dominant on the world stage, Luke's symbolic universe views the Roman world through the critical lens of Israel's tradition. This is a tradition that, as Luke presents it in his infancy narrative, gives particular prominence to the royal house of King David and the town of Bethlehem from which David came (Mic 5:2; Luke 2:4), and contains diverse expectations about the restoration of that royal house through a future

---

14 Luke Timothy Johnson, *The Writings of the New Testament: An Interpretation* (rev. edn; Philadelphia: Fortress, 1986), 12.
15 Some might see it as a weakness of narrative criticism that it can fail to engage seriously with problematic and even morally objectionable elements that may exist in the perspective of the text.
16 Tannehill, *Narrative Unity*, 1.3.
17 On these historical questions, see Raymond E. Brown, *The Birth of the Messiah* (rev. edn; New York: Doubleday, 1993), 412–18, 547–56, 666–68.

anointed king (the royal Messiah, Luke 2:11). Moreover, implicit in these messianic expectations is the conviction that ultimate power rests not with Augustus but with Israel's God, who created the world, promised protection to his people, and whose agent the Davidic Messiah would be.[18]

But Luke's symbolic universe is even more expansive. For Luke's earthly world of emperors, governors, client-rulers, and priests is one into which heaven regularly breaks. The intervention and action of angels permeate Luke-Acts, making it one of the most "apocalyptic" sections of the New Testament.[19] Already by this stage in the narrative, readers of Luke have encountered two angelic visitations, both by the archangel Gabriel, one of the seven archangels who according to Jewish angelology "stand ready and enter before the glory of the Lord" (Tob 12:15; cf. Luke 1:19). Now again an "angel of the Lord" (whether Gabriel or another we are not told) enters our earthly realm to deliver a divine message. At the same point, earth also has a glimpse into heaven, as the shepherds hear the singing of the heavenly liturgy, performed by the heavenly army (Luke 2:13). Angels will continue to intervene both in the life of Jesus (Luke 22:43) and in the lives of his followers (Acts 5:19; 8:26; 10:30; 12:7–10, 23; 27:23). This much richer and deeper symbolic world is only too real for Luke, whereas twenty-first-century Christians may need to rediscover something of this angelic depth in order to enter into that world more sympathetically.

Within this apocalyptic tradition, angelic messages are far more authoritative than any imperial decree. Hence the message conveyed by the angel to the shepherds (Luke 2:10–12) is *the* authoritative message, to be heard and taken to heart by all ideal readers. At the heart of this message is the proclamation that there is a rival claimant to the imperial throne. This child of David's line, not the Emperor Augustus, is the true Savior, whose birth establishes true peace (e.g., Luke 7:50; 8:48; 10:5–6; 19:38, 42; 24:36; but see 12:51). So Luke's symbolic world is both expansive and politically subversive.

Narrative Parallels to the Nativity

Yet Luke's story of the birth, the shepherds, and the angelic proclamation does not stand alone. Scholars have often noted literary parallels to this story elsewhere in his Gospel. A good place to start is within the infancy narratives themselves, since they form a recognizable block within the Gospel for their

---

[18] Darrell Bock makes a good case for Luke being influenced by Old Testament traditions about the Davidic king in his portrayal of Jesus in the infancy narrative: Darrell L. Bock, *Proclamation from Prophecy and Pattern: Lukan Old Testament Christology* (JSNT Supplement 12; Sheffield: JSOT Press, 1987), 55–90. On Luke's view of the Davidic dynasty, see also Leonard Maluf's essay in the present volume.

[19] By "apocalyptic" I mean that strand of Jewish religion that claims heavenly secrets can be revealed directly to humans, whether by dream, heavenly ascent, or angelic visitation.

thematic unity and their imitation of Septuagintal Greek style. The story of the birth and the shepherds forms the first part of what Charles Talbert calls Episode Two in Luke's infancy narrative (Luke 1:57–2:52).[20] There are sufficient narrative echoes of Episode One (Luke 1:5–38) to conclude that literary patterning is at work across these two chapters.

Commentators attentive to the literary structure of the Lukan infancy narratives have often noted the narrative patterning of the story of John and Jesus. Luke the artist is skillfully at work, creating a series of literary diptychs in which panels portraying the Baptist and his greater cousin stand side by side. Here, Luke's account of the birth and naming of Jesus (Luke 2:1–21) directly parallels his story of the birth and naming of John, though not perhaps with the precision that marks the two annunciations to Zechariah and Mary.[21] Within the wider diptych of Luke 1–2, the following parallels may be detected:

Annunciation to Zechariah (1:5–25)	Annunciation to Mary (1:26–38)
Zechariah's canticle (1:67–79)	Mary's canticle (1:46–55)
Birth of John (1:57–58)	Birth of Jesus (2:1–20)
Circumcision/naming of John (1:59–66)	Circumcision/naming of Jesus (2:21)
John's growth in spirit (1:80)	Jesus' growth in wisdom (2:52)

What is highlighted is the close relationship between John and Jesus. There are similarities: both John and Jesus receive the prophetic spirit to proclaim God's word (e.g., Luke 1:15, 80; 3:3; 3:22; 4:14, 18). Yet it is also clear that Jesus is the greater, the Lord and Son of the Most High, whose way John comes to prepare (Luke 1:32, 76; 3:4–6).

But we should not look only to the story of John's birth for parallels to the nativity of Jesus. For Luke's main focus in 2:1–20 is not on the birth as such but on the angelic announcement to the shepherds about that birth, as well as the reaction of the shepherds to this announcement.[22] The scene in which the shepherds encounter the angel closely parallels the two appearances of the angel Gabriel in chapter 1. In formal terms, Luke 2:8–14 is Luke's third annunciation story. All three share a similar pattern, placing the marginal Jewish shepherds alongside Zechariah the Jewish priest and Mary the Jewish mother-to-be as recipients of divine revelation:

- an appearance of an angel of the Lord (Gabriel in the first two)
- a command not to be afraid
- the announcement of a birth (a future birth in the case of the first two)

[20] Charles H. Talbert, *Reading Luke* (New York: Crossroad; London: SPCK, 1982), 31.
[21] Brown, *Birth*, 367–434.
[22] Ibid., 410.

Yet there are also differences among the three accounts. In the annunciation to the shepherds, the typical structure is interrupted by the appearance of a heavenly host (2:13–14). This underscores the heavenly character of this message, and also anticipates the ascension at the end of the gospel and the beginning of Acts, where again the boundary separating earth from heaven is pierced (Luke 24:51; Acts 1:9–11).[23] The reaction of the shepherds is also somewhat different. Unlike Zechariah (who is struck dumb as a result, 1:18) and Mary (who wishes to understand how she could possibly conceive, 1:34), the shepherds ask no question of the angel ("How can this be...?"). Instead, they immediately set out for Bethlehem in the conviction that what the angel announced has indeed come to pass. At the end of their journey, they find "Mary and Joseph, and the child lying in a manger" (2:16). Perhaps the contrast with Mary is not so great after all, however. She too embarks on a journey as a result of the angel's words, at the end of which she also meets a woman with a child (albeit yet unborn: Luke 1:39–56). She magnifies the Lord as a result of that meeting, just as the shepherds glorify and praise God (Luke 1:46; 2:20).

Nor is Luke's narrative patterning confined to the infancy stories. Denis McBride has made the plausible suggestion that, in general shape, if not in exact order or vocabulary, the angelic proclamation of Christ's birth in Luke 2:8–20 parallels the angelic proclamation of the resurrection at Luke 24:1–11.[24] In both cases, for example, the angelic revelation is made to those unable to be legal witnesses—whether shepherds or women—and here McBride follows other commentators in reading later rabbinic evidence about shepherds or herdsmen as reflecting first-century attitudes.[25] In both cases, an angelic interpretation is given of an event or sign (a baby wrapped in bands of cloth; an empty tomb with linen cloths left behind). In both, the testimony of the witnesses provokes a reaction from those to whom they speak (astonishment; disbelief). The parallel becomes even clearer when a clarification in the story of Emmaus is taken into account. Though Luke simply describes the figures at the tomb as "two men in dazzling clothes" (Luke 24:4), verse 23 clarifies the women's interpretation of this event as "a vision of angels," explicitly linking it to the angelic vision over the shepherds' fields near Bethlehem.

---

[23] Some manuscripts famously omit the words "and was carried up into heaven" at Luke 24:51.

[24] Denis McBride, C.Ss.R., *The Gospel of Luke: A Reflective Commentary* (Dublin: Dominican Publications, 1991), 39.

[25] On shepherds as ineligible to give witness in court in the Talmud, see Brown, *Birth*, 420, 673; Richard A. Horsley, *The Liberation of Christmas: The Infancy Narratives in Social Context* (New York: Continuum, 1989; reprint, Eugene, OR: Wipf & Stock, 2006), 102–103.

The Cradle and the Grave

If we take an even broader perspective on the parallel between the birth and resurrection narratives highlighted by McBride—keeping in view the whole birth story, and therefore also the broader narrative of which the appearance at the empty tomb is part—then we are brought back to the possible relationship between the nativity and the death and burial. We have already noted Ghirlandaio's impressive depiction of the nativity with its stone sarcophagus, a vivid example of the powerful link seen by Renaissance artists between the beginning of Christ's story and its end. The manger anticipates the tomb, just as Simeon's prophecy at the Presentation in the Temple will warn of the rejection leading to the cross: "Then Simeon blessed them and said to his mother Mary, 'This child is set for the falling and rising of many in Israel, and to be *a sign* that will be opposed so that the inner thoughts of many will be revealed—and a sword will pierce your own soul too'" (Luke 2:34–35, adapted from NRSV; italics mine). The "sign" that the shepherds witness—of a babe wrapped in bands of cloth and lying in a manger—will be a "sign" to be opposed.

Yet it is precisely this proposed link between the manger and the tomb that is dismissed by Raymond Brown, the distinguished scholar of the infancy narratives, on the grounds that the vocabulary is quite different in the two passages (Luke 2:7; 23:53).[26] Certainly, the Greek words are not as close as some English translations might suggest. The NRSV's "wrapped him in bands of cloth" (2:7) translates the Greek *esparganōsen auton*, while the similar "wrapped it in a linen cloth" (23:53) is a rendering of the quite different Greek phrase *enetulixen auto sidoni*. But vocabulary cannot be the sole deciding factor. A narrative approach would direct our attention also to the similar rhythm and structure of the two verses[27]:

And she gave birth *[main verb]* to her firstborn son and
wrapped him in bands of cloth *[main verb]*
and laid *[main verb]* him in a manger
because there was no place for them in the inn *[further explanatory clause]*

Then he took *[participle]* it [= the body of Jesus] down
wrapped *[main verb]* it in a linen cloth
and laid *[main verb]* it in a rock-hewn tomb
where no one had ever been laid *[further explanatory clause]*

---

[26] Brown, *Birth*, 399.
[27] A point noted, tentatively, by Luke Timothy Johnson, *The Gospel of Luke* (Sacra Pagina 3; Collegeville, MN: Liturgical Press, 1991), 53.

In the reception history of Luke, the potential for such a parallel must have been detected relatively early, for it is reflected in the Latin Vulgate, which uses exactly the same verb *involvit* ("she/he wrapped") at 2:7 and 23:53.

Further support for this parallel is provided by attention to the characters. In the first, the primary actor is Mary, whom Luke has already portrayed as an ideal disciple, willingly cooperating with God's will and pondering the heavenly words in her heart (Luke 1:38; 2:19). In the second, Joseph of Arimathea is introduced as someone "waiting expectantly for the kingdom of God," that is, at least a potential disciple (23:51; cf. 2:25, 38). Indeed, the earlier scene too is marked by the presence of a character named Joseph (2:4), the only other of that name in Luke's Gospel. The invitation to the implied reader then is not only to worship at the manger, but to remain with Christ at the tomb, at the risk of being identified with the crucified.

Revisiting the Shepherds

Finally, let us return to one particular set of characters whose role spans the latter two sections of Luke's nativity story, and who undergo a transformation from passive onlookers to active participants: the shepherds. Commentators continue to disagree as to their precise significance in Luke's nativity story. Romantic images of pastoral simplicity are probably unhelpful. Some contrast the high-status magi of Matthew's version, bearing extravagant gifts of gold, frankincense, and myrrh (Matt 2:11), with the poverty of these shepherds, as representatives of the poor whom Luke's Jesus declares "blessed" (Luke 6:20). Others, drawing upon later rabbinic sources (e.g., *b. Sanhedrin* 25b), regard the shepherds as disreputable or dishonest, thus placing Christ among the outcast even before he begins his public ministry. As Brown notes, however, there is no hint of dishonesty in the shepherds of Luke's story.[28] Perhaps there is some truth in the alternative suggestion that, if not quite dishonest, they would be located on the margins of Jewish society, given that their occupation meant they were unable to participate fully in its religious requirements. Outreach to those on the margins, both rich and poor, will be a feature of Jesus' ministry throughout Luke's story.

Their presence in the vicinity of Bethlehem, however, suggests that Luke has King David in mind. David, after all, had been a shepherd boy at Bethlehem prior to his anointing by Samuel (1 Sam 16:11). Moreover, commentators have detected the underlying influence on Luke 2 of Micah 4–5, with its prophecy of a shepherd–ruler emerging from Bethlehem of Ephrathah.[29] When David's royal successor is born, therefore, it is only natural for him to be greeted by those of his own.

---

[28] Brown, *Birth*, 420.
[29] Ibid., 421–23.

However, the shepherds are not mere observers. Two further comments are relevant, one intertextual, the other intratextual. The intertextual point picks up on echoes between the story of the shepherds' encounter with the angel and the Old Testament commissioning of Moses (another shepherd) at Mount Horeb. The two scenes share several formal characteristics, even though the Lukan story lacks an objection from the shepherds:

1. Appearance of an angel of the Lord.
2. Reaction of the seer(s).
3. Angelic message.
4. [Objection].
5. Giving of a sign.

This parallel with Moses' commissioning is the most striking, not least in the phrase introducing point 5 ("and this shall be the sign for you," Exod 3:12; cf. Luke 2:12), although we might also compare the commissioning of Gideon in Judg 6.[30]

The shepherds, therefore, receive a divine commissioning, akin to that received by Moses at the burning bush, while watching over his father-in-law's flock (Exod 3), or by Gideon at the oak at Ophrah, after which the Lord promised him "peace" (Judg 6). Like Moses and Gideon, the shepherds of Bethlehem are also given a sign (Exod 3:12; Judg 6:17). This suggests that, like Moses and Gideon, and like their own ancestor David, the shepherd–king from Bethlehem, they too have a particular task to fulfill in relation to God's people.

The other comment, picking up on an echo later in Luke's own text, relates to their transformation from passive observers to active players, and helps clarify the character of the commission they have received. As a result of the angelic announcement, they go and "see," then "tell" what they have seen, and finally "return," glorifying and praising God. In other words, they become preachers of the gospel, the *euangelion* that they have just heard from the angel (2:10). Would not an attentive reader of the gospel—not on a first reading but on subsequent readings—detect another echo here of the end of Luke's first volume? As McBride has noticed, they first share the same ministry as the women—perhaps as inadmissible witnesses—who announce (to the absent apostles, 24:10) what they have heard and seen. But they are equally pioneering apostles themselves, anticipating at the birth the mission that will only be possible in the light of Christ's resurrection and ascension.[31] Again, setting two

---

[30] Ibid., 156–57 (applied to the stories of the annunciations to Zechariah and Mary).

[31] Although Luke does not explicitly make this connection, other New Testament writers can speak of Christ's death–resurrection–ascension using the language of "birth" (e.g., John 16:21–22; Col 1:18; Rev 1:5; 12:5).

passages alongside each other may clarify the parallel:

> The shepherds *returned, glorifying and praising God* for all they had heard and seen, as it had been told them (Luke 2:20).

> And they [= the eleven and their companions] worshipped him, and *returned* to Jerusalem with great joy; and they were continually in the temple *blessing God* (Luke 24:52–53).

A significant number of ancient manuscripts make the connection at 24:53 even more explicit, with the longer reading "praising and blessing God" (or in some versions "blessing and praising God").

Concluding Reflections

What has been attempted in this essay—with fairly broad brushstrokes—is an exploration of the potential inherent in Luke's nativity story, as illuminated by the tools of narrative criticism. If similar insights have been detected here to those achieved by artists such as Ghirlandaio, that may well be evidence for similar sympathies and interpretative strategies. To enter sympathetically into the rich symbolic world that Luke's narrative presents, allowing our horizons to be expanded and our imaginations sharpened, is an approach to the text that cannot leave us detached or unmoved. If the contours sketched out here are not wholly wide of the mark, moreover, at least two implications are worth highlighting.

First, Luke's first two chapters can be seen as something akin to a trailer for a film, in which key scenes and characters are flashed momentarily across the screen, anticipating the unfolding plot before the film itself begins. In particular, Luke's birth story proclaims that what the disciples were only able to see in light of the ascension—that Jesus had been made both Lord and Messiah (Acts 2:36)—was already there at the beginning of his earthly life (Luke 2:11). So too was his destiny: the one whose birth brings peace will provoke such a hostile reaction that he will later speak of bringing, not peace, but division (12:51). To be born is for Christ also to be rejected and to die, and so to enter his glory (24:26).

Second, to listen attentively to Luke's nativity story is an invitation to enter into it and become one of its characters. Here the shepherds serve as the particular model for the ideal reader. In their transformation from observers of the angelic appearance to active proclaimers of the gospel, they anticipate the later apostolic mission, and serve as models for all preachers of the good news. If their character as despised and marginal figures is part of Luke's plot, then the challenge to Luke's readers is all the greater. It poses the question: what kind of person does one have to be in order to be able to see an angel, and thus have the courage to identify oneself with the crucified babe of Bethlehem, the sign that will be opposed?

Chapter 3

Prophetic Voices of Elizabeth, Mary, and Anna in Luke 1–2

Barbara E. Reid, O.P.

One of the most prominent images of Jesus in the Third Gospel is that of rejected prophet (Luke 4:24; 13:33–34; 24:19–20). In the opening chapters, however, it is Elizabeth, Mary, and Anna who embody the prophetic mission, and who prefigure the ways in which it will take form in Jesus' life. Later, Jesus' disciples participate in the prophetic mission and continue it after his death and resurrection (Luke 24:48; Acts 1:8). In this essay, I will focus on the ways in which the prophetic women in Luke, particularly in the infancy narratives, can model for contemporary women and men how to articulate an alternative vision of God's reign and mobilize energies for transformative action that will help to bring about that reign. I will also explore how women are silenced in Luke and ways in which women can find their voice in a patriarchal world.

Prophetic Women Ancestors

As Luke sets the stage for his gospel in the first two chapters, three women take prominent roles: Elizabeth, Mary, and Anna. Although only Anna is explicitly called a prophet (Luke 2:36),[1] each of these three women embodies characteristics of a prophet. As Wilda Gafney has shown, Israel's prophets are vessels of divine communication, whose activities include not only declaring oracles, but also "engaging in intercessory prayer, dancing, drumming, singing, giving and interpreting laws, delivering oracles on behalf of YHWH (sometimes in ecstasy, sometimes demonstratively), resolving disputes, working wonders, mustering troops and fighting battles, archiving their oracles in writing, and experiencing visions."[2] Such women prophets are found throughout the canon of the Old Testament. There are five who are specifically named

---

[1] It is preferable to call Anna a "prophet" (as in NRSV), rather than "prophetess" (as in NAB, NJB, NASB), so that she is seen on a par with male prophets.
[2] Wilda C. Gafney, *Daughters of Miriam. Women Prophets in Ancient Israel* (Minneapolis: Fortress, 2008), 6.

as prophets: Miriam (Exod 15:20), Deborah (Judg 4:4), Huldah (2 Kgs 22:14; 2 Chr 34:22), the unnamed woman with whom Isaiah fathers a child (Isa 8:3), and Noadiah (Neh 6:14). In addition, there are references in Joel (3:1–2) and Ezekiel (13:17) to daughters who prophesy, and 1 Chronicles (25:4–6) speaks of Heman who directs his sons and daughters in musical prophecy. The Talmud (*Megillah* 14a) adds Sarah, Hannah, Abigail, and Esther to those women recognized as prophets.

In the New Testament, besides Anna, the four virgin daughters of Philip have the gift of prophecy (Acts 21:9), as well as the women prophets of Corinth (1 Cor 11:5). A false woman prophet appears in Revelation (2:20–23). As Gafney points out, there are "more female prophets in the Hebrew Scriptures than have previously been discussed, and certainly more in ancient Israel than have been included in the Scriptures."[3] The same can also be said for early Christianity. To the first hearers of Luke's Gospel, Elizabeth, Mary, and Anna would have been easily recognizable as prophetic figures, vessels of divine communication of God's new action in Christ.

Prophetic Call (Luke 1:26–38)

We turn first to Mary of Nazareth.[4] The scene of the Annunciation (Luke 1:26–38) is a most familiar story and a popular subject in Christian art. Many painters and writers have focused on Mary's piety, purity, joy, and submission in her encounter with God's messenger. But there is another side to her story. As Luke tells it, Mary is not described as praying (often she is depicted as kneeling at a *prie-dieu*!) but, like the Galilean fisherfolk whom Jesus calls to be disciples (5:1–11), she has an extraordinary encounter with the Divine in the midst of everyday life. She is an ordinary Galilean woman who is making wedding plans when the call comes to do something extraordinary with God's grace. That is how the call usually comes to a prophet—in the midst of everyday life.

Mary, like other prophets, is full of questions and fear. Like Jeremiah who objected that he was too young (Jer 1:6) and Moses who insisted he couldn't speak well (Exod 4:10), Mary cannot fathom how the message she hears from Gabriel could be possible (Luke 1:34). Every prophet realizes that the task is greater than their human abilities. But God always gives assurances of divine assistance. To Jeremiah God insists "Do not be afraid . . . I am with you to deliver you" (Jer 1:8). For Moses, God provides a companion, Aaron, and guarantees, "I will be with your mouth and with his mouth, and will teach you what you shall do" (Exod 4:15). So, too, God assures Mary through Gabriel that the Holy

---

[3] Ibid., 20.
[4] On Mary, see Elizabeth Johnson, *Truly Our Sister: A Theology of Mary in the Communion of Saints* (New York: Continuum, 2003).

Spirit will come upon her and the power of the Most High will overshadow her (Luke 1:35) and that nothing is impossible for God (1:37). Mary is like Isaiah and other prophets, who feel the spirit of God come upon them (Isa 61:1; Ezek 2:2) with a prophetic word, and she freely gives herself over to this power (Luke 1:38).

A prophet who says yes, however, takes a great risk. As Jesus starkly observes in Luke 13:34, Jerusalem regularly kills prophets. Although this is not always literally true, every prophet experiences hostility and opposition. Mary is no exception. While many envision the annunciation scene as wrapped in an aura of joy and delight, there is an undercurrent of terror, upheaval, and scandal in the story. When we recall that in Mary's small village she and her family are known to everyone, and that everyone knows that she and Joseph are formally betrothed but have not yet begun to live together (see Matt 1:18), we can easily imagine the suspicious glances, rumors, and whispering about Mary when it becomes evident that she is with child. Even prophets, who have powerful experiences of God's presence and God's action through them, cannot sustain the struggle alone. And so it is most understandable that Mary leaves home for a time to stay with her relative Elizabeth.

Elizabeth: Companioning Mentor and Prophet of Grace (Luke 1:39–45)

Although we often envision Mary, the younger woman, as going to Judea to help her older relative Elizabeth, the gospel portrays Elizabeth in the role of wise mentor for Mary. Elizabeth has known God and has been faithful many long years. Luke says she has been "righteous" before God, living blamelessly, with integrity, according to all God's commands, all her days (Luke 1:6), despite the fact that she has suffered greatly. In first-century Palestinian culture, a woman who is childless is looked upon with disdain (1:25). We can imagine that behind Elizabeth's back people have speculated all her married life about what sin she must have committed to be so punished by God. Despite all this, Elizabeth, in the unknowing and the anguish, has been faithful and upright in every way. She is just the one to accompany Mary through her difficult days, to help Mary claim her own integrity, and to rejoice in the hope that will be birthed for the world from her freely given "yes."[5]

Many of the male prophets in the Bible are portrayed as solitary figures who act alone (like Elijah in 1 Kgs 19:10), mediating between God and the people. In the Visitation scene (Luke 1:39–45), however, we see a typically female form

---

[5] See further Barbara E. Reid, *Choosing the Better Part? Women in the Gospel of Luke* (Collegeville: Liturgical Press, 1996), 55–85.

of prophetic companionship. Mary and Elizabeth are not lone-ranger figures who take on the whole world all by themselves. These women prophets know their deep need for one another and for shared wisdom. They are like Ruth and Naomi (Ruth 1–4) and Moses' mother and sister and Pharaoh's daughter (Exod 2:1–10), who collaborate together to accomplish God's purposes. They know that the prophetic word arises from the midst of their experience in community, not only in individual intimate communion with God. With intuition and insight, together Mary and Elizabeth abandon themselves into the arms of Holy Mystery, allowing the Divine to envelop them and sustain them in the unknowing.

Both women are portrayed as deeply contemplative, a requisite quality for a prophet. Elizabeth, once she becomes pregnant, stays in seclusion, nurturing the life within her, reflecting on God's grace and favor (Luke 1:24–25). Similarly, Luke twice tells us that Mary treasured everything in her heart, reflecting on the divine ways that were beyond knowing or understanding (2:19, 51). Both women are "filled with the Holy Spirit" (1:35, 41), impelling them to speak prophetically. Elizabeth pronounces blessing on Mary and her child, echoing the words of the prophet Deborah, "Blessed among women be Jael" (Judg 5:24), and of Moses to the Israelites, "Blessed shall be the fruit of your womb" (Deut 28:4).[6] Elizabeth's prophetic blessing also recognizes the child Mary carries as "my Lord" (Luke 1:43), the first in Luke's Gospel to use this frequent title for Jesus.

Proclaiming an Alternative Vision (Luke 1:46–56)

Contemplative oneness with the Divine leads to prophetic proclamation and action. It is on Mary's lips that Luke first articulates a vision for a new world order, one in which those who are made poor are lifted up and those who profit from injustice and oppression of others are toppled from their undeserved thrones (Luke 1:46–55). Mary sings not of how God will reverse the roles and put on top those who had been oppressed. Rather, she envisions God's justice as creating a circle in which all have an equal place at the table; all are in right relation, each one knowing their integrity and preciousness in God's eyes, each one free to love fully. For this to happen, two simultaneous movements are needed: the empowerment of those formerly oppressed, and relinquishment on the part of those holding the power, privilege, and status.

In the Magnificat, we also see an example of the ways in which women characteristically prophesy: with song and dance. There are strong parallels between Mary's song and that of Miriam, her namesake, who led the Israelites

---

[6] See Brittany E. Wilson, "Pugnacious Precursors and the Bearer of Peace: Jael, Judith, and Mary in Luke 1:42," *Catholic Biblical Quarterly* 68 (2006) 436–56.

in singing and dancing after their escape from the Egyptians (Exod 15:1–21).[7] Miriam is identified as a prophet in Exod 15:20, when she leads the singing and dancing with tambourine in hand.[8] In her role as prophet, Miriam leads the people to understand their experience of liberation as a gift from God and to further imagine—and thus be able to achieve—a new future in the land of God's promise.[9] In a similar way, Judith also led her people in a victory hymn after freeing them from the terror of Holofernes (Jdt 16:1–17), as did Deborah, after leading the successful campaign against the Canaanite King Jabin (Judg 5:1–31). These kinds of songs are not sweet lullabies, although our usual docile image of Mary has taken the edge off her words. "They have lost their power to stun and offend."[10] The Guatemalan government, however, recognized their revolutionary potential and banned the public recitation of the Magnificat in the 1980s.

Finding One's Voice (Luke 1:57–66)

Following the Visitation and Mary's canticle, Luke shifts the scene to the circumcision and naming of John the Baptist (1:57–66). There is tension and drama in the scene, as the neighbors and relatives gather for the celebration. Everyone is ready to name the child "Zechariah," after his father. To the astonishment of all, Elizabeth speaks up and declares, "No, he is to be called John." The assembled group protests this choice, essentially saying this had never been done before: "None of your relatives has this name." So they turn to Zechariah, who is still mute, and ask him what name the child is to have. To their amazement, he confirms what his wife has said. With that, Zechariah regains his voice, and he begins praising God.

---

[7] Most likely the whole exodus hymn was originally led by Miriam, and not simply Exod 15:21, which mirrors v. 1. See also 1 Sam 18:7, where the women lead victory songs and dancing. See further George J. Brooke, "A Long-Lost Song of Miriam," *Biblical Archaeology Review* 20 (1994) 62–65; Rita J. Burns, *Has the Lord Indeed Spoken Only Through Moses? A Study of the Biblical Portrait of Miriam* (SBLDS 84; Atlanta: Scholars Press, 1987); Phyllis Trible, "Bringing Miriam Out of the Shadows," *Bible Review* 5 (1989) 14–25; J. Gerald Janzen, "Song of Moses, Song of Miriam: Who is Seconding Whom?" *Catholic Biblical Quarterly* 54 (1992) 211–20.

[8] Drorah O'Donnell Setel ("Exodus," in *Women's Bible Commentary: Expanded Edition with Apocrypha*, ed. Carol Newsom and Sharon Ringe [Louisville: Westminster John Knox, 1998], 30–39, here 36) observes that Miriam's actions and lineage are priestly and proposes that her designation as prophet may be due to male transmitters of the tradition who found this title less objectionable than "priest."

[9] Irene Nowell, *Women in the Old Testament* (Collegeville: Liturgical Press, 1997), 52. For a detailed list of parallels between the songs of Mary and Miriam, see Barbara Reid, *Taking Up the Cross. New Testament Interpretations through Latina and Feminist Eyes* (Minneapolis: Fortress, 2007), 103. Many commentators have also noted the similarities between Mary's canticle and Hannah's song (1 Sam 2:1–10).

[10] Lisa Wilson Davison, *Preaching the Women of the Bible* (St. Louis: Chalice, 2006), 91.

The experience of Elizabeth is like that of many women who attempt to speak out in the church today. She has been given a prophetic word and she knows the truth of it. Luke does not say how Elizabeth came to know the name of the child that had been revealed earlier to Zechariah in the temple (1:13). But it is clear that she is deeply attuned to God and has the name right. The God-given name for the child, "John"—*Yôhānān* in Hebrew—means "YHWH has given grace." This name not only expresses the child's character and the parents' hopes for him, but also captures Elizabeth's own experience of God.

It happens often that women who have a prophetic word are not at first believed, as when Mary Magdalene, Joanna, Mary the mother of James, and the other Galilean women proclaim the good news of the resurrection to the other disciples (Luke 24:9–11).[11] Their words seem like "an idle tale" (NRSV) or "pure nonsense" (NJB). And just as Peter goes to the tomb to verify what the women have reported (24:12), so Zechariah has to confirm Elizabeth's word before it is believed. It is particularly painful for women prophets when their word is dismissed or disbelieved, or accepted only when echoed by a male authority. It is a grave loss for the believing community when women's prophetic gifts are ignored or not welcomed. Moreover, it is very important for women to articulate their experience of God in their own voice and their own language and with their own imagery. Likewise, it is very important for the whole community to hear how God speaks through female experiences. Sometimes, as in the case of Elizabeth, it is only when male voices are silenced that space is made for females to speak. It is also the case that some women need to be encouraged to find their own voice and claim it, so that their valuable contribution can be heard.

A woman friend in the state of Chiapas, Mexico, shared how she was becoming emboldened through attending women's Bible study meetings, so as to express her faith within the group. One day, she attended a large meeting of about three hundred women from all over the region. Others were urging her to share her word in front of the group. She finally stood and was handed the microphone. Never having used one before, she put it to her ear. When they laughed at her she almost lost her nerve entirely, but with the help of a friend, who showed her how to use the microphone, she finally said her piece in a wee, frightened voice. As time went on, she received more and more encouragement and practice, so much so that now she can courageously address crowds of several hundred, with a voice so confident that she does not even need a microphone![12]

---

[11] For ongoing traditions about Mary Magdalene, see Jane Schaberg, *The Resurrection of Mary Magdalene. Legends, Apocrypha, and the Christian Tradition* (New York: Continuum, 2002).

[12] On women as contemporary preachers, see Sarah Ann Fairbanks, "Liturgical Preaching by Women. A New Sign Language of Salvation," in *The Future of Ordained Ministry: The Way Supplement* 83 (1995) 131–40; Beverly Mayne Kienzle and Pamela J. Walker, eds, *Women Preachers and Prophets through Two Millennia of Christianity* (Berkeley: University of California Press, 1998).

Persistent Presence (Luke 2:36–38)

The third in the trio of women prophets that appear in Luke's infancy narrative is Anna, who is found along with Simeon (2:22–35) in the Temple, when
Mary and Joseph bring the child Jesus for the presentation and purification
ritual. Anna's name (Hannah, meaning "grace" in Hebrew) is a kind of femi-
nine version of "John"; as such, she is the very embodiment of the divine grace
that she prophesies. Anna's credentials are impeccable. Her advanced years
give her an authority that comes with age and wisdom. Luke depicts her as having previously been an ideal wife—seven is the perfect number in the Bible,
so a seven-year marriage (despite its shortness) evokes an image of perfection.
It is unclear in the Greek text whether she has stationed herself in the temple
for eighty-four years or whether she herself is eighty-four years old. It is possible that Luke intends the former, creating an allusion to Judith, who lived to
an age of one hundred and five years (Jdt 16:23).[13] If Anna had been married
at fourteen, then spent seven years as a good wife, before her eighty-four-year
vigil in the temple, she would be the same age as Judith. There are other parallels with Judith. She too was a widow (Jdt 8:4) who "fasted all the days of
her widowhood" (Jdt 8:6), and who prayed for the rescue of Israel "while the
incense was being offered in the temple of God in Jerusalem" (Jdt 9:1).

One of the notable characteristics of Anna is that she is a persistent
presence—for more than eight decades she fasts and prays, day and night,
watching and waiting for the propitious moment. A prophet must persevere
through the long, hard mission entrusted to her or him. In the Old Testament
we see several prophets who grow weary of their task and try to abandon it. At
one point Moses complains to God that the burden of his leadership of the
Israelites is too heavy: "Why have I not found favor in your sight, that you lay
the burden of all this people on me?" (Num 11:11). Moses continues, insisting
that he was not the one who gave birth to this ornery people, implying that God
needs to take responsibility for them. He is so miserable that he asks God to do
the favor of killing him at once, so that he no longer has to face such distress
(Num 11:15). God's reply is to give him assistance, by having him appoint seventy elders to help bear the load. Jeremiah also decides at one point that he has
had enough revilement on account of his mission. He says: "The word of the
Lord has become for me a reproach and derision all day long" (Jer 20:8). So he
decides he will no longer speak in God's name; he will hold it all in. But then,
he says, "there is something in me like a burning fire shut up in my bones; I am
weary with holding it in, and I cannot" (Jer 20:9). There is no clue in Luke's text
that Anna ever grew weary of her long years of attuning her ear to God's word.
She exemplifies the persistence and perseverance that characterize a prophet.

---

[13] See J. K. Elliott, "Anna's Age (Luke 2:36–37)," *Novum Testamentum* 30 (1988) 100–102.

The other important prophetic characteristic that Anna embodies is that she discerns the propitious time to speak the authentic word. A false prophet feels compelled to speak on every topic at every moment. A genuine prophet discerns the propitious time to speak the word of comfort or the word of challenge. By means of diligent prayer a prophet attunes her or his ear to God's voice. Anna waits eighty-four years for the moment when God's salvation is revealed in the person of Jesus. And then she doesn't stop speaking of this definitive revelation—to any who will listen, she persists in announcing God's new act of redemption.

Scholars often call attention to the pairing of women and men characters in the Gospel of Luke. The list includes Zechariah and Elizabeth; Simeon and Anna; the healing on a sabbath of a woman bent over (13:10–17) and the healing on a sabbath of a man with dropsy (14:1–6). But there are significant differences in the way Luke portrays Anna compared to his depiction of Simeon. Whereas Luke devotes thirteen verses to a detailed interchange between Simeon and Mary, culminating in Simeon's canticle (which is recited by many Christians at compline each night), he gives Anna only a brief three verses. There is no canticle from her that continues to be sung in the church's liturgy, but only the third-person report that "she spoke about the child to all who were looking for the redemption of Jerusalem" (2:38). Here we see the first instance where Luke silences the voices of women in his Gospel. Beyond the infancy narrative, no woman speaks in the Gospel, except to be corrected (10:38–42; 11:27–28) or disbelieved (24:11).[14] Admittedly, in the Acts of the Apostles, Luke places on Peter's lips at Pentecost the declaration that both "your sons and your daughters shall prophesy" (Acts 2:17, citing Joel 2:28–29), and he tells us that Philip had four daughters who were prophets (Acts 21:9), but he does not preserve for us any of the content of what these female prophets proclaimed. In Luke's presentation, it is Peter and Paul and the male disciples who are entrusted with the role of public proclamation.

Prophet Jesus

The powerful portrayals of female prophets in the infancy narrative prefigure and prepare the way for the prophetic mission of Jesus in the remainder of the Gospel. More than any other evangelist, Luke emphasizes Jesus' role as prophet.[15] When Jesus first announces his mission in the synagogue at

---

[14] See Mary Rose D'Angelo, "Women in Luke-Acts: A Redactional View," *Journal of Biblical Literature* 109 (1990) 441–61. See also Ivoni Richter Reimer, *Women in the Acts of the Apostles: A Feminist Liberation Perspective* (Minneapolis: Fortress, 1995). On Mark's presentation of women, see Susan Miller, *Women in Mark's Gospel* (New York: T&T Clark, 2004).

[15] In the Gospel of Matthew (14:5; 21:11, 46) Jesus is called a prophet, and his words and deeds are said to fulfill those of the prophets who came before him, particularly Isaiah

Nazareth (Luke 4:18–19), he employs the words of the prophet Isaiah (61:1–2) and recalls Elijah's ministry to the widow of Zarephath (Luke 4:25-26) and Elisha's cure of Naaman the Syrian (4:27). Luke then proceeds to portray Jesus' mighty deeds in parallel lines to Elijah and Elisha.[16] The question of Jesus' identity as prophet is central to the discussion about Jesus' relationship to John the Baptist (7:18–35) and to the story of the woman who lavishes great love on Jesus in the home of Simon the Pharisee (7:36–50).[17] Speculating on Jesus' identity, both Herod Antipas (9:7–8) and the crowds (9:18–20) think that "one of the ancient prophets has arisen."

As with all prophets, there is a dual response to Jesus' message and deeds. Those whom he raises up with his liberating vision and his freeing actions praise God and follow Jesus; those whose power, privilege, and status are threatened by his alternate vision of life in the realm of God set themselves in opposition to him. This dual reaction is visible from the first, as Jesus makes his opening declaration of his mission in the synagogue at Nazareth (4:18–19). He first wins approval and amazement (4:22), but then the crowd turns on him, ready to hurl him off a cliff (4:28–29). As the opposition becomes deadly, the theme of Jesus as rejected prophet surfaces as the dominant theological explanation for the crucifixion of Jesus in Luke's Gospel (11:29–32; 13:33–34; 22:64; 24:19, 25, 27).[18]

The figures of Mary, Elizabeth, and Anna have already prepared the way for this message. In various ways, each of these women exemplifies the suffering that a prophet undergoes, even as she knows certainly the truth of what God has revealed to her. Mary, Elizabeth, and Anna are each portrayed as contemplative, entirely devoted to God and to doing what God asks, no matter what the cost. Luke paints these powerful prophetic women in the mold of Israel's prophets, such as Miriam, Deborah, Huldah, and Judith. But at the same time

---

(Matt 1:22; 2:5, 15, 17, 23; 4:14; 5:17; 8:17; 12:17; 13:35; 21:4; 24:15; 26:56; 27:9). There are only three allusions to Jesus as prophet in Mark (6:4, 15; 8:28). In the Gospel of John several references to Jesus as prophet occur (1:45; 4:19, 29; 6:14–15; 7:40–41, 52; 9:17; 12:38). On Jesus in the Johannine tradition, see Sandra Schneiders, *Written that You May Believe. Encountering Jesus in the Fourth Gospel* (rev. edn; New York: Crossroad, 2003).

16 Compare Luke 7:2–10 with 2 Kgs 5:1–14; Luke 7:11–17 with 1 Kgs 17:17–24 and 2 Kgs 4:18–37; Luke 9:10–17 with 2 Kgs 4:42–44. Jesus is also "taken up" into heaven (Luke 9:51; 24:51; Acts 1:9) like Elijah (2 Kgs 2:11). One difference between Jesus and Elijah is that Jesus refuses to "call down fire from heaven" against his opponents (compare Luke 9:54 with 1 Kgs 18:36–38; 2 Kgs 1:9–14).

17 For further discussion of these episodes, see Barbara E. Reid, "Wisdom's Children Justified (Mt. 11.16–19; Lk. 7.31–35)," in *The Lost Coin. Parables of Women, Work, and Wisdom*, ed. Mary Ann Beavis (Biblical Seminar 86; London/New York: Sheffield Academic Press, 2002), 287–305; "The Woman Who Showed Great Love," in *Choosing the Better Part?*, 107–23; "'Do You See this Woman?': A Liberative Look at Luke 7.36–50 and Strategies for Reading Other Lukan Stories Against the Grain," in *A Feminist Companion to Luke*, ed. Amy-Jill Levine (FCNTEC 3; New York: Sheffield Academic Press, 2002), 106–20.

18 Reid, *Taking Up the Cross*, 87–121.

he does not encourage Christian women to take up this mission. Luke who
sees salvation history in clearly delineated epochs of the Law and the Prophets,
then the new age that dawns with Jesus and his followers (16:16), envisions
leadership roles in the Jesus movement as firmly entrusted to the male disciples. Yet he cannot ignore the reality that women such as Lydia and Prisca exercised their leadership as heads of house churches (Acts 16:40; 18:1–4, 18–28;
cf. Rom 16:3–5), instructed eloquent preachers (Acts 18:26), and continued
prophesying faithfully (Acts 2:17; 21:9).

Conclusion

Many women who try to speak a prophetic word in today's church encounter
opposition, disbelief, and attempts to silence them. In the stories of Elizabeth,
Mary, and Anna in Luke 1–2, there are many aspects that can give hope and
courage to women in a world and church that continue to struggle with patriarchal authority. Each of these female prophets is portrayed as contemplative,
as being well attuned to the word of God, and utterly committed to acting on
that word, not for themselves alone, but for the salvation of the whole community. Each one encounters opposition, silencing, dismissal, yet each persists in
her loyalty to God and to the divine purposes. In this, they also prefigure the
acceptance by the least, and the opposition by the powerful toward prophet
Jesus. These faithful women invite us to reflect on how the prophetic mission of Jesus continues to be embraced today by faithful women, who take to
heart the prophecy of Joel 2:28–29, repeated on Pentecost: "your sons and your
daughters shall prophesy" (Acts 2:17).[19]

---

[19] For further reflection, see Mary Catherine Hilkert, *Naming Grace. Preaching and the
Sacramental Imagination* (New York: Continuum, 1997); Katharine Rhodes Henderson,
God's Troublemakers. How Women of Faith are Changing the World (New York: Continuum,
2006); Dorothee Sölle, *The Silent Cry. Mysticism and Resistance*, trans. Barbara and Martin
Rumscheidt (Minneapolis: Fortress, 2001); Kenneth E. Untener, *The Practical Prophet:
Pastoral Writings* (New York: Paulist, 2007).

Chapter 4

Zechariah's "Benedictus" (Luke 1:68–79): A New Look at a Familiar Text

Leonard J. Maluf

The Benedictus of Zechariah, the father of John the Baptist in the Gospel of Luke, is a familiar text for many Christians, being often recited at Morning Prayer. Most commentators have interpreted Zechariah's utterance (Luke 1:68–79) as a messianic hymn, with a brief allusion to the child John as fore-runner of the Lord in vv. 76–77. What grounds this interpretation is mainly the conviction that the "horn of salvation" in v. 69 can only be a reference to Jesus, Messiah, and descendant of David.[1] A fresh look at the Greek text raises doubts, however, as to whether this interpretation can be sustained. Some features in the first part of the Benedictus are in fact difficult to rec-oncile with an interpretation of the text that sees here a Christian Messiah, and the hymnic character of Zechariah's utterance is also less evident than is frequently assumed.[2] Since my interpretation differs from conventional renderings of the Benedictus at a number of points, I will offer my own (fairly literal) translation of the Lukan text, and then proceed with com-mentary that explains my translation choices, while at the same time pro-viding a new understanding of the passage as a whole. To set our text in its proper context, I include the immediate literary framework—a single gospel verse at each end.

---

[1] Richard J. Dillon, "The Benedictus in Micro- and Macrocontext," *Catholic Biblical Quarterly* 68 (2006) 457–80. For Dillon, not only does the identification of the "horn of salvation" with Jesus require no proof, it hardly needs to be stated (note his oblique language when he discusses Luke 1:69 on p. 462). The author provides a fairly comprehensive summary of scholarly discussion on the Benedictus in the last century or more.

[2] Ibid., passim, takes absolutely for granted that the Lukan text is a song or hymn. In doing so, he follows a well-established pattern in the commentary tradition, only recently show-ing some signs of weakening: cf. Warren Carter, "Zechariah and the Benedictus (Luke 1, 68–79). Practicing what he preaches," *Biblica* 69 (1988) 239–47, esp. 241; Albert Vanhoye, "L'intérêt de Luc pour la prophétie en Lc 1,76; 4,16–30 et 22,60–65," in *The Four Gospels 1992*, ed. Frans Van Segbroeck *et al.*; 3 vols (FS Frans Neirynck; BETL 100; Leuven: Peeters, 1992), 2.1529–48, esp. 2.1529.

Zechariah's Benedictus (Luke 1:68–79)

⁶⁷And Zechariah his [John's] father was filled with the Holy Spirit and he
prophesied, saying:
    ⁶⁸Blessed is [the Lord]³ the God of Israel,
    because he visited and made redemption for his people,
    ⁶⁹and he raised up a horn of salvation for us
    in the house of his servant David,
    ⁷⁰as he spoke through the mouth of the holy ones,
    his prophets from of old—
    ⁷¹*a salvation from our enemies*
    and from the hand of all who hate us—
    ⁷²to show mercy to our fathers,
    and to remember his holy covenant,
    ⁷³the oath he swore to Abraham our father, to grant us—
    ⁷⁴without fear, delivered from the hand of our enemies—
    to serve him ⁷⁵in holiness and righteousness before him
    all of our days.

    ⁷⁶But *you too*, child, will be called prophet of the Most High,
    for you will go before the Lord to prepare his ways,
    ⁷⁷to give his people knowledge *of a salvation,*
    in the forgiveness of their sins,
    ⁷⁸through the bowels of the mercy of our God,
    in which the Daystar from on high will visit us,
    ⁷⁹to shine on those who sit in darkness and the shadow of death,
    to guide our feet into the way of peace.
⁸⁰Now the child grew and became strong in spirit, and he was in the wilderness till the day of his manifestation to Israel.

Introductory Observations

I acknowledge, first of all, that the graphical devices I have employed (such
as indentation, capitalization, italicization, division into poetic lines and strophes) do not stem from the author of the Gospel. At least the oldest manuscripts we possess of the Greek text of the Benedictus (the original autograph
has not survived) lack any hint of poetic articulation or versification. I have
presented the text in poetic format only because usage in the Church's liturgy,
where its function and format have been aligned to that of Old Testament

---

³ The word "Lord" is absent here from a third-century papyrus (P4) and the fifth-century
Washington Codex.

psalms, has habituated most readers to reading the Benedictus in this way. For convenience of reference, I have also included standard verse numbering as it appears in printed Bible editions.

There is no space here to enter into a full-length discussion of the literary genre of the Benedictus, except to suggest that the passage is not so evidently a song, hymn, psalm, or even prayer as most commentators assume (partly, no doubt, under the influence of long-standing liturgical usage).[4] Unlike most of the Old Testament texts used as "canticles" in the Catholic Office of Lauds, a "song" genre for Zechariah's utterance is not supported by any indication in the text of Luke. What the Gospel text says explicitly is that Zechariah "spoke, blessing God..." (1:64), and that he "prophesied, saying..." (1:67). In its original context, then, the passage is more *prophetic proclamation* than it is song, hymn, or prayer.

As for the articulation of the Benedictus into two parts (vv. 68–75; 76–79), even this principal division is not indicated graphically in the two great fourth-century Bible manuscripts—Vaticanus (B) and Sinaiticus (S). As we shall see, however, it is eminently justified by the sense. Each of the two parts comprises a single lengthy sentence, with multiple subordinate clauses, reproducing the complex syntax of the Greek original. Hence the presentation of the passage in two parts will serve the clarity of my commentary.

The framing verses in its Gospel context (Luke 1:67, 80) are rarely considered pertinent to the meaning of the Benedictus, which is often assumed by scholars to be a pre-existent "hymn," inserted belatedly into its present place in the Gospel narrative.[5] A different perspective emerges under my own assumption that Luke composed the words of Zechariah precisely for the context in which they appear.[6] The emphasis on Zechariah as "father" of John the Baptist in v. 67 is then seen as connected to the first part of the Benedictus, where the "fathers" of Israel are explicitly and emphatically recalled (vv. 72–73). Similarly, v. 80, which immediately follows the Benedictus, is seen to connect

---

[4] For a fuller discussion of the genre of the Benedictus, see chapter two of my thesis extract, *The Prophecy of Zechariah: A Study of the Benedictus in the Context of Luke-Acts* (Rome: Pontifical Gregorian University, 2000), 43–68.

[5] Raymond E. Brown, *The Birth of the Messiah: A Commentary on the Infancy Narratives of Matthew and Luke*, rev. edn (New York: Doubleday, 1993 [orig. 1977]), 347. The hypothesis did not originate with Brown, and it has been repeated in many Lukan commentaries that have appeared since he wrote.

[6] That the apostolic speeches in Acts are largely Lukan compositions, created precisely for the narratives in which they appear, is a widely held view today. Scholarly opinion may some day arrive at a comparable assumption regarding the "canticles" of Luke's infancy narrative. In fact, since the beginning of the twentieth century, there have always been some who thought that Luke wrote the Benedictus; see Adolf Harnack, "Das Magnificat der Elisabeth (Luc.1, 46–55) nebst einigen Bemerkungen zu Luc. 1 und 2," *Sitzungsberichte der königlich preussischen Akademie der Wissenschaften zu Berlin* 27 (1900) 1–19, esp. 15–19. Harnack's arguments in favor of Lukan authorship of the Magnificat and Benedictus have never been effectively refuted, in my opinion.

especially with its second part, since the verse speaks only of the "child," who has been addressed in v. 76, and whose prophetic role and mission is presented in the following verse.

This literary framework of the Benedictus thus provides some support for a reading of the text as moving from consideration of Israel's past, represented by the fathers of Israel (and father Zechariah), to a prophetic glimpse of Israel's future, represented by the child John, who will be forerunner to Christ and prophet to a new generation of Israel, at the dawn of the messianic age. The turning point comes between v. 75 and 76, where we can imagine a dramatic pause, when the priest–prophet turns from musing on the nostalgic past of Israel and the fathers so as to direct his gaze forward—toward a new and wonderful future for this same people to be inaugurated by his son John.

A similar turn from orientation toward the past to forward-looking expectation occurs in the broader context of the Benedictus, namely, in the story of the birth, circumcision, and naming of John (Luke 1:57–66), to which the Benedictus is appended. In this story, neighbors and relatives of the devout priestly family cling to the patterns of their past when they rush to call Elizabeth's newborn son "Zechariah," after his father. The mutually supportive interventions of the child's parents, however, override this conventional choice, so as to comply with a revelation from heaven, made prior to his conception (Luke 1:13), which assigned to the child a new name and destiny: "John shall be his name." This turning from instinctive nostalgia for the old to embrace the heaven-inspired new in the story of John's birth and naming is then reflected in the twofold structure of the Benedictus.

The First Part of the Benedictus

Such an overview of the Benedictus in context as I have just sketched assumes that the first part of the text is about the past history of Israel, understood as the product of divine concern and salvation for a chosen nation. Because of this divine care, the people of Israel have then been free to devote themselves in return—in holiness and righteousness—to the daily worship of their God. What is portrayed in this reading of Luke 1:68–75 is *the salvation of the righteous.*

Previous commentators, however, have routinely taken these verses to refer instead to Christ and his saving mission—an almost universally accepted reading that rests primarily on what has appeared to be a solid, albeit veiled, messianic reference in v. 69.[7] Indeed, once the identification of the "horn of salvation" in the House of David with Jesus is assumed or accepted, the

---

[7] I. Howard Marshall, *The Gospel of Luke* (NIGTC; Exeter: Paternoster, 1978), 91 ("a mighty Savior"); cf. Brown, *The Birth of the Messiah,* 371.

interpretation of this verse exercises a decisive influence on the way the remaining verses of Luke 1:68–75 (the first part of the Benedictus) are read and interpreted. Taken in themselves, however, these verses may be taken to provide a thematically focused summary of Israel's past—amounting at the same time to a multidimensional portrait of the people's traditional "salvation" understanding, which formed the basis of its historical faith and religious practice.

The christological reading of this part of the text, on the other hand, produces the strange result that the Messiah is alluded to and his mission described in vv. 68–75—*prior to the reference to his forerunner in v. 76!* The logic of the text as a whole suffers in this traditional reading, even if the expectation that the text will follow a strictly chronological scheme may appear unnecessary. A fresh look at what Luke is doing in the first part of the Benedictus is in any case possible. Might v. 69 not best be understood as a direct reference to a saving intervention by Israel's God that took place in Old Testament times? Is the interpretation of the "horn of salvation" as a reference to Christ quite as self-evident as is usually assumed?

The present essay will address these questions in a three-step process. First, I will show why a christological reading of Luke 1:69 is unlikely from an exegetical point of view, and indeed problematic for a Christian reader. Second, I will propose an alternative reading of this verse: the "horn of salvation" is the Davidic House or Dynasty itself, viewed as emblematic of the God of Israel's ongoing, saving commitment to his people.[8] And third, commenting briefly on the text as translated and presented earlier, I will show how well the other verses of this part of the Benedictus can be shown to fit in with a non-christological reading of v. 69: in the context of praise and proclamation, they together survey Israel's past history in such a way as to highlight a salvation-type common to a number of this story's crucial moments—a type that stands in partial, though pointed, contrast to the "salvation" of the Christian era portrayed in vv. 76–79.[9]

---

[8] The perspective of Luke 1:68–75 would thus deal with salvation-history, not christological prophecy. We may compare the Lukan review of Israelite history in Acts 7:2–53.

[9] In her insightful essay "Pugnacious Precursors and the Bearer of Peace: Jael, Judith, and Mary in Luke 1:42" (*Catholic Biblical Quarterly* 68 [2006] 436–56), Brittany E. Wilson has argued cogently that a similar contrast to the one I detect (as developed by Luke in the Benedictus) is present in the words addressed to Mary by Elizabeth in Luke 1:42: "Blessed are you among women," when these words are read in their larger narrative context. The Old Testament texts that are echoed in this verse (Judg 5:24 and Jdt 13:18) speak of women warriors in Israel's past who are called "blessed" when they "enact God's will for Israel through violent, even gruesome, means" (p. 442). The author pointedly notes that "whereas Jael and Judith are violent aggressors, Mary is a peaceful listener and doer of God's word" (p. 456). The "new age" dimension of Luke's thinking in his infancy narrative is likewise detected by Wilson in these words of blessing uttered by Elizabeth to Mary, read in their larger context: "Indeed, Mary ushers in a new age, in which women are called most blessed for their acts of peace rather than for their acts of violence" (p. 438). See also the author's apt comments on the second part of the Benedictus, with its message of peace for Israel's future (p. 454).

Moreover, Luke's Benedictus has parallels with Matthew's infancy narrative. If perhaps Luke knew and used Matthew's Gospel, we can regard the Benedictus as containing Luke's profound meditation on Matt 1:21, where the angel of the Lord comments on his name: "you will call his name Jesus, because he will save his people from their sins."[10] This heavenly interpretation of the name of Jesus says what salvation for the messianic era *is*: Luke will create a literary diptych (a two-paneled presentation) that highlights this novel notion of salvation *through the device of contrast* with the salvation idea that informed Israel's regular understanding of its own glorious past (as expressed particularly in its Torah, Prophets, and Writings).

The same use of contrast here at work may also be detected in Luke 4:24–27. Old Testament texts evoked in these words of Jesus in the Nazareth synagogue tell of prophets who were sent to persons outside of Israel. This strange case of Jewish prophets commissioned to act graciously on behalf of Gentiles is highlighted in Luke's retelling through the device of antithesis: Elijah and Elisha were *not* sent to many in Israel who suffered similar afflictions. In Luke 4 it is the contrast with the norm, *not explicit in the Old Testament texts themselves*, that is developed by Luke and that effectively brings out the novelty of the universal messianic mission of Jesus portended by these prophetic stories. Similarly, in Luke 1:68–75, Luke spells out what is only implicit in the Matthean text that establishes the meaning of the name Jesus: "He will save his people (*not from their enemies—as in Old Testament times—but*) *from their sins*" (Matt 1:21). In the three sections that follow I will further develop this idea of the first part of the Benedictus as a foil for highlighting a novel, Christian understanding of salvation: *salvation in the forgiveness of sins*—which will guide the feet of faithful Jews toward the path of peace.[11]

---

[10] In its Gospel context, the Benedictus stands between the story of the circumcision and naming of John and that of Jesus (cf. Luke 1:57–66, 2:21). The prophetic utterance looks back to the one and forward to the other. Luke's use of Matthew has been suggested by various scholars such as William R. Farmer, *The Synoptic Problem: A Critical Analysis*, second edn (Dillsboro, NC: Western North Carolina Press, 1976); and Michael D. Goulder, *Luke: A New Paradigm*, 2 vols (JSNT Supplement 10; Sheffield: JSOT Press, 1989).

[11] The second part of the Benedictus is a powerful expression of the "dawn" (*anatolē⁻*) of a new age of peace. As is well known, the age of Caesar Augustus (cf. Luke 2:1) had been hailed by Roman writers, particularly Virgil, in similarly glowing terms. Remarkable parallels with Luke 1:76–79 in Virgilian literature have yet to be fully explored, such as Virgil's *Culex*, lines 24–41. The paragraph begins with the words: "*Et tu, ... sancte puer*" ("and you, ... holy boy"), addressed to the child Augustus, and goes on to contrast the poem of joy and light about to unfold with those traditional epics that dealt with "Jove's gloomy wars." The parallels here to the two parts of the Benedictus, as interpreted here, are remarkable. Cf. also *Oriens* in line 30 and Luke 1:78! These parallels with Luke 1:76–79 are closer even than those of Virgil's oft-cited fourth Eclogue (4.18–19), which is discussed by Brown, *The Birth of the Messiah*, 566–70.

Is the "Horn of Salvation" (Luke 1:69) an Allusion to Jesus?

This expression is clearly the crux of the interpretation of the Benedictus as a whole, and especially of its first part (Luke 1:68–75). Since the time of Origen, most Christians have interpreted the "horn of salvation" as a self-evident reference to Christ; rarely was trouble taken to justify this identification. Despite this long history of interpretation, the issue of the reference in v. 69 deserves further consideration, for several reasons:

1. Jesus is not referred to elsewhere in the New Testament, or in early Christian literature, as a "Horn of Salvation." It is not, therefore, self-evident that the phrase in question is an early christological title, as many have said. Only if its context in the Benedictus demanded a reference to Jesus here would this interpretive option be compelling.
2. The term "horn" by itself is not normally used by New Testament authors *in connection with Jesus*. The only exception to this observation is Rev 5:6, where the Lamb, standing as it were slaughtered, is said in passing to have seven horns and seven eyes. To be sure, the Lamb here is the risen and glorified Christ. However, the horn imagery is not further developed, and seems in fact to have little echo in the remainder of the passage. In any case, no actual equation is here made between "horn" and Jesus, and there is no reason to suspect that a familiar, early Christian title for Jesus is employed, or even obliquely reflected in this passage.
3. The exact phrase "horn of salvation" (*keras sōtērias*) never occurs *as a personal, messianic reference* in the Old Testament. In the only two (parallel) Greek Old Testament texts where the words appear (2 Sam 22:3; Ps 17[18]:3 LXX), they serve either as a symbolic description of God or as a name by which God is addressed.[12] It is clear, therefore, that Luke did not intend to reproduce an exact Septuagintal usage here: "horn of salvation" cannot logically be taken as a name or description of God in the syntax Luke gives it (*"the God of Israel raised up a horn of salvation [= God] for us"*). The question remains open as to what exactly Luke did intend by this expression; but it is not possible to determine its reference in Luke simply through a study of Old Testament usage of the phrase.
4. The term "horn" (*keras*) as used metaphorically in relevant Old Testament texts derives from the *brute animal world*: it is the fear-provoking "horn" on

---

[12] Strictly speaking, the expression used in the Septuagint is *not* exactly identical to that found in Luke 1:69. In both Old Testament texts, the expression found is not "horn of salvation" (*keras sōtērias*) but "horn of *my* salvation" (*keras sōtērias mou*).

the head of certain mammals, particularly the bull or the rhinoceros.[13] The imagery is that of aggressive strength and (particularly military) might: the power to defeat an enemy by utterly destroying him.[14] It is hardly self-evident that Luke would have seen this as appropriate imagery for the salvation delivered by a Messiah, whose mission he describes in the second part of the Benedictus as bringing peace (1:79; cf. 2:14). Moreover, this mission takes place "through the bowels (*splagchna*) of the mercy of our God" (1:78). Indeed, the Greek term *splagchna*, or "spleen," used here in a metaphorical sense, refers to a very different internal body part, this time taken from the *human world*, and with a symbolism that is antithetical to that of the external hardware atop the head of a bull. In fact, used metaphorically, the term *splagchna* implies the dynamism of heartfelt compassion, which, among other things, inspires movement toward forgiveness, reconciliation, and peace (1:77–79).[15]

5. The fact that the expression "horn of salvation" occurs following the verb "raised up" (Greek *egeirein*) in Luke 1:69 is taken by some to require a personal reference for the expression. Indeed, with God as subject, the verb *egeirein* most frequently has a personal object in the Septuagint and New Testament.[16] This initially plausible objection to my thesis may be met in two complementary ways. First, any person named in this verse is (in my view) David rather than Christ. Second, the continuation of the text does not in fact confirm *a directly personal reference* for the expression "horn of salvation" in Luke 1:69. Normally, when the verb "raised up" has a person as direct object, we expect to find a pronoun—often a relative pronoun—in the immediately following verse (e.g., Acts 3:15, 22; 5:30–31; 13:22) that confirms the personal reference. This pronoun introduces a clause that indicates something further about the person alluded to in the original statement: God raised up X, *who* did such and such a thing, or *to whom* a

---

[13] For the literal sense of the term *keras*, or its verbal equivalents, see especially Exod 21:28–29 LXX. The literal meaning of *keras* also shines through powerfully in Deut 33:17, even though the poetic context here moves the discourse to the level of metaphor.

[14] For this metaphorical use of *keras* and its verbal cognates, see especially Ps 43 (44):5 LXX: *en soi tous echthrous hēmōn keratioumen*, "in you [by your power] we will gore our enemies"; also Deut 33:17; Ps 148:14. These three texts are probably the closest Old Testament parallels to the entire context of Luke 1:69–71.

[15] For the (quite literal) centrality of the term *splagchna* in the second part of the Benedictus, see Maarten J.J. Menken, "The Position of SPLAGCHNIZESTHAI and SPLAGCHNA in the Gospel of Luke," *Novum Testamentum* 30 (1988) 107–14, here 112. Other Lukan texts that employ this root to magnificent effect are Luke 7:13; 10:33 (with "the Samaritan" as subject); 15:20 (where the implied subject is God). In the New Testament letters the term *splagchna* refers to compassion associated with forgiveness, reconciliation, and peace (Col 3:12–13; Phlm 7; Phil 1:8; 2:1; 1 John 3:17).

[16] In itself, however, the verb *egeirein* in the Septuagint often has a non-personal (or not directly personal) object. See, e.g., Prov 10:12; 11:16; 15:1; 29:22; 1 Esdr 5:44; Jer 28 (51):11 LXX ("*the spirit* of the king of the Medes" is object here, with God [Lord] as subject).

promise was made. The follow-up phrase to v. 69 in the Benedictus (found in v. 71) is instead *a definition of salvation* as "salvation from our enemies and from the hand of all who hate us." This suggests that in v. 69 the expression "horn of salvation" is intended immediately and primarily to evoke (not a person, but) *a salvation type or notion* (associated with, or epitomized by, David and his House), which is then spelled out and defined in v. 71. To paraphrase what is implied in the horn imagery in Luke 1:69, we might then translate the phrase: "a powerful salvation," or better still: "a salvation *of formidable potency*" (and *not* "a mighty Savior," as so often appears in popular translations of the Benedictus).

This argument against a directly personal reference in Luke 1:69 would also undercut the objection that the term "horn" by itself does occur once or twice in Old Testament texts as a personal reference to a future, messianic descendant of David (cf. Ps 131[132]:17 LXX and possibly Ezek 29:21). The objection is based on fact, but not quite relevant to our passage. In these Old Testament texts, where the term "horn" patently refers to *a personal descendant of David*, such a personal reference is also confirmed by an immediately appended clause containing a pronoun with backward reference. Thus, Ps 131[132]:17-18a LXX reads: "There I will make a horn to sprout for David; I have prepared a lamp for my anointed. His enemies I will clothe with shame." Here we note the possessive pronoun "his" (in the phrase "*his* enemies"), which confirms the personal reference, through the images of a horn and a lamp, in the previous verse. By way of contrast, no such pronoun follows the reference to "horn of salvation" in Luke 1:69. Instead, the expression is expanded upon through a *definition of a salvation-type* in v. 71. Once again, therefore, Old Testament usage is not a decisive guide for the interpretation of "horn of salvation" in the syntax of Zechariah's Benedictus.

More even than by any of the facts and arguments mentioned earlier, a personal allusion *to Jesus* in Luke 1:69 becomes highly problematic when v. 71—which defines divine deliverance as "salvation from our enemies and from the hand of all who hate us"—is properly seen as explaining the salvation mentioned in v. 69, and perhaps also the "redemption" of v. 68.[17] It is extremely unlikely that Luke would have viewed the words of v. 71 as an apt definition of

---

[17] The approach of those who interpret this part of the Benedictus as referring to Christ has traditionally been to rely on the hypothesis of pre-Lukan origin or to spiritualize the "enemies" from whom Jesus is supposed to save. There is, however, nothing in the text that supports such spiritualization. On the contrary, if we suppose that Luke himself is the author of the text, he is using a whole cluster of conventional terms and concepts that relate to very real experiences of salvation in the Old Testament, where the enemies were real and human—dehumanized, to be sure, in some parts of the literature, but not spiritualized.

the salvation Jesus came to deliver. But is there a viable alternative reading of
Luke 1:69? It is to this question that I now turn.

Luke 1:69 as a Reference to David and his House

The verse ("and he raised up a horn of salvation for us in the house of his
servant David") is intriguing, because in one sense it contains no translation
difficulty at all: every Greek word in the sentence is perfectly lucid as to its
"meaning," and the syntax of the phrase is likewise without apparent interpretive challenge. It is the *reference* of the verse and its constitutive parts (not its
meaning) that remains open to divergent interpretive possibilities. If, however,
we take seriously the fact that this part of the Benedictus is in praise of the
"God of Israel" (v. 68a), then it makes good sense to see Luke 1:69 as *a continuation of a recital of benefits bestowed by their God on this people, Israel,* of whom the
priest Zechariah is a natural representative in Luke's narrative. The use of
aorist-tense verbs (generally employed for past narrative) throughout the first
part of the Benedictus suggests—if it does not quite demand—this orientation
toward Israel's history.[18] And since it may be argued that "salvation" is the main
theme of the text as a whole, we are led to expect in particular *the benefits of
divine salvation to Israel* (in accordance with the definition of salvation given in
v. 71) as the text's primary focus.[19]

My proposal, then, is that the reference in Luke 1:69 is to David himself and
his house, or dynasty, viewed as a benefit given by God to Israel—a media-
tion of divine "salvation" from enemies that threatened the people's existence
at a crucial moment in their history in the early days of the Israelite monarchy. To clinch the validity of this reading would require an exposition of the
Benedictus, in all of its parts as they relate to v. 69, read with this understanding. Such a closer reading will be previewed in a third step later, where I will
treat the text's opening verses in some detail. At this stage of my argument, I
focus more directly on the particular verse in question and on its syntax: can
Luke 1:69 itself be taken to refer to an important moment in the history of
Israel when the people's God intervened through the prophetic word (cf. v. 70)

---

[18] The main verbs in the second part of the Benedictus, on the other hand, are all in the
future tense. I am assuming here that the well-known text-critical problem in v. 78 is
resolved in favor of the future reading: *episkepsetai* ("will visit"). So, rightly, Dillon, "The
Benedictus," 467, n. 25, and many other commentators. The idea of "prophetic aorists"
in vv. 68–69 is an approach taken by those who already assume that the first part of the
Benedictus relates to Christ. But the prophetic aorist approach hardly represents the most
natural reading of the text, and it also suggests a pre-Lukan origin of the Benedictus, for
which there is no historical or documentary evidence.

[19] For "salvation" as the main theme of the Benedictus, see François Rousseau, "Les
Structures du Benedictus (Luc 1.68–79)," *New Testament Studies* 32 (1986) 268–82, especially 282 n. 16.

to establish a dynastic entity that could provide "salvation" for Israel, a bulwark against enemies that threatened its national existence? I think that the following points deserve consideration:

1. Luke views David in a variety of ways, *and not uniquely as an ancestor, prophet, or even type of Christ.*[20] On more than one occasion in his Acts of the Apostles, Luke even goes so far as to draw an explicit contrast between David and Jesus (cf. Acts 2:25–36; 13:36–37). In terms of his positive evaluation of David, it is crucial above all to recognize that, for Luke, David *has a salvation-historical role that stands on its own* and that does not involve specific reference or orientation to Christ—except perhaps in terms of large salvation-historical patterns, which might also involve contrast. Non-christological assessments of David occur in Acts 7:45–46 (David's role concerning the "tent of witness" and the temple) and especially in Acts 13:22, 36 (David as implicated in the history of God's special care for the people of Israel, which began with the time of their sojourn in the land of Egypt). In the context of Acts 13:22 David is said to have been chosen by God *to do all his will.* This means that David served God's purposes for his people, Israel, in his own time (cf. Acts 13:36), which according to the biblical story followed the era of the Judges and of Saul (cf. Acts 13:19–21) in the history of Israel. The perspective in this Acts sermon, like that for which we are arguing in the first part of the Benedictus, involves salvation-history. Luke moves on then, in the following verse of Acts (13:23), skipping over a thousand-year period, to highlight the Savior, Jesus, "of this man's [David's] posterity," whom God has now (i.e., in Paul's time) brought to Israel. Notice that in Acts 13:23 Luke explicitly refers to Jesus, the Savior of Israel, as coming from this man's (David's) seed. In the following verse, we find the Greek term "his" (*autou*) that picks up on the personal reference to Jesus in 13:23 ("Before *his* coming, John had preached a baptism of repentance"). Nothing like this clarity of personal reference, with supporting syntax of subsequent reference (using a Greek pronoun), occurs in Luke 1:69–70. Instead, v. 69 is best read as a parallel to the perspective *of the previous verse* in Acts (13:22), where the reference is *to David himself and his own role in salvation-history*, long before the time of John the Baptist and Jesus.

2. The prepositional phrase "in the house of his servant David" is often rendered by commentators "from the house of his servant David." The Greek preposition *en* ("in"), however, hardly carries the meaning "from." It appears therefore that commentators who paraphrase in this way are trying to make the text say something here that it does not say. In other words, such a translation wants to convey the idea that v. 69 speaks of a particular descendant

---

[20] Mark L. Strauss, *The Davidic Messiah in Luke-Acts: Promise and Its Fulfillment in Lukan Christology* (JSNT Supplement 110; Sheffield: Sheffield Academic Press, 1995).

of David, though it is not clear that it does so. The Greek language is quite capable of expressing the meaning "from" (using *apo*, Acts 13:23; Luke 2:4; or *ek*, Luke 1:27; 2:4), but that is not what Zechariah actually says in our verse. Only if we assume in advance that the "horn of salvation" is a reference to Jesus are we inclined to thus revise the text in paraphrase. My proposal is that in this context the preposition *en* should be given its normal rendering, but with the somewhat uncommon sense: "consisting in." Although this usage of the preposition *en* is unusual, remarkably it occurs again in the second part of the Benedictus itself: "a salvation (consisting) in the forgiveness of their sins" (v. 77).[21] This meaning of *en* is attested elsewhere in the New Testament as well.[22]

On this understanding, the verse as a whole is thus properly rendered: "And he raised up for us a horn of salvation (consisting) in the house (or dynasty) of his servant David." The most pertinent Old Testament background text here is the last part of 1 Chr 17:10 LXX: "Moreover, I declare to you that the Lord will build you a house." These words are to be spoken through the mouth of God's holy prophet Nathan to God's servant, David (cf. 1 Chr 17:4), and the close association between David himself and his House is then echoed in the king's prayer: "Who am I, O Lord God, and what is my house, that you have brought me thus far?" (1 Chr 17:16 and cf. 17:22-27). In fact, these references occur in a chapter where numerous themes echoed in the early verses of the Benedictus appear, including that of the destruction of Israel's enemies.[23] As noted earlier, the perspective of Luke 1:69 is very close to that found, differently expressed, in Acts 13:22: "and when he had removed him (Saul), he raised up David to be their king; of whom he said in testimony: 'I have found in David the son of Jesse a man after my heart, who will do all my will.'"

---

[21] In both v. 69 and v. 77, there is a similar pattern in the Greek: verb + accusative noun + *sōtērias* ("of salvation") + dative word/phrase + *en* ("consisting in") + dative noun + genitive phrase.

[22] A similar usage appears in Eph 2:15 (*en dogmasin* = "consisting in ordinances"), and perhaps 1 Cor 4:20 ("consisting in speech...consisting in power"). For this meaning of the Greek preposition *en*, see Frederick W. Danker, *A Greek-English Lexicon of the New Testament and Other Early Christian Literature*, third edn (Chicago: University of Chicago Press, 2000), 330 (*en* as "marker of specification or substance").

[23] As is well known, 1 Chr 17 closely parallels 2 Sam 7, which can also be regarded as Old Testament background for Luke 1:69. However, the idea of the Lord building a "house" for David is most explicit in 1 Chr 17:10, and the phrase that contains these words does not, in fact, appear in the parallel verse in the Greek of 2 Sam (2 Sam 7:11). Moreover, the specific verses regarding David's *son* in this passage (1 Chr 17:11–14), and in the parallel verses of 2 Sam 7, are *not* echoed in Luke 1:69, though elsewhere in Luke, where the reference is to Jesus, parts of these verses, or the parallel verses in 2 Sam 7, are indeed alluded to by Luke (cf. Luke 1:32–33 and 2 Sam 7:12, 16). We can thus say that Luke distinguishes carefully in these Old Testament texts between what is said about David and his House, on the one hand, and prophecies made, in an isolated group of verses, that relate to *a specific son of David and to his "eternal" reign*, on the other. Only the latter are applied by Luke to Jesus.

3. One last feature of Luke 1:69 would benefit from closer attention, because its implications are commonly ignored in the commentaries. It is the small Greek pronoun *hēmin* ("for us"), whose grammatical meaning is perfectly clear, but where once again we find a problem of *reference*. Since most Christians encounter the Benedictus in the context of liturgical use, the "us" in this verse is spontaneously taken as a self-reference to the Christian community. Such a reference makes little sense, however, if the verse is read in its context in the Gospel of Luke. Indeed, in its Lukan context the speaker is the Jewish priest Zechariah, who would naturally represent the people whose God is being praised in this solemn prophetic utterance. Zechariah the priest could therefore refer to "us" as the beneficiary of the protection afforded by the "horn of salvation," the Dynasty of King David, raised up by God for the salvation of Israel. This solidarity of a Jewish "us" that transcends generations and that unites the present with the past appears in at least one other Lukan text, since the Sadducees later say to Jesus: "Teacher, Moses wrote *for us*" (*hēmin*: Luke 20:28). This Jewish solidarity occurs with fair frequency also in the Old Testament, particularly in liturgical or covenant-renewal contexts, where the community of Israel implicitly acknowledges sharing its identity as a people with that of its ancestral past (Exod 12:27; 13:14–15; Deut 6:20–25; 26:5–10; Josh 24:5–7). The term "us" in Luke 1:69 therefore serves as an equivalent of "Israel" and "his people" in v. 68.[24]

Points made thus far establish the *possibility* of reading Luke 1:69 in a salvation-historical perspective, as a reference to the time of David—a time of divinely provided security (salvation) for Israel through the Davidic house or dynasty. This possibility, however, cannot stand on its own. Only if the verse, thus understood, makes good sense in the context of the Benedictus as a whole, and especially of its first part, would this interpretation invite more serious consideration. In the next and final section of my essay, I will illustrate how such a demonstration would proceed through a more detailed commentary on the opening verses of the Benedictus, read in this perspective.

The Benedictus: An Analysis of Its Opening Verses

The text begins with a formula that introduces the two parties in covenant relationship, God and Israel. The genitive construction ("the God of Israel") already

---

[24] A similar sequence of equivalent terms occurs in the second part of the Benedictus and in many Old Testament texts as well. See Hos 11:1–2: "When *Israel* was a child, I loved him, and out of Egypt I called *my son*. The more I called *them*, the more they went away from me." The sequence in Hosea is *Israel* → *my son* → *them*. In the opening verses of the Benedictus (Luke 1:68–69), we find *Israel* → *his people* → *us*.

sums up God's fundamental commitment to his people, which will be developed in the following verses. Although the words "Blessed [be, or is] the God of Israel," or a similar formula, are found in the Old Testament, most notably as an appendage to four of the smaller Psalm "books" that make up the whole Psalter (Pss 40:14[41:13]; 71:18[72:18]; 88:53[89:52], 105:48 [106:48] LXX), Luke places them in an overall syntax that more closely resembles comparable expressions *in narrative portions of the Greek Old Testament.* Most pertinently, the opening phrase of the Benedictus echoes the usage found in Exod 18:10 and in 1 Kgs 1:48.

In the first comparable text, Jethro, priest and father-in-law of Moses, exclaims: "Blessed [be] the Lord, who has delivered you out of the hand of the Egyptians" (Exod 18:10). Since Luke 1:68b ("he visited and made redemption for his people") most likely refers—and not merely alludes—to the Exodus story, the parallel of 1:68a with this Exodus text is remarkable indeed; it differs only in that Zechariah is more removed in time from the original event and is therefore giving a more comprehensive overview of Israel's salvation story than was possible for Jethro in the framework of Exodus. I therefore translate v. 68b: "he visited and made redemption for his people" rather than "he *has* visited...," which would suggest an event of the *recent* past.[25]

In another text, 1 Kgs 1:48, a similar formula is used by David in his last hours of life, confirming that God has indeed built him a House, in accordance with his promise (cf. 1 Chr 17:10), by allowing him to see his son Solomon firmly established on his throne: "Blessed [be the] Lord the God of Israel, who has given today from my seed [one] to sit on my throne, and my eyes witness it." The opening verse of the Benedictus thus echoes Old Testament texts in which Israel's God is praised for his saving interventions—at the time of the Exodus, as well as at the time of the rise of David's house (cf. Luke 1:69).

The second part of Luke 1:68 gives the first of a series of motive clauses, explaining why Israel's God is praised and glorified: *because he visited and made redemption for his people.* The words "visited" and "redemption" are not accidental. Both are *key words* whose roots are found in the Greek translation of the story of the Exodus from Egypt as told in the Hebrew Scriptures (primarily the Book of Exodus) and that epitomize *two distinct moments* of this divine saving intervention that gave birth to Israel as a people.

God's "visit" is the event of his *taking notice of his people* in the distress of their enslavement to the Egyptian Pharaoh. Both God's "visit" to (or "taking notice

---

[25] A long discussion could be devoted to the nuances of English usage in translating Greek aorist verbs (mostly used for past narrative). I would simply note here that the translation of the Magnificat cannot be used as a decisive guide for how the apparently comparable aorist verbs in the Benedictus should be rendered. The Benedictus is about "the God of Israel," whereas Mary speaks in praise of God *her Savior.* By Zechariah's time, Israel's relationship with God is centuries old, and hence the aorist verbs used by the pious priest may require different treatment in translation than those found in the Magnificat that allude to recent events in the life of Mary.

of") his people (the cognitive dimension of the event, which precedes God's active intervention) and the great redemptive act itself are foretold to the people of Israel by "God's holy ones, his prophets from of old" (Luke 1:70)—in this case the patriarch Joseph (cf. Gen 50:24 LXX), Moses, and Aaron (Exod 3:16; 6:6–7). (Note how the pieces of the first part of the Benedictus are already beginning to come together to form a coherent whole, based closely on the story of Israel as told in the Jewish Scriptures.) The cycle that goes from God's announcing through his holy one (Joseph) that he would "visit" his people (Gen 50:24) and the acknowledgement by the people that God had in fact followed through on this "visit" (Exod 4:31)[26] is already complete in the story of Exodus before the theme of *redemption* is broached for the first time (Exod 6:6).

This theme of redemption is similarly introduced *by a prophetic word* (Exod 6:6; cf. Luke 1:70) prior to its eventual execution by God and acknowledgment by Israel (Exod 14:30–31). The tendency of most commentators to amalgamate the two verbal expressions in Luke 1:68, as though they were parallel references to the same specific event, is mistaken: instead, the word "and" (*kai*) here indicates a syntax of proper coordination, and the references are to two distinct moments within the overall story of the Exodus—God's taking notice of his people in their slavery and distress, and God's subsequent mighty act of deliverance of Israel through the waters of the Red Sea.

A similar inclination to amalgamate is found in most commentaries on Luke 1:69, which is understood as interpreting the preceding phrase (God has visited and redeemed his people *by raising up a horn of salvation*). Instead, the *kai* ("and") that introduces v. 69 is likewise best understood as making a proper coordination: the verse moves on to speak of a later phase of Israel's history, which likewise involved a divine saving intervention. This time God's salvation was mediated by David and his House, as foretold to Israel through the mouth of an anonymous holy prophet: "The Lord has spoken concerning David: 'By the hand of my servant David I will save my people from the hand of the Philistines'" (2 Sam 3:18 LXX). Since much of this essay has already focused on Luke 1:69, I will move forward now to the following verse.

I have already hinted at the importance of v. 70 as an integral part of the Benedictus, with its reference to the holy prophets through whom, in the Old Testament books, God regularly announced his future saving interventions (cf. Isa 43:12). Commentators have too hastily assumed that because prophecy and fulfillment is involved here the context must be christological; hence v. 70

---

[26] Note how this acknowledgment of God's visit to Israel in Exod 4:31 leads immediately to the worship of God, which is the theme of v. 75 in the Benedictus. This "visitation" is also distinct from the "visit" of God predicted for the future in the second part of the Benedictus. The Benedictus is thus a tale of two divine visitations, one referred to by an aorist (past) tense verb, and one by a future. Luke knows also of a third divine visitation, when God "visited" to take a people to himself from among the Gentiles, as James of Jerusalem acknowledges in Acts 15:14.

is often taken to confirm a christological reading of v. 69. This is a mistake, based on a lack of attentive reading of the Old Testament texts that are Luke's primary guides in this verse. The use of the prophetic voice to foretell divine interventions is (in Luke's understanding) by no means an exclusively christological phenomenon. The Old Testament is full of stories of such prophetic announcements, *complete with the narrative of their fulfillment in the history of Israel itself*. Moreover, a similar perspective appears in Acts 7:17, which recounts the fulfillment of God's promise to Abraham to give his descendants the Promised Land (Gen 17:8).

In particular, the events of God's "visit" to Israel, God's "redemption" of Israel, and God's supplying Israel with a "horn of salvation" in the Davidic House (cf. Luke 1:68–69) are in each case anticipated in the biblical story by a prophetic word. Joseph, Moses, Aaron, an anonymous prophet, and Nathan are specific, prophetically inspired persons involved in these concrete instances. None of them is mentioned by name in the Benedictus, because it is the *theme* of God's prophetic word preceding God's saving action as such that interests Luke here. Similarly, none of the historical "enemies" of Israel is named (such as Egypt or the Philistines), since it is the general theme that is important for Luke. Whereas salvation for Israel in the pre-Christian era involved the destruction of Israel's enemies,[27] for the messianic age *it is from sin* that those are saved who sit in darkness and in the shadow of death, and this salvation leads to the way of peace (Luke 1:78–79).

The focus on the "mouth" of God's holy prophets (v. 70) echoes in particular the story of Moses being called to his prophetic role in Exod 4. In Exod 4:10–16 God responds by challenging Moses' reluctance to embrace the prophetic task: "Who has made a human being's mouth? Who makes him mute, or deaf, or seeing, or blind? Is it not I, the Lord? Now therefore, go, and I will be with your mouth and teach you what you shall speak" (Exod 4:11–12). The passage may be read in its entirety for full effect, but a rich background for our New Testament story already appears in these two verses. God is the one who makes mute (cf. Zechariah in Luke's infancy story) and who will open the mouth of his prophet to proclaim his salvation (Luke 1:64; cf. Ezek 3:27).

The importance for Luke of the theme of prophetic announcement that precedes God's great saving interventions is further confirmed by the opening Greek phrase in Luke 1:76 (*kai su de, paidion*), which is usually mistranslated to read simply: "And you, child..." (e.g., NRSV and NAB). As Albert Vanhoye has

---

[27] While this theme appears in numerous Old Testament texts, it is stated with extraordinary clarity and pith in the Wisdom of Solomon: "This was the expectation of your people: the salvation of the righteous [nation] on the one hand, and the destruction of [its] enemies, on the other" (Wis 18:7). Note that this concept explicitly involves the salvation *of the righteous*, which, together with its many associated notions, stands in striking contrast to the salvation *for sinners* that is the subject of Luke 1:76–79.

rightly observed,[28] the text should rather be rendered: "But you *too*, child..." The linking function is carried in this verse by the Greek particle *de* ("and," or more probably "but"). The mildly adversative connotation reflects the fact that the salvation to be announced by the prophet John will differ strikingly from that which characterized the Old Testament stories of divine salvation. Since the term *de* is the linking element in the phrase, the *kai* is not coordinative here ("and"), but rather adverbial ("too"): "But you *too*, child, will be called prophet of the Most High."

The implication of v. 76 is that *Luke still has very much in mind the theme of prophetic announcement* from v. 70 when he begins to write the second half of his diptych that is the two-part text of the Benedictus. In Luke's view, John will be the prophet who announces God's new salvation, just as prophets of old regularly mediated the message of salvation prior to God's earlier saving interventions.[29] "Salvation" is not a vague theological abstraction for Luke, but refers rather to specific divine interventions recorded in Scripture. What Paul refers to as "*this* salvation" in Luke's Acts of the Apostles (13:26) is the Christian reality involving the forgiveness of sins, which was prepared for and prophetically proclaimed through the preaching of John (cf. Acts 13:23–24), prophet of the Most High, in Luke's understanding (cf. Luke 1:76–79).

In my analysis, the mention of deliverance from enemies in v. 71 amounts to a definition of the salvation-type common to specific moments of Israel's past history: principally that of the exodus, and that of the establishment of the Israelite monarchy with David.[30] The term "salvation" (*sōtēria*) in this verse is thus in parallel with the idea contained in "made redemption" (v. 68) and in "horn of salvation" (v. 69). The idea of "salvation from enemies" who are threatened by the Davidic horn hardly fits the era and mission of Christ, where *love* of enemies is the new and revolutionary challenge issued to followers of Christ (Luke 6:27–36; cf. Matt 5:31–48; 1 Thess 5:15; Rom 12:17–21; 1 Pet 3:9). On the other hand, the destruction of Israel's enemies is integral to the Old Testament stories of God's saving presence to Israel in its moments of need, as described by the biblical writers. Verse 71 thus epitomizes the way "salvation" was understood in the time before Christ so as better to bring out the novelty of the new salvation (v. 78) proper to the Christian era. A similar contrasting

---

[28] Vanhoye, "L'intérêt de Luc," 1529–31.

[29] This syntactical observation also removes the ground from a common scholarly opinion that sees the two parts of the Benedictus as emanating from two unrelated sources. A unity of authorship for the Benedictus is strongly indicated here, even if my interpretation of the text as a whole remains open for discussion.

[30] Luke 1:69 refers directly to God's gift to Israel of the Davidic House as a bulwark of salvation against the nation's enemies. However, the language used in the verse also reflects phraseology found frequently in the Book of Judges, in connection with leaders raised up by God as "saviors" of Israel (cf. Judg 2:16, 18; 3:9, 15). Hence Luke may also intend a passing allusion to this earlier period of the Judges even as he writes directly about the rise of David and his dynasty (cf. Acts 7:45; 13:19).

diptych of salvation-types, symbolized by the divergent responses of two evildoers hanging one on each side of the crucified Jesus, is dramatically portrayed
toward the end of Luke's Gospel. These two texts, the Benedictus in Luke
1:68–79 and the crucifixion narrative in Luke 23:35–43, contain, respectively,
the first and last clusters of "salvation" terminology found in the Gospel of
Luke.[31]

The final four verses of the first part of the Benedictus (vv. 72–75) can be
regarded together as an expanded view of the salvation events alluded to in
the opening verses. This view now encompasses the prehistory of these events
in the original promise of God to Israel's patriarchs and their aftermath in the
practice of piety and divine worship, still ongoing in the activity of the priest
Zechariah himself (Luke 1:5–10), which was in each case the goal of God's saving interventions on Israel's behalf.

Prior even to the mediated word of God that came to Israel through the
mouth of its holy prophets (v. 70), proclaiming God's imminent saving interventions, was God's ancient and directly communicated covenantal promise to
Abraham and the patriarchs of an abundant posterity and of a homeland for
the nation that their posterity would become (Gen 12:2–3; 15:13–16; 17:4–8).
It is not so much this word of promise, and in particular the oath and promise
to Abraham itself, that is recalled in vv. 72–74a as it is *the remembrance of this
promise* that motivated God's saving intervention at the time of the exodus.
Once again, Luke is inventing nothing here, but simply following the story of
salvation as told in the Jewish Scriptures. In that story, it is the memory of an
original promise to Abraham that is said to motivate God's action at the time
of the Exodus (Exod 2:24; 6:2–4). For the house of David, there is also a kind
of covenant remembering by the God of Israel, this time a covenant made with
David that is acknowledged by Solomon in the context of his great prayer at
the time of the dedication of the temple (1 Kgs 8:23–24). Though the primary
reference in the Benedictus is to the covenant made with Abraham, and therefore to the remembrance of this covenant at the time of the exodus, the theme
of God's remembering his covenant is first introduced (v. 72b) in a slightly
more general way, which may possibly allow for an allusion to the covenant
with David as well.[32]

A similar (perhaps deliberate) ambiguity of reference appears in the theme
of the *worship of God* in vv. 74–75. The primary reference is to the motivation or
goal of God's great act of deliverance in the exodus: this was not only a salvation

[31] For a detailed discussion of Luke 23:35–43 from this perspective, see Maluf, *The Prophecy
of Zechariah*, 74–88.
[32] Verse 72a ("to show [or, showing] mercy to our fathers") seems to be a hinge line, linking the previous verses of the Benedictus with those about to follow. The ambiguity of
the expression "our fathers," which could refer to the patriarchs *or* to the generations of
Israel, or their male representatives, at the time of the exodus and that of the rise of the
Davidic monarchy may thus be intentional.

from humiliating service to Israel's enemies, but also a salvation *for* the worship or service of Israel's God, as the story is told in the Old Testament.[33] But the saving intervention of the Deity that was mediated by the rise of David and his House is also closely connected, in the biblical story, to the worship of God. Indeed, David's son Solomon was to build a house for God where Israel could worship in grand style (2 Sam 7:13), after being liberated from its enemies.[34] By not mentioning either the temple or any of the specific place settings for the worship of God in the Exodus story (such as the mountain or the desert) in Luke 1:74–75, the author of the Benedictus leaves this verse open to evoke the goal of both of the great divine interventions that are referred to in vv. 68–69: God saves his people Israel in general so that they will have the freedom to worship him in holiness and righteousness, as the priest Zechariah is doing in his own time.

But the most important Old Testament background for Luke 1:74–75 is almost certainly a famous incident of Israelite history that took place some time between the two great acts of divine deliverance alluded to in Luke 1:68–69, the time of the entry of Israel into the Promised Land under Joshua. The solemn covenant renewal ceremony that is recorded in Joshua 24 is amply echoed in the language of Luke 1:74–75. Here, the people are put on the spot by Joshua as to whether they will serve the gods of the nations in Canaan or remain faithful to the God of Israel. More than once the people affirm their intention to persevere in the worship of their God, and the incident terminates with a verse differently located in the Septuagint and in the Hebrew text: "And Israel worshipped (served) the Lord all the days of Joshua and all the days of the elders that lived as long as Joshua, and all that knew all the works of the Lord which he worked for Israel" (Josh 24:29 [31]). The closeness of the language here to that of Luke 1:74–75 hardly needs to be stressed.

Conclusion

In an article published four decades ago, Douglas Jones summarized his own comments on the first part of the Benedictus as follows: "The first section of the Benedictus has thus celebrated the coming of the Messiah in terms derived mainly from the Old Testament, and according to ideas and conceptions which

---

[33] See Exod 3:12; 4:23; 7:16; 8:1, 20; 9:1, all of which texts in the LXX contain the Greek term *latreuein* ("to serve/worship"), with God as object, just as in Luke 1:74c.

[34] See the Hebrew of 2 Sam 7:11, and notice the passing allusion to the period of the Judges in this verse. The Greek translation of this verse somewhat confusedly suggests that David himself will build a house for God. The original promise of God is better preserved in the Hebrew text of 2 Sam 7:11, and in the parallel Greek verse in 1 Chr 17:10.

never go beyond the Old Testament hope."[35] The present essay has attempted to supply a reason for this apparent anomaly: the terms in the first part of the Benedictus are derived from the Old Testament, and never go beyond the Old Testament hope, precisely because they are intended to evoke not the messianic era but the story and the notion of salvation that were current in the Old Testament itself. The interpretive crux of this text segment of the Benedictus, as we have seen, is Luke 1:69. This verse is best read as a reference to the rise of David and his House, viewed in the context of the God of Israel's most generous gifts of salvation to his people, announced in advance through the mouth of his holy prophets. In Luke's day this conception of salvation as deliverance from Israel's enemies would have had a nostalgic appeal for many Jews, but would not, in Luke's view, coincide with the most recent revelation mediated through the prophet John the Baptist. For the new messianic era, salvation was to be defined as *salvation (consisting) in the forgiveness of sins*, which leads to reconciliation and peace among peoples.

---

[35] Douglas Jones, "The Background and Character of the Lukan Psalms," *Journal of Theological Studies* 19 (1968) 19–50, here 33.

Chapter 5

The Significance of the Inn for Luke's Infancy Narrative

Nicholas King, S.J.

There is a popular story of a small boy who exacted a terrible vengeance on the producer of the school's nativity play when he was not selected for the starring role of Joseph, but instead had to make do with playing the innkeeper. He brought the entire proceedings to a shuddering halt when Joseph and the heavily pregnant Mary banged on his door asking for a bed for the night, simply by beaming a welcome and saying, "Yes—come on in; there's plenty of room!"

Now that story evidently depends on the traditional translation of a particular expression in Luke 2:7. The Greek phrase *en tō katalymati* has usually been translated "in the inn" (NRSV, NAB, NIV). Hence, "there was no room for them in the inn" is understood as the reason why Jesus was laid in a "feeding-trough" or "manger." Recently, however, there has grown up what we may call a revisionist interpretation: *katalyma* is a place where horses and other animals are unharnessed, and in this sense it can certainly mean an "inn."[1] But Luke has another word at his disposal for "inn," namely *pandocheion*, which is the place to which the Samaritan in Jesus' parable takes the wounded traveler (10:34).[2] So, the argument runs, *katalyma* is not an inn, but the guest room of the house (the meaning of the word in 22:11). On this interpretation, Mary and Joseph were not being left outside in the cold, but given both privacy and warmth in the animals' quarters, because there was no space in the guest room.[3] We are therefore to read this episode not as indicating the suffering and rejection that Jesus' family endured, but as a sign of how well they were received. So established has this view become that an Oxford theologian felt able to say recently, and dismissively, on a British radio program that "no room at the inn" is a "Victorian myth." In fact, it is a good deal older than the reign

---

[1] The related verb *katalyō* means literally "unharness the pack animals," and hence "lodge" or "find lodging" (as in Luke 9:12 and 19:7). In this chapter all biblical translations are mine unless otherwise noted.

[2] Richard A. Horsley, *The Liberation of Christmas: The Infancy Narratives in Social Context* (New York: Continuum, 1989; reprint, Eugene, OR: Wipf & Stock, 2006), 104.

[3] Joel B. Green, *The Gospel of Luke* (NICNT; Grand Rapids: Eerdmans, 1997), 128–29.

of Queen Victoria, since the Vulgate translates the Greek expression *en tō kata-lymati* with the Latin phrase *in diversorio* ("in the inn"). The time has perhaps come to take another look at the translation and significance of the phrase.[4]

In Defense of the Traditional View

On the one other occasion when Luke uses the word *katalyma* (22:11), it clearly means somewhere to dine ("the *katalyma* where I am to eat the Passover with my disciples"). The place is further described (22:12) as *anagaion mega estrōmenon*, which is probably best understood as "a big upstairs room, ready furnished." However, when the word appears in the Septuagint, it is occasionally quite clearly a lodging or inn (Exod 4:24; cf. 1 Macc 3:45). In Jer 14:8 it is a resting-place of some kind; at 1 Sam 1:18 it is a guest room; and in Jer 25:38 (LXX 32:38) it is an animal's lair. So *katalyma* is a rather versatile term, and "inn" seems a perfectly sensible translation as a first attempt in Luke 2:7.

There is a further question: is this "revisionist approach" an appropriate way to understand the text? It seems to me that it shows a lack of sensitivity to what Luke is doing here, and I propose to argue first for an approach based on the history of interpretation—that this is in fact how the community at which Luke's infancy narrative is aimed has, down the centuries, read this phrase; and second, for a placing of this Greek phrase in the wider context of Luke-Acts as a whole, and what Luke is trying to do (following the approach of redaction criticism, if you will).

My first point does not need much defending. I cannot find any evidence for the revisionist reading (= "guest room") until relatively recently. The second is a more interesting point, and I should like to spend the rest of this essay argu-ing that Luke uses chapters 1 and 2 of Luke-Acts rather as a composer will use an overture, to play themes that will appear later, so that they are already to some extent in the hearer's head. One of these themes in the present case is Luke's view that God's Messiah, and his eventual followers, encounter many obstacles and difficulties (Acts 14:22), but that because the Holy Spirit is driv-ing the narrative, everything will in the end be well. This phrase, then, *ouk ēn autois topos en tō katalymati* ("there was no room for them in the inn"), fits precisely into that Lukan theme; and we remember the two evildoers who were crucified with Jesus, how one of them defended Jesus against the other (23:41), using precisely a cognate of the word *topos*: "he has done nothing *atopon* (out of

---

[4] For discussion of this phrase, see Joseph A. Fitzmyer, *The Gospel according to Luke I–IX* (Anchor Bible 28; New York: Doubleday, 1980). 408; Eugene LaVerdiere, "No Room for Them in the Inn," *Emmanuel* 91 (1985) 552–57; A.J. Kerr, "'No Room in the Kataluma,'" *Expository Times* 103 (1991–92) 15–16; J.W. Olley, "God on the Move—A Further Look at *Kataluma* in Luke," *Expository Times* 103 (1991–92) 300–301; Raymond E. Brown, *The Birth of the Messiah*, rev. edn (New York: Doubleday, 1993), 399–401, 670–71.

place)." So what our phrase implies is that Jesus and his parents are powerless in contrast to the apparently effortless power of Augustus and Quirinius.

In Luke 2:7 the gospel writer is suggesting that God always surmounts the obstacles put in place by human beings; and the hearer may already know, or will do by the end of the two-volume work, that the gospel about Jesus will eventually find its way to Rome, of all places. Luke's second volume concludes by narrating how the gospel reaches Rome in the person of Paul, apparently in custody; and the very last word of the whole journey will be *akōlytōs* ("in an unhindered way"): "Paul remained two whole years at his own expense; and he offered hospitality to all those who made their way to him, proclaiming the kingdom of God, and teaching all about the Lord Jesus Christ, with utter openness, unhindered" (Acts 28:30–31).

It is of a piece with this, to be sure, that, as is well known, Luke uses the language of the "faithful remnant" of the Old Testament, particularly in those very thematic songs from the infancy narrative, the Magnificat and the Benedictus, with their emphasis on God's reversal of the way the powerful do things.

What we shall do in the remainder of this brief essay is to point to certain other features of Luke's infancy narrative that likewise create the atmosphere in which it is possible to read *ouk ēn autois topos en tō katalymati* precisely as "there was no room for them in the inn." What Luke is doing in these two chapters is to suggest that God, who is hardly mentioned explicitly here in the text, but lies just below the surface of every verse, is the one who is at work, and that no human agency, no setback, is going to thwart the divine project.

A Charming Picture of God's Action

The first way to see this is by observing Luke's ability to paint a beguiling picture; there are several examples of this throughout Luke-Acts. It is no accident, but a matter of fact in the history of interpretation, that no biblical author has inspired more paintings than Luke, and that legend often gives him the status of artist.[5] He has an astonishing gift for depicting a scene. One of his most often-painted scenes in Luke's infancy narrative is the Annunciation to Mary.[6] It is a captivating scene, with Luke's characteristically deft brush strokes; for our purposes, the point to note is the subdued presence of God from the very beginning, in the divine passive "in the sixth month, the angel Gabriel was

[5] See Ian Boxall's chapter in the present volume, as well as Heidi J. Hornik and Mikeal C. Parsons, *Illuminating Luke: The Infancy Narrative in Italian Renaissance Painting* (Harrisburg, PA: Trinity Press International, 2003), esp. 14–23.

[6] See, for instance, John Drury, *Painting the Word: Christian Pictures and their Meanings* (New Haven, CT: Yale University Press, 1999), 40–59, on annunciation paintings by Duccio, Filippo Lippi, and Poussin.

sent" (1:26). No need to ask who did the sending—but God is not named here. Characteristically, the person to whom Gabriel is sent is mentioned last in the sentence, after Galilee (which is itself perhaps among the least significant portions of Rome's empire), Nazareth (an utterly unimportant hill town, as we may recall from Nathanael's dismissive comment in John 1:46), and Joseph (whose only apparent significance is that he is "of the house of David"). Moreover, Mary's name is only mentioned after Luke has recorded her status as a "virgin," and a betrothed virgin was rarely of high social status in first-century Palestine.

Despite this implied downgrading of Mary, it is nevertheless to her that the astonishing two-word address is uttered, *chaire kecharitōmenē*, which you can translate "rejoice, favored lady," or in more casual mode, "cheer up, you lucky thing," or in traditional Catholic diction, "hail, full of grace" (Luke 1:28). The first of these two Greek words is a regular form of greeting in the ancient world, but its root meaning is "rejoice," and it is worth noting that Luke is very much the gospel of "joy" (*chara*), which in Luke-Acts is a sign of the presence of the Holy Spirit (Luke 10:21; Acts 13:52). Likewise, in our infancy narrative, the shepherds, themselves representatives of the marginalized, are told that the good news that they are hearing is "great joy" (2:8, and compare the outbreak of joy offered to Zechariah at 1:14).

The second Greek word in the angel's greeting is connected with the noun *charis*, which means "divine favor," "grace," "unconditional gift," "graciousness," "attractiveness," and takes on immense theological weight in the writings of Paul. It even sounds a bit like the words for "joy" and "rejoice," and is probably cognate with them. Certainly the Greek assonance adds to the effect on us, the hearers of the story, as we imagine ourselves in the place of Mary, who is the hearer in the narrative. The angel now amplifies this statement as he continues (1:30), "you have found *charis* with God," offering this as a reason for her not to be afraid. And, interestingly, the only other use of this word in the infancy narrative refers to Jesus, "the grace of God was on the [little child]" (2:40, cf. 2:52). This is the child for whom there was no place in the *katalyma*.

A Picture Painted by Contrasts

Another way in which this artistic author operates is by contrast. The most eye-catching example in the infancy narrative is that between Zechariah and Mary, or rather between the story of the annunciation and birth of John the Baptist and that of Jesus.[7] In both cases, God's inescapable purposes are fulfilled by devout and obedient human beings (though Zechariah gets punished

[7] See the chart in Brendan Byrne, *The Hospitality of God: A Reading of Luke's Gospel* (Collegeville: Liturgical Press, 2000), 20.

for demanding evidence, 1:18, 20), and in both cases Luke paints an unforgettable picture of the angel Gabriel announcing what God's purposes are. Strikingly, though, it is Zechariah, not Mary, who seems the more important figure when Luke's hearers first meet them.[8] Zechariah is given an ancestry, as is his wife, and a status ("a priest," 1:5), whereas Mary, as we have seen, is no more than "a virgin." Zechariah is doing his priestly job (1:8–9), and "the people" (a very important entity for Luke) are "praying outside at the hour of sacrifice" (1:10).

Nevertheless, it is Mary who is of more interest to Luke, and while Zechariah's son will be "great before the Lord…and filled with the Holy Spirit…and will return many of the sons of Israel to the Lord their God…to make ready a people prepared for the Lord" (1:15–17), Mary's son, by contrast, "will be great and will be called Son of the Most High…and he will rule over the house of David for ever" (1:32–33). The contrast is deftly painted, and the message unmistakable: God is at work, and in precisely the way we should not expect. Most hearers in the ancient world would have expected Zechariah and his offspring to be the significant players in this contrast of opposites.

The same is true of two other contrasting pairs whom Luke allows us to glimpse in the infancy narrative. He starts the infancy story proper with a reference to Herod: "in the days of Herod King of Judea," and immediately proceeds to speak, not of Herod, but of "a certain priest, Zechariah by name" (1:5). It is this Zechariah, not the paranoid and homicidal Herod the Great, whom Luke wishes to present as significant to his hearers.

A further such contrast we have already hinted at. Look at the solemn opening of chapter 2: "It happened in those days that a decree went out from Caesar Augustus for the whole world to be enrolled…when Quirinius was governor of Syria" (2:1–2). Most of the hearers of the Gospel would have been in no doubt that Luke is doing serious history here. Once again, however, the contrast is with the apparently utterly insignificant "Joseph from Galilee…with Mary his fiancée—who was pregnant" (2:4–5), and it is this irregular couple in whom Luke is interested. For a similar example of an unexpected trick played on us by Luke, see the list of disreputable potentates in 3:1–2, and then contemplate to whom "the word of God came."

On the Way

So the important people in Luke's narrative are not necessarily the most obvious ones, but those who find no place in the *katalyma*. This fits well with

---

[8] Bruce J. Malina and Jerome H. Neyrey, "Honor and Shame in Luke-Acts: Pivotal Values of the Mediterranean World," in *The Social World of Luke-Acts: Models for Interpretation*, ed. Jerome H. Neyrey (Peabody, MA: Hendrickson, 1991), 25–65, esp. 47.

another very significant, and often neglected, element of Luke's story. It is the fact that the whole of Luke-Acts is a journey, from Galilee (to Jerusalem and back), through Samaria and Judea, to Jerusalem (several times), and eventually to "the ends of the earth" (Acts 1:8), which presumably we reach in Athens (Acts 17) and Rome (Acts 28).[9] This gives the whole story a provisional feel, signaled in an unobtrusive but (once you have seen it) unmistakable way by Luke, through his use of the Greek verb *poreuomai*. This word, which often means something stronger than "go," can be translated as "proceed," "march," "go one's way," "live," "conduct oneself," or "walk." It is fairly rare in Matthew and John, and not found at all in Mark, other than the "long ending" of that Gospel. Luke, however, uses it and its compounds ("go with," "go into," "go out of") 108 times in his two volumes, and this is surely no accident. It is Luke's view that the word of God is on a journey, and therefore has not yet come safely into harbor; but it will achieve its destination despite all the obstacles that the opponents of God may place in its way.

Look at the ways in which Luke deploys the word in the infancy narrative. At 1:6 it evokes a Hebrew background, when Luke uses it to describe Zechariah and Elizabeth as "both just before the Lord, and *walking* blamelessly in all the commandments and decrees of the Lord." Here it echoes a Hebrew verb (*hālak*) which means "walk" or "conduct one's life" (cf. Gen 17:1). The next use of the word occurs after Mary has already indicated (Luke 1:38) that she too will walk in the Lord's way. Now she puts it startlingly into practice: "Mary arose in those days and *journeyed* with haste into the hill country" (1:39). She has not been commanded to do so, but the hearer is in no doubt that she is doing exactly what she should be doing.

The next time we encounter the word is in 2:3–4, when it describes the general effect of Caesar Augustus' decree ("everyone went to be enrolled"). Interestingly, and perhaps significantly, Luke avoids reaching for this favored verb when he describes the movement of the shepherds from their fields to Bethlehem. Instead, we hear them say, "Let us come through as far as Bethlehem" (2:15), and in 2:16 Luke reports that "they came in a hurry" (this last word echoes Luke's account of Mary's journey to the hill country, 1:39).

Finally, the word reappears at 2:41, where it describes the annual pilgrimage journey of Jesus' parents to Jerusalem. Here it combines the notion of obedience to God's commands with the journey on which the Gospel has embarked.

---

[9] Dennis M. Sweetland, *Our Journey with Jesus: Discipleship according to Luke-Acts* (Good News Studies 23; Collegeville: Liturgical Press, 1990). For this theme in the Third Gospel, see David P. Moessner, *Lord of the Banquet: The Literary and Theological Significance of the Lukan Travel Narrative* (Minneapolis: Fortress, 1989); Charles H.H. Scobie, "A Canonical Approach to Interpreting Luke: The Journey Motif as a Hermeneutical Key," in *Reading Luke: Interpretation, Reflection, Formation*, ed. Craig G. Bartholomew, Joel B. Green, and Anthony C. Thiselton (Grand Rapids: Zondervan; Milton Keynes: Paternoster, 2005), 327–49.

It is worth noting in this context, though space does not permit us to examine the matter in greater depth, that the Gospel's action shifts scene no less than nine times in the first two chapters of Luke, so that by the time the hearer gets to chapter 3, we are already aware (at some level) that this is very much a "journeying," provisional Gospel. This is the context in which we are to understand the *katalyma* in which there was no place for the infant Savior.

Filling and Fulfilling

There is another technique that Luke employs to indicate that God is at work, and it is our contention that the *katalyma* is a part of his overarching intention. It is his use of the idea of fulfillment. Luke opens his account, even before the infancy narrative is properly underway, by describing it as "a narrative of the things that have been fulfilled among us" (1:1). In case we had any doubt that he wishes to imply that it is God who is at work here he tells Theophilus, the addressee of both volumes, of his aim: "that you should know the infallibility of the words (or 'things') regarding which you have been catechized" (1:4).

Luke has a number of tactics that serve his overall strategy of fulfillment, the sense of God being in charge. There are three verbs in particular, *plēroō*, *plērophoreō* (1:1), and *pimplēmi*, which all have the meaning of "fill" or "fulfill." So Gabriel tells Zechariah that his son "will be filled with the Holy Spirit from his mother's womb" (1:15); and indeed that same mother, we learn at 1:41, is "filled with the Holy Spirit." The word can also mean "fulfilled," as at 1:23, where "the days of [Zechariah's] liturgy were fulfilled" is the only possible translation, or "Elizabeth's time to give birth was fulfilled" (1:57), or Mary's "days were fulfilled for her to give birth" (2:6), or Jesus' "eight days were fulfilled for him to be circumcised, and he was called by the name 'Jesus' which he had been called by the angel before he had been conceived in the womb" (2:21). Every single phrase in that verse might be said to serve Luke's strategy of indicating that God is in charge. Finally, we notice Luke's language: "when the days of their purification were fulfilled" in 2:23, and in 2:40 how Jesus was "filled with wisdom."

And there are other pointers here. Look, for example, at the noun *teleiōsis*, a word from a different root, but still hard to translate other than as "fulfillment," in 1:45, the verb *teleō* ("complete") in 2:39, another verb *teleioō* (also "complete") in 2:43, and the related noun *telos* ("end") used in 1:33 ("of his kingdom there shall be no end"). All of these reinforce the sense that God is in charge, overcoming every obstacle in the completion of the divine project. There is also Luke's use of the two Greek terms for "word," *rhēma* and *logos*. Notice, for example, Mary's response to Gabriel, "let it happen to me according to your *rhēma*" (1:38), and compare Luke's use of "as he said/spoke" in 1:55, 70. Similarly, there is the apparently mysterious "sign" to the shepherds (2:12), whose only function is to get fulfilled (though no "fulfillment" word occurs here), in the wrapping of Jesus in swathing bands at 2:7, and the placing in a manger at 2:16. Once again the hearer, almost unconsciously, gathers that everything will happen as God has ordained. There is, in consequence, a sense at every point in the infancy narrative that wherever you touch it, the story is governed by God. Something of the sort is evident in 2:25–26, with Simeon's promise from the Holy Spirit, and in 2:49, where Luke places on Jesus' lips the apparently insignificant Greek word *dei* ("it is necessary"), which is in Luke-Acts one of the indicators that the divine plan is unstoppably at work—for a striking example, see the story of the road to Emmaus (24:26).[10]

A Subtle Use of Indicators of Time

So Luke has multiple ways of letting his hearers know that God is at work; and this helps to fill out the background against which *katalyma* has been tra-ditionally understood as "inn." We may mention just one last characteristic brush stroke, Luke's subtle employment of indicators of time. It was notable in the previous section how often "fulfill" and "days" came together in the same sentence—here Luke is offering us a clue that we are not simply talking of convenient chronological identifiers, but of God's time. The use of the word "day" is one such indication: "in the days of Herod the King" (1:5) is followed very closely by a description of Zechariah and Elizabeth as "advanced in their days" (1:7), and it is a very slow hearer who has not grasped, first, that Herod's days are unimportant to Luke, and second, that this old and childless couple are going to produce a baby, all because God is so improbably at work. Look at the way in which "day" is used at 1:20 (prophecy will come true), 1:23 (a loyal servant of God completes his duty), and 1:24 (the improbable conception comes to pass). Clearer than this is Luke's use of "month," in particular to draw together the closely linked stories of Elizabeth–John and Mary–Jesus: "in the sixth month" (1:26), "this is the sixth month for her who was called barren" (1:36), and "Mary stayed with her about three months" (1:56), presumably tak-ing the story to the moment of John's birth.

We might add to this Luke's use of "year" (in 2:36, 37). After we have learned that Anna (like Elizabeth and Zechariah) is "advanced in many days," Luke adds a detail whose precise significance is obscure, unless we are meant to understand that God is at work here, delaying the moment of this admirable lady's delight ("she had lived with her husband for seven years from her virgin-ity, and she was a widow until eighty-four years" (2:36–37). This is then fol-lowed, almost immediately, by the appearance of the same word to emphasize

---

[10] Byrne (*Hospitality*, 37) observes that in 2:49, Jesus' future is "determined by a divine imper-ative, expressed here for the first time by the characteristic Lukan 'must' (Greek: *dei*)."

the Jewish piety of Mary and Joseph: "his parents would journey every year to Jerusalem for the feast of the Passover" (2:41). Finally, the occurrence of "years" in the very next verse indicates, presumably, that Jesus had reached the right age to make the pilgrimage.

There is another word in Greek that can be translated as "right time" or "window of opportunity." The word is *kairos*, and Luke uses it of the fulfillment of Gabriel's words to Zechariah (1:20); and he uses it again, this time replete with menace and meaning, at the end of the temptation of Jesus, when "the devil left him until the *kairos*" (4:13). Greek has a second word for time, however, *chronos*, or "clock-time," as it is often understood; and Luke manages to invest even this word with divine purpose when "the time was fulfilled" for Elizabeth to produce her son (1:57).

Last, there is Luke's use of the word "today." It appears only once in the infancy narrative, in the story of the angel's appearance to the shepherds (2:11); but it is an important idea for Luke. See, for example, the all-important use of it in Jesus' "mission statement" at the synagogue at Nazareth: "today this Scripture is fulfilled" (4:21). It appears several times in Luke, notably twice in the Zaccheus story (19:5, 9), and, regally, on Jesus' lips in 23:43.

So it seems that even Luke's use of indicators of time may serve as deft strokes of this artist's brush to give a context against which his Gospel, both volumes of it, is to be heard and understood and translated.[11] That context is God's inescapable purpose, which comes up against refractory humanity and other obstacles, but, in the end, according to Luke, will find its mark.

Conclusion: What Luke Is Trying to Do

Luke's endeavor is, with delicate shades of his palette, to express what God is doing in Jesus. The infancy narrative ends, significantly enough, with this sentence: "And Jesus was growing in wisdom and age/size before God and before human beings" (2:52). This sentence is characteristic of the entire infancy narrative; God is the central character, but you would not know that as you read the sentence, which concentrates instead on the one who is unmistakably human, and who has to grow. Luke has expressed this, and shaped our reading of all the rest of his two volumes, in a performance of great subtlety. The whole story, he signals, is driven by God, effortlessly surmounting all obstacles, no matter how daunting they may seem.

Two key sentences, which carry an implicit instruction for hearer and translator, come in 2:19, 51b; and it is in their light that we are to read the infancy

---

[11] For an up-to-date rendering of the New Testament, see Nicholas King, *The New Testament, Freshly Translated* (Stowmarket, Suffolk: Mayhew, 2004).

narrative, and, in consequence, the whole work to which these chapters are the overture:

> 2:19 [after the visit of the shepherds in Bethlehem]:
> "Mary was watching (*synetērei*) all these things/words, comparing them in her heart."

> 2:51 [after the painful rediscovery of Jesus in Jerusalem]:
> "His mother was watching (*dietērei*) all the words/things in her heart."

So those of us who would presume to translate or interpret the text have to imitate Mary here, whom Luke is certainly offering as a model performer of this mystery. We have far more to do than merely thumb through the latest complete lexicon of the Greek language or consult commentaries. What we are invited to do is to develop a sensitivity to what the author thinks he or she is doing, and, implicitly, an accountability to the audience for whom the author supposes himself to be writing. Theophilus may have a few questions to put to us at the end of the performance.[12]

---

[12] My thanks are due to Professors Chris Rowland and Markus Bockmuehl, Revd Dr Helen-Ann Hartley, and Dr Patricia McDonald for taking the trouble to read this essay and offering some very helpful comments and insights.

Chapter 6

Matthew 1–2 and Roman Political Power

Warren Carter

For many contemporary hearers, the story of Jesus' birth has nothing to do with politics. If the story is heard at all in the context of the contemporary western Christmas—often driven by consumerism, marked by sentimentality, secularized by its own cast of characters, and focused on families and feasting—the story of the birth of a cute baby provides at most a religious tinge for domestic celebrations, with hardly a perspective on political structures and agenda.[1] Yet at least three observations indicate that Roman imperial power plays a central role in Matthew's narrative.

The first factor concerns the Gospel's storyline. The account of Jesus' birth, or more accurately, the account of his conception (Matt 1:18–25), sets in motion the Gospel's plot that will culminate in the story's main character being put to death on a Roman cross.[2] The Gospel's opening chapters explicitly anticipate Jesus' death by using language that will reappear prominently in the crucifixion story. For example, the magi inquire about the one born "king of the Jews" (2:2), the same phrase that the governor Pilate uses in questioning Jesus (27:11).[3] The "chief priests and scribes," who now advise Herod (2:4), later instigate Jesus' death with their ally Pilate (26:3, 57). The verb that designates their "assembling" to advise Herod (2:4) identifies their later actions four times in assembling to plan and execute Jesus' death (26:3, 57; 27:62; 28:12), as well as the actions of the Roman soldiers (27:27) and the crowds (27:17, 20). The magi "deceive" or "mock" Herod by not returning to him with news about Jesus' birthplace. The same verb appears four times as an action done to Jesus as he is put to death (20:19; 27:29, 31, 41). In this way, Jesus' birth and subsequent death by Roman crucifixion are closely linked. To follow Jesus crucified by Rome is to follow one who disturbs any political system with

---

[1] James Tracy and Richard Horsley, *Christmas Unwrapped: Consumerism, Christ, and Culture* (Harrisburg: Trinity Press International, 2001).

[2] Warren Carter, *Matthew: Storyteller, Interpreter, Evangelist*, rev. edn (Peabody: Hendrickson, 2004), 132–53.

[3] On Pilate, see Warren Carter, *Pontius Pilate: Portraits of a Roman Governor* (Interfaces; Collegeville: Liturgical Press, 2003); also "Pilate and Jesus: Roman Justice All Washed Up (Matt 27:11–26)," in Warren Carter, *Matthew and Empire: Initial Explorations* (Harrisburg: Trinity Press International, 2001), 145–68.

searching questions about its vision of society, its personnel, and the impact of its practices and policies.

And second, Roman imperial power pervades the world of Jesus' birth, as well as the world of the folks for whom Matthew's Gospel was written, nearly a hundred years later around 90 CE.[4] Roman power secured the empire's hierarchical social structure and maintained elite status, wealth, and power in various ways. Leading personnel like governors, based in provincial cities, ruled provinces and made alliances with local urban elites. Roman control and presence were manifested through buildings, statues, images on coins, and festivals. The ruling classes garnered wealth, resources, and production from the rest of the population through taxes, tributes, rents, loans, and slavery. Rhetoric and justice asserted elite values and control. Provincial elites expressed their own compliance and fostered the allegiance of non-elites through local imperial cult observances that provided numerous opportunities for most to participate. Religion and politics were not separable entities. Roman imperial theology emphasized the gods' choice of Rome. The gods had commissioned Rome as their agent to manifest the divine will, purposes, and blessings. Roman rule thereby enjoyed divine sanction. And naturally it was expressed in military power. Legions, including locally recruited troops, maintained order, enforced compliance, and deterred revolt. While Rome did not target followers of Jesus with empire-wide persecution, harsh socioeconomic realities made daily life difficult and precarious for most people. This is the everyday world that pervades Matthew's story and is the world addressed by the Gospel, perhaps written in Antioch, the capital city of the province of Syria, around 90 CE.

Third, the Gospel tells this story of Jesus at a time soon after a fresh assertion of Roman power. Between 66 and 70 CE, some Judeans and Galileans revolted against Roman rule, only to be mercilessly crushed in 70 CE as Jerusalem was burned and the temple destroyed. The loss of city, temple, and priesthood meant not only the task of significant reformulation for post-70 Judaism, but also a fresh awareness in Jewish communities throughout the empire, and especially in nearby regions such as Syria, of the challenging task of negotiating Roman power. Matthew's Gospel, with the story of its main character crucified by Rome, participates in that task of negotiation as it seeks to guide followers of Jesus in their daily lives within the Roman Empire.

These three observations indicate that twenty-first-century readers of Matthew's story of Jesus' origins would do well to be attuned to the imperial realities that Matthew's Gospel assumes but that are not often evident to us. I will make clear some of these imperial realities in the following discussion.

---

[4] Warren Carter, *Matthew and the Margins: A Socio-Political and Religious Reading* (Maryknoll: Orbis; Sheffield: Sheffield Academic Press, 2000), 1–49; Carter, *Matthew and Empire*, 9–53; John Riches and David C. Sim (eds), *The Gospel of Matthew in its Roman Imperial Context* (JSNT Supplement 276; London: T&T Clark, 2005).

I will argue that Matthew's story of Jesus' origins guides followers of Jesus by revealing the Roman Empire to be at odds with the divine purposes yet subject to them for the time being. Jesus' followers are to manifest God's saving plan at work in the midst of the empire. Matthew offers these followers reassurance and guidance for living in the dangerous empire until God's purposes are enacted to end Roman power.

The Genealogy (Matt 1:1–17)

It was customary in Matthew's world to define an elite hero by associating him with prestigious and virtuous (usually male) ancestors who had wealth, power, and status. For example, in his biography of his father-in-law Agricola, governor of Britain, Tacitus outlines the elite status and power of Agricola's two grandfathers, his father, and his mother (*Agricola* 4).[5] While some of the ancestors named in Jesus' genealogy are prominent and virtuous figures with power, wealth, and status—Abraham, David, Solomon, and other kings—many lack these features. David is hardly a paragon of virtue in all respects. Neither were the kings Rehoboam, Abijah, Joram, Ahaz, and Manasseh (1:7–10). Many of those named in verses 12-16 are nobodies, about whom there are no surviving traditions.

Matthew's genealogy makes the somewhat unconventional move of including five women (Tamar, Rahab, Ruth, the wife of Uriah, Mary; 1:3–6, 16). There have been numerous suggestions about the contribution of these women. Certainly there is no merit in the old tradition, dating from at least Jerome in the fifth century, that the women were sinners; the men are hardly sinfree. More helpful are the Gentile connections of some of the women (Rahab, Ruth) along with the recognition of their sexual roles and socioeconomic and cultural powerlessness outside conventional male-dominated society in which they actively further God's purposes.[6] These women, to be sure, also prepare for Mary's role in conceiving and birthing Jesus.

With its somewhat unusual genealogy, the Gospel sets Jesus' origins within Matthew's version of the biblical story concerning God's interactions with the nations and Israel. For Matthew, basic to these interactions is God's promise to Abraham to bless all the peoples of the earth (Gen 12:3; 22:18). Abraham is named in the Gospel's first verse and Jesus is linked to him with the identification of "son of Abraham."[7] Abraham stands at the head of the genealogy,

---

[5] Maurice Hutton and William Peterson, *Tacitus: Dialogus, Agricola, Germania* (LCL; New York: Macmillan, 1914), 173–75.

[6] Carter, *Matthew and the Margins*, 58–61; Raymond E. Brown, *The Birth of the Messiah*, rev. edn (New York: Doubleday, 1993), 71–74, 590–96.

[7] Warren Carter, "Matthean Christology in Roman Imperial Key: Matthew 1:1," in *The Gospel of Matthew in its Roman Imperial Context*, ed. Riches and Sim, 143–65.

casting his shadow over its first section (Matt 1:2–6a). He is also highlighted in the genealogy's summary (1:17). God's promise to Abraham to bless all people with a just and abundant life provides a vision of life as God intends it to be. The vision is, for example, elaborated for Israel in Deuteronomy 28–29 in terms of fertility, food, physical wholeness, and security.

That vision of life is, however, challenged by some named in the genealogy. Kingly descendants from David, for instance, are charged with the task of representing God's just and good purposes. But many of the kings named in 1:6–11 do not live out the royal job description entrusted to David and articulated in royal Psalms such as Psalm 72. Solomon employs exploitative and oppressive means to enhance his own wealth (1 Kgs 1–11).[8] His son Rehoboam continues the practices (1 Kgs 12–14). Manasseh specializes in false worship and injustice (2 Kgs 21:1–18).

God intervenes in 587 BCE with the defeat of Jerusalem by the Babylonian empire. Reference to exile in Babylon marks the end of the genealogy's second section and beginning of its third section (Matt 1:11–12, 17). This exile names an event in which Babylonian imperial power was asserted over Judea and Jerusalem, in which the city was defeated, and leading citizens were relocated to Babylon. The term that Matthew uses for this "exile" (*metoikesia*) appears three times in the Greek text of the Hebrew Bible in contexts that interpret this event theologically (2 Kgs 24:16; 1 Chr 5:22; Ezek 12:11). That is, Babylonian exile is seen to play a part in God's purposes, namely the punishment of kings for failing to represent divine justice and to lead the people in faithful worship and service of God. This perspective interprets Babylonian imperialism as an instrument of God's punitive purposes (1 Kgs 9:6–9).

But the tradition also evaluates Babylon's empire in another way. Subsequently God judges Babylon for oppressing the chosen people and ends its empire. God uses the Persian ruler Cyrus to accomplish this purpose and to set Judeans free from Babylonian rule, so as to return home after 539 BCE (Isa 44:21–28; 45:1, 15b). Verses 12–16 in the Matthean genealogy show that Babylon did not have the final word. There was life after and beyond the exile. This last section indicates that no imperial power can thwart or divert the divine purposes, and no imperial power is stronger than God. Ultimately God overcomes Babylon.

Evoking these various perspectives on how God uses Babylonian imperial power has important implications for Matthew's readers under Roman control. The Babylonian references create an analogous relationship between Babylon and Rome, between the events of 587 BCE and of 70 CE. Matthew seems to see the disastrous events of 66–70 CE when Rome overran Jerusalem as parallel to the fall of Jerusalem to Babylon in 587 BCE. Just as God made use of Babylon to punish Jerusalem in 587 BCE, so God has used Rome to punish

[8] Warren Carter, " 'Solomon in All His Glory'; Intertextuality and Matthew 6:29," *Journal for the Study of the New Testament* 65 (1997) 3–25.

Jerusalem in 70 CE. Matthew makes this perspective explicit in the Gospel, especially when Jesus enters Jerusalem (21:12–13, 18–19, 41).[9] Matthew also edits the parable of the wedding feast from the traditions of Jesus' sayings to include a reference to Jerusalem's destruction (22:7) and to condemn the city's leaders (21:45; 22:7).[10] The link with Babylon interprets the disaster of 70 CE in terms of God's punitive purposes.

But a further link exists between Babylon in 587 BCE and Rome in 70 CE. After God has used Babylon to punish the people with exile, God then judges the Babylonian empire to be at odds with the divine purposes for the world (Jer 51:64). God neither endorses Babylon, nor sanctions its way of life, nor blesses its way of ordering the world. It is contrary to the divine plan for the world. So God brings the Babylonian empire to an end and the people return home. A further, hopeful dimension of the parallel between Babylon and Rome emerges. Just as Babylonian power did not last, neither will Rome's. Just as God saved the people from Babylon, God will save them from Rome. While imperial power at times serves or enacts the divine purposes, ultimately it is at odds with God's plan and subject to God's saving or liberating work. Just as Babylon was destroyed, so will be Rome. Or to put it in other terms, God will outmuscle Rome's empire to establish His empire.

This is, to be sure, a dangerous message for an imperial power such as Rome. That is why the genealogy—and the Gospel—do not state it openly, in the form of direct and open "God will get Rome" rhetoric. Instead the message of Rome's inevitable downfall is conveyed much more covertly by using "insider knowledge."[11] That is, these references to Babylon evoke Hebrew Bible traditions that present a particular theological perspective on Babylon. As with all the names in the genealogy, these traditions are not elaborated but rely on the readers' cultural knowledge to elaborate the cryptic references. The Gospel's audience is expected to know about the Babylonian defeat of Jerusalem and exile, as well as the end of Babylonian power and return from exile after 539 BCE (referred to in Matt 1:11–12, 17). The audience is also to draw a parallel between Babylon and Rome. Similar connections are made in other Jewish texts like *4 Ezra* and *2 Baruch*, written about the same time as Matthew and also concerned to make sense of the tragedy of 70 CE. The repetition of the references to Babylon in 1:11–12, 17 also draws attention to their importance.

But if 70 CE was about God using Rome to punish the rulers and people for their sins, how will God bring about the hopeful act of saving the people from their sins and from Rome, the punisher of those sins?

---

[9] Carter, *Matthew and the Margins*, 418.
[10] Ibid., 435–36.
[11] For ways in which the powerless employ self-protective, covert resistance to power, see James Scott, *Domination and the Arts of Resistance: Hidden Transcripts* (New Haven: Yale University Press, 1990).

Being Saved from Sins (Matt 1:18–25)

In 1:18–25 Matthew narrates the conception and commission of the yet unborn Jesus to carry out this task of saving the people.[12] In a dream, an angel announces Mary's pregnancy to Joseph and instructs him, "you will call his name Jesus, for he will save his people from their sins" (1:21). The name Jesus sums up the baby's mission or life's work, "to save his people from their sins." In Matthew's view, these sins have been punished in the fall of Jerusalem in 70 CE.[13] But what does this commission involve and how will Jesus carry it out? Are the sins—from which Jesus is to save—personal, individual, and internal sins, or is he concerned with all sin, anything and everything in the world that is contrary to God's good and just purposes, including Roman imperial power? Verses 18–25 begin to offer some clues.

First of all, the name "Jesus" is the Greek form of the Hebrew name "Joshua" which means "the Lord saves."[14] Matthew again assumes that hearers of the Gospel story know that the most famous Joshua in the biblical story was the successor of Moses. Joshua completed the people's liberation from Egypt by overcoming Canaanite power and occupying the Promised Land. This link with Joshua and the struggle over the land with the Canaanites suggests that Jesus' saving task is much more extensive than only personal and individual sins.

Moreover, the scope of Jesus' "saving from sins" is clarified by v. 23. Here Jesus is linked with the prophetic word of Isa 7:14 and given an additional name and mission: Immanuel, "God with us." Putting Matt 1:21 and 1:23 together, his task or commission is to manifest God's saving presence. Evoking Isaiah 7–9 is another instance of disguised knowledge that the Gospel's readers are supposed to know.[15] The chapters concern a threat to Judah and King Ahaz from the northern powers Israel and Syria, as well as from the Assyrian empire. Isaiah assures Ahaz that God will protect Judah and points to the imminent birth of a child named Immanuel as a sign of the continuation of the Davidic line. But Ahaz does not trust the word, and punishment at the hands of Assyria follows. Ahaz's sin is not just a personal matter; it concerns how life on the earth is ordered. Yet Isaiah also promises that God will save the people from Assyria (Isa 9:1–2; cited by Matthew in 4:15–16). So despite using Assyria to punish, God does not sanction or bless Assyrian imperialism as a permanent or acceptable way of ordering the world.

It is important to note that Matthew's evoking of Assyrian imperial power in 1:23 matches the perspectives on Babylonian imperial power evoked by the genealogy in 1:11–12, 17. God makes use of an imperial power to punish the

---

[12] Carter, " 'To Save His People from Their Sins,' " in Carter, *Matthew and Empire*, 75–92.
[13] Carter, *Matthew and the Margins*, 34.
[14] Brown, *The Birth of the Messiah*, 131.
[15] Carter, "Evoking Isaiah," in Carter, *Matthew and Empire*, 93–107.

people. Then God saves the people from that power because it is contrary to the divine purposes. Again a parallel with Rome's empire is implicit.

Four crucial affirmations about God's saving ways and Jesus' role in them become clear in 1:18–25. First, this saving will take place in Jesus. The *how* of that saving is not yet clear and we will have to read further through the Gospel to gain an answer. But the continual evoking of imperial powers indicates that the *extent* of Jesus' saving commission is to restore all of human life to participate in God's good and just purposes.

Second, it is clear that imperial power does not have divine sanction as a way of ordering the world. God uses it but does not bless its permanent establishment. In fact, its oppressive structures that benefit ruling elites while damaging most of the population (as Matthew's second chapter will demonstrate) are contrary to God's purposes expressed in the promise to Abraham to bless all the peoples of the earth. Jesus' saving from sins is set in this systemic, global context.

Third, Jesus' commission to manifest God's saving presence addresses a central question with which post-70, post-temple Judaism wrestled: how to encounter God's saving presence after the fresh assertion of Roman power and after the destruction of Jerusalem and its temple? Both Roman and Jewish authors declared that God had abandoned the temple (and the people) when it was destroyed in 70 CE (Josephus, *Jewish War* 5.412; Tacitus, *Hist.* 5.13). In contrast, Matthew's answer is that God has not abandoned the people and is not absent from them. Rather, God's saving presence is encountered in the midst of Roman power in Jesus, in the community that follows him (18:20; 28:20), and in his words and teaching (24:35; 28:19–20).

And fourth, Roman imperial theology claimed that the gods had made Rome to be the agent of their will, rule, and blessings.[16] By linking and contrasting Jesus' mission to save from sins with imperial powers such as Assyria and Babylon (set in parallel with Rome), the Gospel makes the first of several claims that Rome's world is not blessed by the gods, that it is in fact sinful in its rejection of God's purposes promised to Abraham, and that God's saving plan and presence are being manifested in their midst through God's agent Jesus.

The Empire Strikes Back through Herod (Matt 2:1–23)

What happens, then, when God's saving presence is asserted in the Roman-dominated world? The empire strikes back. Matthew's second chapter demonstrates the realities of Roman imperial power in a collision between King Herod, the face of Roman imperial power in Judea centered in Jerusalem, and

---

[16] Carter, "Roman Imperial Theology," in Carter, *Matthew and Empire*, 20–34.

the new-born Jesus. In doing so, the chapter exemplifies the perspectives on imperial power established in the first chapter.

The opening verse of chapter 2 asserts Jesus' birth, thereby confirming the efficacy of the angel's announcement in 1:20–21 and demonstrating God's purposes at work in the Roman world. The birth takes place "in Bethlehem of Judea in the days of Herod the king" (2:1). This opening verse brings together two conflicting visions of kingship. The reference to "Bethlehem" identifies a small village marginal to the center of power (Jerusalem), but one that nevertheless has an important history. At Bethlehem David was anointed king (1 Sam 16:1–13). The link with David recalls the royal tradition whereby the faithful king was to represent God's justice, "defending the cause of the poor of the people, giving deliverance to the needy, and crushing the oppressor" (Ps 72:4). Matthew's first chapter has already linked Jesus with this tradition as "son of David" through Joseph (1:1, 17, 20). To manifest God's saving presence is to enact divine justice for all people—not good news for the Roman Empire committed to an unjust status quo marked by domination and submission.

King Herod, however, embodies the "everyday" vision of imperial "business-as-usual." He was Rome's puppet or client king, "king of the Jews" because Rome said so (Josephus, *Ant.* 16.10.2 #311). He is a classic example of Rome's use of alliances with local elites to secure imperial power. As a shrewd and astute ruler, he maintained his own authority, even while there were changing political fortunes in Rome. He undertook grand building projects including temples for Roma and the emperor Augustus in Caesarea Maritima, yet he also rebuilt the temple for Israel's God in Jerusalem. His brutality maintained the hierarchical status quo against any threat. The genealogy has already evoked a history of kings who have failed to live out God's purposes (1:6b–11). Herod belongs in this line of resistance to the divine will.

Predictably, then, the announcement of the magi that they have discerned in the heavens a star signifying one born as "king of the Jews," results in Herod being alarmed "and all Jerusalem with him" (2:3). The only legitimate monarchs in Rome's empire were client–kings appointed by Rome. Contrary to the Christmas cards and Sunday school pageants, magi were neither kings nor, necessarily, "wise men." Turning up in Herod's major city to inquire about a new king, when the present one is very much alive and brutal, is not especially wise by any standards. And nor is it very wise to announce that they have come to "pay homage" (*proskyneō*) to the new king. The term "paying homage" denotes allegiance and was a political as well as religious term expressing submission to a ruler. The magi offer no such allegiance to Herod and thus occupy an ambivalent role. As priestly and courtly figures they have access to Herod as king, yet as those who engaged in the old (and at times despised) practice of studying the stars to discern significant events on earth, they bring news disturbing to the status quo.

Herod responds with fear and immediately gathers his Jerusalem allies, "the chief priests and scribes of the people" (2:4). We commonly think of these characters as "religious leaders" and see this as a meeting between political and religious personnel over a religious matter. But such an understanding and division between religious and political matters and personnel is anachronistic for the first century.[17] The chief priests were, according to Josephus, the rulers of Judea (*Ant.* 20.10.5 #251). Here they are Herod's allies; together they constitute the Rome-allied elite, members of the governing class based in the Jerusalem temple who uphold the hierarchical society under Rome's rule. As we have seen from Herod's fearful response in 2:3, the question about being "king of the Jews" is not specifically, let alone exclusively, a religious one. The political and religious dimensions of the question are intertwined.

Herod specifically inquires about where the "Christ" is to be born (2:4), using the term meaning "anointed." It refers to a tradition among some, but by no means all, Jews that looked for a figure sent or "anointed" by God to establish the divine purposes. There was no universal or monolithic expectation for *the* Messiah.[18] Traditions were diverse as to what sort of mission this figure would have and how it might be accomplished. One important element shared by several different forms of the expectation, though, involved this figure replacing Roman power and its allies with God's purposes, sometimes even doing so peacefully. Herod thus asks a politically charged question.

The Jerusalem leaders respond by evoking traditions about David from Micah 5, even though the passage does not use the term "Christ" or "Messiah." According to most interpreters, Micah 4:1–5:15 again evokes Babylonian imperialism, referring to the sixth-century time of desperation when Babylon had overthrown Jerusalem and its inhabitants had been exiled to Babylon (Mic 4:10–11; see Matt 1:11–12, 17).[19] God resists (while also imitating) the imperial aspirations of the nations (Mic 4:11). Gentiles (like the magi) will come to Jerusalem to worship God, and Jews and Gentiles will live according to the divine purposes. God will provide a ruler, a shepherd from Bethlehem—a reference to the line of David and a king who will replace the rule of imperial powers such as Rome and govern with compassion and justice (see Ps 72). These words found in Micah, probably arising in the time after the exile, now serve to interpret what God is doing in Jesus' birth. It is not good news for an imperial power such as Rome, but great news for those suffering under Roman rule.

Yet interestingly, these Jerusalem leaders neither connect the Scriptures to Jesus nor act in any way on the basis of them. As part of the power structure, they do not recognize God at work and so do not order their lives accordingly.

---

[17] See Anthony J. Saldarini, *Pharisees, Scribes, Sadducees in Palestinian Society: A Sociological Approach* (Wilmington: Glazier, 1988).

[18] John J. Collins, *The Scepter and the Star: The Messiahs of the Dead Sea Scrolls and Other Ancient Literature* (New York: Doubleday, 1995); Joseph A. Fitzmyer, *The One Who Is to Come* (Grand Rapids: Eerdmans, 2007).

[19] Carter, *Matthew and the Margins*, 78; Collins, *The Scepter and the Star*, 24.

This is Matthew's negative evaluation of these leaders and part of his explanation for their punishment in the events of 70 CE.

The rest of the chapter outlines Herod's attempt to destroy this shepherd ruler. It thereby reveals and catalogs some of the standard ways that imperial powers operate. First, there is secrecy as Herod summons the magi (Matt 2:7). Then there is manipulation as he turns pilgrims into spies, sending the magi to find the child and report back to him. Third, there are lies as he declares he wants to "worship him" (2:8) when in fact he wants to murder him (2:13). Then, finally, when spies and lies fail, there is murderous violence as Herod's soldiers kill "all the male children in the region of Bethlehem two years and under" (2:16). While it is commonplace to imagine (and to depict in numerous paintings) thousands being slaughtered, Bethlehem and its region were small and so there would not have been many infants in this age range.[20] To be sure, even one such death is one too many. And the narrative notes the "wailing and loud lamentation" inflicted on the population by Herod's murderous and selfish defense of his power and the elite-dominated status quo (2:18). Here again, Matthew's quotation of Jer 31:15 about weeping in Ramah evokes the earlier suffering arising from the Babylonian imperial conquest of Judah in 587 BCE.

But in this dangerous imperial world, God intervenes to protect Jesus and his commission to manifest God's saving presence. In 2:12 God sends a dream, warning the magi not to return to Herod. They comply; whenever imperial power is asserted, resistance takes place in all sorts of forms. Then again in a dream, an angel instructs Joseph to take Mary and Jesus to Egypt (2:13). The repeated use of the term "the child" instead of the name "Jesus" underlines the vulnerability of Jesus as the angel also reveals Herod's purpose "to destroy him" (2:13).

Being in Egypt, however, thwarts Herod's efforts to kill Jesus in Bethlehem. Yet the final and much greater defeat for Herod comes in the narrative's three references to the king's death (2:14, 19, 20). The repetition underscores his failure to kill Jesus and his own vulnerability to God's intervention.[21] Another angelic appearance to Joseph in a dream guides Joseph, Mary, and Jesus back to Judea (2:19–21).

But, as Matthew notes, "Archelaus ruled over Judea in the place of his father Herod," news that causes Joseph to fear (2:22). The death of Herod is not the end of imperial power and its danger. His son Archelaus continues the alliance with Rome and is the new face of Roman power. But again God intervenes and Joseph is guided to Galilee. Admittedly, this is ultimately not an escape from imperial power. Joseph returns to "Galilee under the Gentiles," a land

---

[20] Brown, *The Birth of the Messiah*, 204–205.
[21] Josephus narrates Herod's painful death (*Ant.* 17.7.5–17.8.1 ##168-192), regarding it as just punishment for the king's crimes (*Ant.* 17.7.5 #168).

of "darkness and the shadow of death," a land that God gave to the people but now under Roman control, ruled by Rome's ally and agent Herod Antipas (Matt 4:14–16, citing Isa 9:1).[22] In this place Jesus will carry out his commission to manifest God's saving presence (Matt 1:21–23).

Implications of Matthew Chapter 2

Several dimensions of this presentation in Matthew's second chapter merit further discussion. The first is very troubling. While God intervenes through dreams, angels, and the faithful compliance of Joseph and Mary to protect Jesus from Herod's murderous violence, it is not so for the infants around Bethlehem. When Herod's violence destroys them, God does not intervene to protect them. That is, Jesus is spared at the expense of the deaths and misery of others.[23] The incident raises the haunting question that while Jesus is to manifest God's saving presence, God does not save these infants from imperial power. The scene has become an example of the ongoing destruction and pain empires always cause in pursuit of their self-benefitting goals, whether in first-century Judea or in twenty-first-century Iraq. The task of resisting and ending imperial power is daunting and dangerous indeed, even for God.[24]

Second, the chapter shows the empire and its allies committed to violence as its dominant way of being and means of defending its world.[25] In Matt 2:16 the violence is overtly physical in the murder of the young children. But what is also to be recognized is that the whole imperial system, dominated by a small percentage of elite persons who extract resources and cheap labor from the rest of the population, is violent in its violation of human dignity and freedom. Rome and its elite allies forcibly extracted production through taxes and tribute. The practice of *angaria* requisitioned labor, transport (animals and people), supplies, and lodging from subject peoples, especially for military purposes (so Matt 5:41).[26] The resultant socioeconomic hardship, combined with verbal abuse and social snobbery,[27] exercised denigrating and dehumanizing power.

---

[22] Carter, "Evoking Isaiah," in Carter, *Matthew and Empire*, 93–107.

[23] Admittedly, at the end of the Gospel Jesus also dies at the hands of the same imperial authority.

[24] See the discussion of Alejandro Alberto Duarte, "Matthew," in *Global Bible Commentary*, ed. Daniel Patte (Nashville: Abingdon, 2004), 350–60.

[25] Warren Carter, "Construction of Violence and Identities in Matthew's Gospel," in *Violence in the New Testament*, ed. Shelly Matthews and E. Leigh Gibson (New York: T&T Clark, 2005), 81–108.

[26] Walter Wink, "Beyond Just War and Pacifism: Jesus' Nonviolent Way," *Review and Expositor* 89 (1992) 197–214; "Neither Passivity nor Violence; Jesus' Third Way (Matt 5; 38-42 par.)," in *The Love of Enemy and Nonretaliation in the New Testament*, ed. Willard M. Swartley (Louisville: Westminster John Knox, 1992), 102–25.

[27] Ramsay MacMullen, *Roman Social Relations 50 B.C. to A.D. 284* (New Haven: Yale University Press, 1974).

Jesus forbids meeting Roman imperial violence with violence in the present (5:38–42; 26:51–53). Violence is the preserve of God in the final eschatological destruction of Roman power (24:27–31).[28] But that does not mean passivity or unquestioning compliance in the meantime. Rather, nonviolent, active, yet protective resistance is to mark imperial negotiation.

Third, within the actions and words of Matthew's second chapter are echoes of the accounts of Moses in Egypt and of the exodus from Egypt.[29] Both narratives involve Egypt. Both the infant Moses and the infant Jesus are endangered by powerful rulers. Both Moses and Jesus have the task of saving a people. They experience exile as well as God's protection. Male children are attacked. The tyrant dies. In Matt 2:15 the citation from Hos 11:1 refers, in its original context, to Israel as God's son (Exod 4:22) being delivered from Pharaoh's oppressive and enslaving power in Egypt. There are verbal similarities between the account of Jesus' return from Egypt (Matt 2:19–21) and Moses' return to Egypt (Exod 4:19–20). As with the references to Babylonian exile and Assyrian power in Matthew's first chapter, the evoking of Moses is cryptic, covert, subtle, and subversive.

The echoes of the Moses–Exodus account underscore the pervasive reality of imperial power as well as God's control over it. Herod is a Pharaoh look-alike both in his resistance to the divine purpose and in God's thwarting of him. Just as Herod is "deceived" or "mocked" by the magi (verb *empaizō* in 2:16), so is Pharaoh by Moses and Aaron (Exod 10:2 LXX). Just as God has overcome Egyptian power and preserved Jesus from Roman imperial might, so God's saving presence will be manifested to free all people from Roman power.

Another echo adds further depth to the presentation of Jesus saving people from their sins in the Roman imperial world. God's thwarting of Herod and of Pharaoh, as well as the references to the thwarting of Assyria and Babylon noted earlier, indicate a pattern by which empires and rulers interact with God. The short Psalm 2 provides an example of how rulers typically behave in relation to the divine plan. As Ps 2:2–3 notes, they conspire and plot against "God and his anointed (king)." But God laughs at them and brings their power to nought, establishing God's designated king and purposes (Ps 2:4–11). What was true of Pharaoh and Egyptian power, of Assyrian and Babylonian rule, of Herod and Pilate who cannot keep Jesus dead, is true of Roman power. God has the last word.

And finally, Matthew's second chapter shows that in the midst of imperial power there are people whose lives, marked by courage and faithfulness,

---

28 Warren Carter, "Are There Imperial Texts in the Class? Intertextual Eagles and Matthean Eschatology as 'Lights Out' Time for Imperial Rome (Matt 24:27–31)," *Journal of Biblical Literature* 122 (2003) 467–87.
29 Brown, *The Birth of the Messiah*, 113–16; Dale C. Allison, *The New Moses: A Matthean Typology* (Minneapolis: Augsburg Fortress, 1993), 142–44.

participate in God's alternative ways of being. While the political elite in Jerusalem resist God's initiative, those who are marginal and of little account (as far as this center is concerned) participate in what God is doing. The magi, whose question about one born "king of the Jews" has greatly disturbed the holders of power in Jerusalem, remain undeterred by the power structure in accomplishing their quest to find him and pay homage. In offering their gifts, the magi are guided not by the particularities of the Scriptures but by what they discern in the created world (Matt 2:9–10). Their actions recall traditions that anticipate Gentiles coming to worship God in Jerusalem (Mic 4:1–4; Isa 60:1–6). But they also subvert the traditions. These magi are not kings and they do not find Jerusalem to be a place of worship. Instead, they offer their worship, encountering God's saving presence, within a house in the small and powerless village of Bethlehem (Matt 2:11). Then in a courageous act guided by a dream, they defy Herod's instructions to return to him with knowledge of Jesus' whereabouts (2:8, 12).

Also faithful and courageous are Joseph and Mary, entrusted with the task of protecting Jesus from a king who wants to kill him. Joseph has demonstrated his faithfulness in obeying the angel's instruction to marry the pregnant Mary even though (it would seem to any onlookers) she has dishonored him in conceiving a child that is not his (1:20–25). Likewise, Mary has exhibited profound courage. Pregnant (with no reference in Matthew to her consent) and betrothed, she is culturally, socially, economically, and religiously marginal. Passages such as Sir 23:22–26 and Wis 3:16–19; 4:3–6 pronounce male curses on and articulate hostile attitudes toward a woman (and her child) in such circumstances.

Sir 23:22–26 (NRSV): [22] So it is with a woman who leaves her husband and presents him with an heir by another man. [23] For first of all, she has disobeyed the law of the Most High; second, she has committed an offense against her husband; and third, through her fornication she has committed adultery and brought forth children by another man. [24] She herself will be brought before the assembly, and her punishment will extend to her children. [25] Her children will not take root, and her branches will not bear fruit. [26] She will leave behind an accursed memory and her disgrace will never be blotted out.

Wis 3:16–19 (NRSV): [16] But children of adulterers will not come to maturity, and the offspring of an unlawful union will perish. [17] Even if they live long they will be held of no account, and finally their old age will be without honor. [18] If they die young, they will have no hope and no consolation on the day of judgment. [19] For the end of an unrighteous generation is grievous. (See also Wis 4:3–6.)

The empire reinforced a patriarchal society presided over by the emperor as *pater patriae*, "father of the fatherland." The male-dominated imperial order exercised control over domestic life since households were understood to be the basic unit of a political entity. Women were identified in terms of their relationships with significant males. Reproduction was controlled so as to ensure clear lines of descent.[30]

In these circumstances and guided by angelic appearances and dreams (2:13, 19, 22), Mary and Joseph faithfully and courageously journey as refugees to Egypt and later return to the land of Israel and then Galilee to protect Jesus. Consistently there is a close similarity between the language employed by the angel to instruct Joseph, and that which occurs in the following verse to narrate Joseph's obedience. So in Matt 2:13, the angel commands, "Get up, take the child and his mother, and flee to Egypt, and remain there until I tell you..." Verse 14 narrates Joseph's obedience: "Then Joseph got up, took the child and his mother by night, and went to Egypt..." A similar correspondence is evident in 2:20 and 21. Through Joseph's and Mary's actions, the saving presence of God revealed in Jesus is protected and furthered in the dangerous and threatening world of empire.

Conclusion

These opening chapters of Matthew's nativity story are deeply enmeshed in the Roman imperial world. Rome's empire is not the background for a "religious story" that has nothing to do with politics. Rather it is the foreground, the very world with which the story is engaged. Further, it is the object of the story. Jesus' presence in this imperial world enacts a mission that will challenge and transform it, even while in part it ironically imitates aspects of the imperial world. The story evaluates imperial power negatively and begins to depict an alternative way of being that both contests and imitates imperial power.

The story thus challenges its readers and hearers to consider the way in which political power is used in their own worlds. Who benefits? Who gets hurt? Who pays the cost? What sort of world do we want? And it challenges us to set about living accordingly, thereby manifesting the saving presence of God that enacts the divine vision announced to Abraham to bless all the peoples of the earth.[31]

---

[30] On kinship in ancient patriarchal societies see K.C. Hanson, "Kinship," in *The Social Sciences and New Testament Interpretation*, ed. Richard L. Rohrbaugh (Peabody: Hendrickson, 1996), 62–79.

[31] For further discussion of New Testament texts negotiating Roman power, see Warren Carter, *The New Testament and the Roman Empire: An Essential Guide* (Nashville: Abingdon, 2006).

Chapter 7

Making Sense of the Matthean Genealogy: Matthew 1:17 and the Theology of History

Benedict T. Viviano, O.P.

Upon opening the New Testament, many readers are discouraged by its first page, the genealogy of Jesus (Matt 1:1–17). It seems at first glance to be a dry list of names, framed by some titles. Modern books do not usually begin in such an austere fashion. What first struck readers of old translations was the repetition of the verb "begat." The information that this sort of a list is a typical way to begin a book in the Near East—whether ancient (such as the biblical book of First Chronicles) or modern—is cold comfort. Even the idea that Matthew by this genealogy is trying to condense the whole of the Old Testament (Hebrew Bible and deuterocanonical books) as the indispensable background to the gospel story of Jesus only helps a little.

The thesis of this essay is that the evangelist Matthew is here, in the three-part structure he provides for his genealogy, presenting the reader with the partial outline of one of the earliest recorded theologies of history. He is thereby further signaling to the alert reader that with the birth of Jesus a new era of salvation history has begun. The three-part structure is summarized by Matthew at the end of the genealogy: "Therefore all the generations from Abraham to David [are] fourteen generations, and from David to the exile of Babylon [are] fourteen generations, and from the exile of Babylon to the Christ [are] fourteen generations" (Matt 1:17). This verse is a statement not only about dividing the past into historical periods but also about Christology, the role of Jesus in God's plan. These are subjects worthy of an adult person's attention. It is a mistake to relegate the infancy narratives to the children's nursery. They are full of adult themes and interests. To be sure, this does not rule out a child's interest in stars, camels, and gifts—though the camels come from Isaiah (60:6), rather than from the text of Matthew.

Let me explain. Students of my generation learnt a simple three-part division of the past into historical periods: ancient, medieval, and modern. This structure is supported by a certain ideology, stemming from Voltaire, and is not neutral. But people need some sort of structure to break up the endless flow of the historical continuum. Otherwise history is rejected as meaningless—or in Oliver Wendell Holmes' phrase, "one damned thing after another."

Wherever people have experienced a major upheaval in history, they become hungry for some sort of overall explanation. Thus, after the French Revolution and the wars of Napoleon the philosophies of history offered by Hegel and Schlegel were eagerly devoured, and their works were widely translated.[1] The same thing happened after World War I, when Oswald Spengler's turgid *Decline of the West* became an international bestseller.[2] Again, after World War II people bought and read Arnold Toynbee's *A Study of History* (in abridged form) to find out the meaning of the drama through which they had just lived.[3] After the sudden collapse of Communism in Eastern Europe and the end of the Cold War (without even a shot being fired), Francis Fukuyama was the first in the field to offer an explanation of what had happened and its future implications (*The End of History and the Last Man*).[4] His vision was so optimistic that it threatened the Pentagon's activities. To save their budget (it is alleged), Samuel P. Huntington wrote *The Clash of Civilizations* and thereby, with a little help from Osama bin Laden, created some of the impetus for the long war in Iraq.[5] In brief, people hunger for explanations of major events, explanations that relate them to significant happenings of the past and, to the extent possible, also foresee the future. In other words, they want a philosophy or a theology of history.

Now the Bible contains an extensive theology of history, viewed as salvation history.[6] In its Christian canon, the Bible itself is structured as a story that stretches from a beginning (creation and fall), through mid-point (Jesus Christ crucified and risen), to an end (the future coming of Christ in glory, bringing the kingdom of God in its fullness to the new earth). The Bible contains a long history, stretching well over a thousand years. Little wonder then that around the time of Matthew both Jews and Christians tried to find for it a structuring principle or a form of division into historical periods.

The simplest of these is a two-part pattern based on two eons or epochs: "this world (*aiōn*)" and "the world (*aiōn*) to come." "World" is the older translation of a word that has a spatial meaning (= world) but also a temporal sense (= eon).[7] This two-part pattern occurs both in the Gospels and in Paul, but especially frequently in the rabbis. However, there is also a five-part pattern based on the visions in Daniel 2 and 7. It is developed from the scheme of four ancient Near

---

[1] G.W.F. Hegel, *The Philosophy of History* (New York: Dover, 1956); Friedrich von Schlegel, *The Philosophy of History* (London: Bohn, 1835).

[2] Oswald Spengler, *The Decline of the West*, 2 vols (Oxford: Oxford University Press, 1926–1928).

[3] Arnold Toynbee, *A Study of History*, 12 vols, abridged in 2 vols (New York: Oxford University Press, 1946, 1957).

[4] Francis Fukuyama, *The End of History and the Last Man* (New York: Free Press, 1992).

[5] Samuel P. Huntington, *The Clash of Civilizations and the Remaking of World Order* (New York: Free Press, 1996).

[6] Oscar Cullmann, *Christ and Time* (Philadelphia: Westminster, 1964; orig. 1946).

[7] The Greek word *aiōn* often represents the Hebrew term '*ōlām*.

Eastern empires known to the author of Daniel (Babylonian, Mede, Persian, and Greek), with the addition of a final age.[8] This five-part scheme was received in the Book of Revelation and has a long history of influence.[9]

A Seven-Part Division of History

The most developed scheme of biblical periodization is, however, a seven-part "system." There are variants of this scheme, especially in Judaism,[10] but in Christian writings the seven ages or periods usually run as follows:

1. From Adam to Noah.
2. From Noah to Abraham.
3. From Abraham to David.
4. From David to the Exile.
5. From the Exile to Jesus.
6. From Jesus to his Second Coming.
7. From the Second Coming to the End of the World.

This seven-part scheme calls for a number of comments, but let us come to the point at once. This scheme seems to be known to the evangelist Matthew. In my view, he presupposes it as known to the more learned of his readers.[11] He proceeds to extract three or four of the seven stages, and he insists upon them in several ways. He begins with two christological titles that structure the whole Gospel in some sense, but certainly structure the genealogy: "The book of the origin of Jesus Christ, son of David, son of Abraham" (Matt 1:1). Matthew then goes on to give a list of names (from the third, fourth, and fifth ages in the seven-part scheme), running from Abraham to David, from David to the Babylonian exile, and from the exile to Joseph, Mary, and Jesus. He concludes with a summarizing verse, already cited, that is decisive for our argument. "Therefore all the generations from Abraham to David [are] fourteen generations, and from David to the exile of Babylon [are] fourteen generations, and from the exile of Babylon to the Christ [are] fourteen generations" (Matt 1:17).

---

8   The earliest Christian commentator on Daniel, Hippolytus of Rome (third century), replaced the Greek empire with the Roman one, and this became the common interpretation until the nineteenth century.

9   Mariano Delgado, Klaus Koch, and Edgar Marsch, eds, *Europa, Tausendjähriges Reich und Neue Welt* (Freiburg: Universitätsverlag, 2003).

10 Hermann L. Strack and Paul Billerbeck, *Kommentar zum Neuen Testament aus Talmud und Midrasch*, 6 vols (Munich: Beck, 1922–1961), 3.824–27.

11 On the reader's task of filling the gaps in a story, see Meir Sternberg, *The Poetics of Biblical Literature* (Bloomington, IN: Indiana University Press, 1985), 186–90.

Repetition is a biblical form of emphasis. Matthew is insisting on something, but he does not say explicitly what it is. To be sure, readers have always understood that the genealogy relates Jesus to (and roots him in) the history of Israel, the chosen people of God. (They may not always have rejoiced in this fact but they have understood it.) Our thesis, to repeat, is that Matthew is also providing a theology of history. In this theology each stage of biblical revelation has its place and meaning. With the coming of Jesus called Christ (1:16), a new stage of salvation history has begun. While mentioning only the middle three stages, Matthew presupposes the early stages from Adam to Noah to Abraham as known, and elsewhere he names Noah (24:37–38), although he never mentions Adam by name.

Implications of the Seven-Age Scheme

Now that the main point has been made, there is a place for some comments on the scheme in seven stages, and then for some of its implications as these have been worked out by early Christian exegesis. Particular attention will be given to ancient writings that divide sacred history into thousand-year periods, beginning with Revelation (20:1–10) and Second Peter (3:8–13). This approach is called chiliasm (Greek *chilia* = thousand) or millenarianism (Latin *mille anni* = a thousand years). Such an approach has often had a bad reputation in the Catholic Church. It is widely thought to be an area reserved for crackpots, but that may be unfair.

The scheme of thousand-year periods was constructed by the authors of Second Peter and Revelation through a combination of two biblical passages: the seven days of creation as recounted in Genesis 1, plus the Psalmist's concept: "A thousand years in your sight are like yesterday when it is past, or like a watch in the night" (Ps 90:4). By combining these two elements, each day of creation was taken to refer to a thousand-year period of history. The fact that the intervals between each of the periods did not always amount to a thousand years exactly (e.g., the time between David and the exile, or between the exile and Jesus) did not seem to trouble some of those who adopted the scheme. Nevertheless, Matthew is cautious in speaking of fourteen *generations*, not of thousand-year periods.[12]

Matthew 1:2–17 is perhaps an original fusion of two different schemes: (a) a world week of seven millennial "days," that is, seven thousand-year periods of

---

[12] Alfred Wikenhauser, "Das Problem des tausendjährigen Reiches in der Johannes-Apokalypse," *Römische Quartalschrift* 40 (1932) 13–25; idem, "Die Herkunft der Idee des tausendjährigen Reiches in der Johannes-Apokalypse," *Römische Quartalschrift* 45 (1937) 1–24; idem, "Weltwoche und tausendjähriges Reich," *Theologische Quartalschrift* 127 (1947) 399–417.

salvation history; (b) a scheme of generations grouped or broken up by major figures or events: Adam, Noah, Abraham, David, the Exile, Jesus. The major figures or events give historical labels to each of the millennial "days" and thus make them more concrete and meaningful.

The three sets of names in Matthew's genealogy should yield a total of forty-two names. (For why they do not, see later.) If we add the ten generations from Adam to Noah (Gen 5:3–31) and the ten generations from Noah's son Shem to Abraham (Gen 11:10–26), plus the forty-two generations from Abraham to Jesus (Matt 1:2–17), we arrive at a total of sixty-two generations from Adam to Jesus.[13] This total figure calls to mind the sixty-two weeks mentioned in Dan 9:25. One hesitates to pursue this link for a number of reasons. First, there is the evident difference between generations of named figures and weeks. Second, the sixty-two weeks of Daniel 9 come in a larger context of seventy weeks, divided into sixty-two, seven, and one, all part of Gabriel's visionary message (Dan 9:24–27). In its original intent, this passage, renowned for its difficulties, probably refers to the period between the return from exile under Zerubbabel (along with the high priest Joshua) and the death of Onias III, the deposed high priest murdered in 171 BCE. The sixty-two weeks are a round number to describe the period from the return down to Antiochus IV. As such, this scheme does not fit perfectly with Matthew's text. He deals with the same period in the fourteen generations of the third section of his genealogy.

Jesus and Moses

Matthew does not mention Moses in this genealogy, even to locate the lifetime of "Nahshon son of Aminadab" (Num 1:7; 2:3; cf. Matt 1:4). From a Jewish viewpoint this is a breathtaking omission. After all, Moses is traditionally regarded as the human author of the Torah, the instruction divinely revealed on Sinai. The Torah or Pentateuch remains to this day the canon within the canon for observant Jews, and the main reading at the weekly service. The Torah is by far the most important part of the Hebrew Bible in the traditional Jewish scale of values. Thus, for Matthew to omit Moses here could seem to Jewish readers as leaving out the most important human figure in biblical history. To be sure, Matthew is offering a genealogy of a Judahite, a son of David, not of a Levite. But the genealogy is also trying to shape a view of salvation history. In this context the omission of Moses has a decentering effect. This is so, even though Matthew's Gospel shows no

---

[13] See later for St. Augustine's understanding of this point.

hostility to the Torah of Moses (5:17–20; 23:23).[14] Indeed, Moses is named seven times in Matthew (8:4; 17:3, 4; 19:7, 8; 22:24; 23:2). Moreover, the Law is mentioned nine times, but it is often associated with the prophets, as if to soften the legal focus.[15] But the genealogy's emphasis is elsewhere, on David and Abraham as forebears of Jesus.

Some scholars believe that the structure of Matthew's Gospel suggests that he presents Jesus as a new Moses. In a short essay published almost a century ago, Benjamin W. Bacon noted that after each of five major discourses in Matthew (7:28; 11:1; 13:53; 19:1; 26:1) a phrase occurs that marks the end of the discourse.[16] The phrase runs: "Now when Jesus had finished saying these things…" (*kai egeneto hote etelesen ho Iēsous tous logous toutous*). The last time the phrase occurs (26:1), the word "all" is introduced before "these things," as if to suggest that the time for speaking is over. Now begins the final combat (suffering, death, and victory over death), after which there is a short but important parting statement, the Great Commission (28:18–20). The closing formula of the five discourses reminds us of Deuteronomy's description of Moses (Deut 31:1; 32:45), and suggests that Jesus was in some respects like Moses.[17] From these textual facts, Bacon developed the hypothesis that Matthew intended to write a Christian Pentateuch in which narrative preceded each of the five discourses. This hypothesis was well received for a long time, but it left readers uneasy that this structure left out Matthew's final chapters (26–28), dealing with the death and resurrection of Jesus. Most scholars could not imagine that Matthew intended such a thing.[18]

Although scholars after Bacon tried various makeshift solutions, with Pierre Benoit proposing a seven-act drama[19] and Edgar Krentz suggesting a three-part division,[20] the best proposal so far is a chiastic one based on the

[14] Dale C. Allison, *The New Moses: A Matthean Typology* (Minneapolis: Fortress, 1993), 182.
[15] Alexander Sand, *Das Gesetz und die Propheten* (Biblische Untersuchungen 11; Regensburg: Pustet, 1974).
[16] Benjamin W. Bacon, "The Five Books of Matthew against the Jews," *The Expositor* 15 (1918) 56–66.
[17] Allison, *New Moses*, 192.
[18] Even if a few daring scholars (influenced by redaction criticism) might have thought that Matthew did indeed intend a decentering or shift of accent from the paschal proclamation to a semi-Pelagian works righteousness, they were careful not to say this in print.
[19] Pierre Benoit, "Matthieu," *Bible de Jérusalem* (Paris: Cerf, 1950; rev. edn, 1961). The seven acts are listed in Benoit's *Jerusalem Bible* translation annotations: the preparation (chaps 1–2); the formal proclamation (chaps 3–7); preaching by signs and missionaries (chaps 8–10); the obstacles to the kingdom (11:1–13:52); the Church in embryo (13:53–18:35); the crisis (chaps 19–25); the coming of the kingdom through suffering and resurrection (chaps 26–28).
[20] Edgar Krentz, "The Extent of Matthew's Prologue," *Journal of Biblical Literature* 83 (1964) 409–14. Krentz's three-part division is based on the repeated phrase "from then Jesus began" (*apo tote ērxato ho Iēsous*: 4:17; 16:21). This gives the division: 1:1–4:16; 4:17–16:20; 16:21–28:20. This division dissolves the five discourses into the paschal message.

alternation of narrative and discourse, thereby building on the insight of Bacon:

Chapters 1–4: Birth and beginnings (narrative = N);
   5–7: **Sermon on the Mount** (discourse = D);
     8–9: Authority and invitation (N);
       10: **Mission** (D);
         11–12: Rejection by this generation (N);
          13: **Seven parables of the kingdom** (D);
        14–17: Acknowledgement by the disciples (N);
      18: **Community rules** (D);
    19–22: Authority and invitation (N);
  23–25: **Woes and apocalypse** (D);
26–28: Death and resurrection (N).

In this analysis all twenty-eight chapters are embraced in a meaningful whole, centered on the parables of the kingdom.[21] But this chiastic solution, like the solutions of Benoit and Krentz, has failed to impose itself on many scholars.[22]

Jesus and Joshua

Meanwhile, in the neighboring field of Old Testament studies, James A. Sanders had a brilliant intuition, which he set down in a brief book titled *Torah and Canon*.[23] He thereby launched a whole new approach to the Bible called canon criticism. In his little book, his strongest idea was this. Originally, the Hebrew foundation story was a Hexateuch, a six-part work that concluded with Joshua and the conquest of the Promised Land by force. Sometime later, the rabbis decided to divide the sacred books differently. Genesis to Deuteronomy became the Pentateuch, while Joshua was placed with the early prophets. For Sanders, this was a blessing for both Judaism and Christianity. It provided them with a foundational text that was not essentially bound up with a violent conquest of a particular territory. This new arrangement was better suited to a Judaism that, for millennia, had to survive outside the land—like Moses. And it suited Christianity better with its sense of universal mission,

---

21 Charles H. Lohr, "Oral Techniques in the Gospel of Matthew," *Catholic Biblical Quarterly* 23 (1961) 403–35.
22 William D. Davies and Dale C. Allison, *A Critical and Exegetical Commentary on the Gospel according to St Matthew*, 3 vols (ICC; Edinburgh: T&T Clark, 1988–1997), 1.61–72.
23 James A. Sanders, *Torah and Canon* (Minneapolis: Fortress, 1972; second rev. edn, Eugene, OR: Cascade, 2005).

its emphasis on nonviolence and love of enemies, its orientation toward the future eschatological gift of the kingdom of God and toward eternal life with God in heaven.

So far, so good. But what if Matthew had another idea? What if he accepted the Hexateuch as his model? That is my suggestion. To accept this proposal, that Matthew intended to structure his gospel book into six sections, it would be important to remember first that Joshua in Greek is spelled Jesus. For Matthew, on this view, the new Joshua (Jesus), by his suffering and death, by his mortal combat, conquered the great enemy (death), and entered the promised land of the risen life with the heavenly Father. Matthew's sixth book would consist in his chapters 26–28, which conclude with the Great Commission (28:18–20). These compact final verses affirm that Jesus is the Son of Man to whom all authority on heaven and earth has been transmitted (cf. Dan 7:13–14; Matt 11:27). He (the Emmanuel) will be with us in this, the sixth age, as well as in the final seventh age (Matt 1:21; 18:20). That is why these verses have been called an anticipated second coming of Jesus (cf. 27:51–53).[24]

A possible objection to this proposal is that we do not know enough about the currency of the Hexateuch model at the time of Matthew. After all, some have proposed an Enneateuch model, carrying the Torah through three more books for a total of nine, adding to the previous six the Books of Judges, Samuel, and Kings. (The last two are reckoned as single books in the Hebrew computation.) Both Hexateuch and Enneateuch offer multiples of Matthew's beloved triad, and a normal reckoning counts six contrasts between the Law of Moses and Jesus' teaching in Matt 5:21–48. However, Joshua son of Nun, Moses' successor, seems to play no role in Matthew (contrast Acts 7:45; Heb 4:8; 11:30–31), and so the suggestion is not without its difficulties.

On the other hand, almost as soon as the Christian Church began to enter into polemical debate with the Synagogue, the story of Joshua (Jesus son of Nave in the Septuagint spelling) became an ideal type of Christ. Joshua was contrasted with Moses in his victory over Amalek, in his crossing of the Jordan (a prefigurement of baptism), in his receiving the second law (Deuteronomy), and in his conquest of the land (the fall of Jericho was interpreted as a symbol of the end of the world).

Matthew in fact does not mention Joshua in the genealogy, even though "Nahshon son of Aminadab" (Num 10:14; cf. Matt 1:4) was his contemporary (Num 11:28). He does, however, include mention of Rahab in Matt 1:5. Rahab became a type of the Church, especially as a type of the pagans who are incorporated into the *ecclesia*, the people of God, and thus spared in the destruction that befell Jericho. In the New Testament she is an ancestor of Jesus

---

[24] John P. Meier, *Matthew* (Wilmington, DE: Glazier, 1980), 369.

(Matt 1:5), and then is contrasted as a model of salvation by works (Jas 2:25) and as a model of salvation by faith (Heb 11:30–31).[25]

The fact that Rahab is mentioned in Matthew's genealogy (1:5) is the anchor for the basic idea that Matthew was well aware of the contents of the Book of Joshua. The fact that he chose not to render the Joshua–Jesus typology more explicit matches his general literary discretion. He does not use footnotes—they had not yet been invented. He is telling a story and giving instructions to the church. With regard to structure he leaves discreet hints in the five conclusions to the great discourses (7:28; 11:1; 13:53; 19:1; 26:1), but he does not hit the reader over the head. Even more is this discretion and restraint present in the last three chapters of the gospel. The biblically literate reader is, however, free to interpret the silences.

From the Coming of Jesus to the End of the World

In the seven-stage scheme the sixth age (between the first and second comings of Christ) is sometimes called the time of the Church, the time of the Holy Spirit, the time in which we live now. In the Acts of the Apostles the risen Christ gives the apostles the Spirit as a foretaste of the full realization of the Kingdom, as the gift for this interval (Acts 1:6–8). To be sure, theologically the Spirit is present at all periods of history, from creation (Gen 1:2) to the end of the world and beyond. But the New Testament presents the time after Easter as a period of a special outpouring of the Spirit (Pentecost). On the other hand, the number six can suggest a time of evil just before the fulfillment, which is thus associated with the number seven. This could account for some of the disappointing, even sinful, aspects of the last two thousand years.

In the seven-part scheme, the seventh age would involve the coming (*parousia*) in glory of the Son of Man. His coming involves judgment (Matt 25:31–46) and governing the world in justice and peace (Matt 24:3, 27, 37, 39; 1 Cor 15:23; 1 Thess 2:19; 3:13; 4:15; 5:23). Judging here includes the Hebrew sense of the verb *shāphat*, as in the Book of Judges, where charismatic leaders such as Deborah, Gideon, and Samson do indeed judge cases, but also lead in battle and govern the people.

Readers may reasonably ask where this seventh age is suggested in the genealogy. The answer is surprising. If we return to our key structuring verse (1:17), we recall that Matthew insists on the number fourteen three times. Now when

---

[25] The Joshua typology, already found in the *Letter of Barnabas* (12:7–10; 17:14), is greatly developed by St. Justin Martyr (*Dialogue with Trypho* 49, 70, 75, 89–90, 113–14), St. Irenaeus, Tertullian, St. Hippolytus, St. Clement of Alexandria, Origen (who devoted a commentary to the Book of Joshua), Eusebius, St. Cyril of Jerusalem, and St. Zeno of Verona. Cf. Jean Daniélou, *From Shadows to Reality: Studies in the Biblical Typology of the Fathers* (Westminster, MD: Newman, 1960), 227–28.

we actually count the names we do find fourteen names (or generations) in the first two lists but only thirteen in the third list. Why is this? Several suggestions have been made, but only one is of major theological significance. It was cautiously made by the late Swedish scholar Krister Stendahl in 1962. The thirteenth name is Jesus, "who is called the Messiah [or Christ]" (1:16, 17). For Stendahl, the missing fourteenth name is also Jesus Christ but now as Son of Man in his glory, "at his coming (*parousia*) at the end of time. We...have here the strong futuristic eschatology of the early church."[26] This suggestion would seem farfetched and improbable if it did not fit so well with Matthew's Jewish-Christian outlook, which includes an interest in eschatology, apocalyptic, and salvation-historical thinking. Matthew's broad outlook points to the universal significance of Jesus as he comes first in humility and suffering and then in his glory in the future, anticipated already by his Easter resurrection.

From Adam to Abraham

There is another perplexing omission in Matthew's genealogy. If Matthew knew the seven-part scheme (as we assume he did), why did he omit the first two parts: from Adam to Noah, and then from Noah to Abraham? What is clear from Matt 1:1 and 17 is that Matthew is striving for a christological concentration on Abraham and David as ancestors of the Jews. Matthew makes no mention of Jesus as a second Adam (cf. 1 Cor 15:45) or as son of Adam (Luke 3:38).[27] There is also no developed Christian tradition of calling Jesus son of Noah, but both Noah and Adam count as ancestors of Jesus in Luke's genealogy (Luke 3:36, 38).

We may note here a significant salvation-historical statement concerning the virtuous, murdered, son of Adam (= Abel), found in Matt 23:35 and Luke 11:51, that is, in the Sayings Source (Q): "so that upon you may come all the righteous blood shed on earth, from the blood of righteous Abel (Gen 4:8, 10) to the blood of Zechariah son of Barachiah..."[28] This verse is an extract from

---

[26] Krister Stendahl, "Matthew," in *Peake's Commentary on the Bible*, ed. Matthew Black and H. H. Rowley (Edinburgh: Nelson, 1962), 769–98, here 770–71. For this futuristic eschatology, see Matt 24:29–31 (and its parallels in Mark and Luke), as well as Acts 2:20; 3:20–21.

[27] Admittedly there is an allusion to Adam and Eve (unnamed) in Matt 19:4: "Have you not read that the one who made (*ktisas*) at the beginning 'made them male and female'?" However, the idea of Christ as second man or last Adam is a Pauline notion (1 Cor 15:45, 47).

[28] Here we may briefly notice some of the problems connected with the reference to "the blood of Zechariah son of Barachiah, whom you murdered between the sanctuary and the altar" (Matt 23:35). There is some debate as to which Zechariah is meant. Zechariah son of Berechiah son of Iddo is the eleventh of the twelve minor prophets (Zech 1:1; cf. Ezra 5:1), but he is not known to have been slain except in the diffuse post-biblical tradition that all the prophets suffered violent ends; cf. Odil Hannes Steck, *Israel und das gewaltsame Geschick der Propheten* (WMANT 23; Neukirchen: Neukirchener Verlag, 1967). Zechariah, the son of the priest Jehoiada, may be the person meant (2 Chr 24:20–22), because he was

the climax of the woes (Matthew 23; Luke 11) and very likely goes back to the historical Jesus. The verse reflects a perspective of eschatological judgment in which the whole human history of unjust suffering, from the first to the last murder of the innocent in the Hebrew Bible, will be set right by God. The verse tries to embrace the whole of biblical history. In this respect it represents a precedent in the preaching of Jesus himself for the comprehensive historical perspective that Matthew attempts in his genealogy. But it takes its start from the story of Adam, Cain, and Abel at the beginning of Genesis. So Matthew knows the story too, even though he chooses not to mention it in his genealogy.

As we continue to answer the question, why did Matthew omit the first two stages in the scheme (Adam and Noah), we may also suggest a pedagogical reason. Adding the first two steps, even with only ten names in each of these two sections, would have made the genealogy too long for Matthew's taste. It would have damaged his pattern of fourteen names per section, as well as the triadic pattern. As the adage says, "All good things come in threes" (*omne trinum perfectum*), so Matthew loves triads.[29] Moreover, brevity is the soul of wit, and many regard the genealogy as too long even in this briefer form.

Another reason for the omission of the first two stages might be Matthew's literary coquetry. Like other biblical authors, of both testaments, he employs what has been called the "foolproof method" of biblical composition.[30] This means that he has written his gospel in plain prose, with much narrative that any reader or hearer can understand. This ready intelligibility provides the basis for the measure of truth in the old Calvinist doctrine of the perspicuity of Scripture. This doctrine holds that any believing reader can and should read the Scriptures daily; with the help of the Holy Spirit, the reader will derive spiritual profit from the reading. This is well and good but it is not the whole truth. The biblical authors added subtle tests of skill for their more learned readers and copyists—those initiated into the professional secrets of the guild of scribes. These tests have proven a source of endless delight and fascination to studious readers down through the centuries. These readers are asked to apply their background knowledge of the Bible and its accompanying tradition to a particular composition.

---

stoned to death in the court of the Temple by order of the king who had been offended by his preaching. Some commentators think that it is a third Zechariah, son of Baris (or in some manuscripts, Baruch), known from Josephus, *Jewish War* 4.5.4 ##334–344. Of these three options, probably the first fits best here, since Matthew refers twice in this chapter (23:30, 37) to the tradition that the prophets were killed. Note finally that in the Septuagint of Isa 8:2, two reliable witnesses support Isaiah: the priest Uriah (cf. 2 Kgs 16:10–16) and Zechariah son of Barachiah (whereas in the Hebrew he is the son of Jeberechiah).

[29] Davies and Allison, *St Matthew*, 1.62; cf. Dale C. Allison, "The Structure of the Sermon on the Mount," *Journal of Biblical Literature* 106 (1987) 423–35.

[30] Sternberg, *Poetics*, 50–56. We can compare what has been said of the novelist Anthony Trollope's style: "plain British boiled beef."

Apocalyptic Origin of the Seven-Part Division of History?

This last point leads us naturally to the difficult question: how old is the seven-age scheme of history? Could Matthew have known of it? Was it sufficiently well known that he could reasonably expect some of his readers to know about it and to see an allusion to it in his genealogy?

Already in the 1920s, Paul Billerbeck proposed that *1 Enoch*'s Ten Week Apocalypse was the closest pre-Christian parallel to Matthew and his most probable source.[31] We will proceed as though this were correct, but with fear and trepidation, given the difficulties in dating and determining the text and translation of *1 Enoch*. To be sure, what is properly characteristic of the apocalyptic theology of history is *numbered* periods as parts of the divine plan. Apart from Genesis 1 and the history by generations in the Pentateuch and in the historical books of the Hebrew Bible, this reckoning of numbers may be said to begin already with Jeremiah's prophecy of a seventy-year exile (Jer 25:11-12; 29:10; Zech 1:12). This figure of seventy years is then reflected on in 2 Chr 36:22-23 and in the influential Dan 9:24-27. The latter passage in Daniel teems with ambiguities of translation, but these are concerned with the Messiah rather than with the numbered periods.[32] It is from this background that *1 Enoch* most likely takes its start.

The Apocalypse of Weeks appears in *1 Enoch* 93:1-10; 91:11-17, where the Ethiopic text has these sections in reverse order.[33] The Qumran Aramaic fragments provide textual evidence for the scholarly rearrangement.[34] In this case the basis for the rearrangement is simple. It is based on a list of ten "weeks" or historical periods in the history of Israel. Seven refer to Israel's past history, three to the present messianic age and to future judgments. However, in 91:15, the text speaks about "the tenth week in the seventh part." This can be taken to mean that the

[31] Strack and Billerbeck, *Kommentar zum Neuen Testament*, 1.43–45 (on Matt 1:17).

[32] D.S. Russell, *The Method and Message of Jewish Apocalyptic* (Philadelphia: Westminster, 1964), 224–29; Paul Volz, *Jüdische Eschatologie von Daniel bis Akiba* (Tübingen: Mohr, 1936); Joseph Bonsirven, *Palestinian Judaism in the Time of Jesus Christ* (New York: Holt, 1964), 205–25. On the implications of Dan 9:24-27 for messianism, see Joseph A. Fitzmyer, *The One Who is to Come* (Grand Rapids: Eerdmans, 2007), 60–64.

[33] Most of *1 Enoch* has been dated anywhere from 250 BCE to 50 CE. This long book is not a unity that was written at one date by one author but the product of an Enoch "school" that continued into two more works known as *Second Enoch* and *Third Enoch*. The parts of *First Enoch* that most concern us are found in considerable fragments in Aramaic at Qumran, so certainly before 70 CE, and probably composed around 170 BCE. The Aramaic fragments are important because the complete text, preserved only in Ethiopic (Ge'ez) has suffered some textual disturbance in the crucial chapters 91 and 93. Scholars have long suspected this dislocation and rearranged the chapters accordingly.

[34] J.T. Milik, *The Books of Enoch: Aramaic Fragments* (Oxford: Clarendon, 1976); George W.E. Nickelsburg, *1 Enoch 1: A Commentary on...1 Enoch, chaps. 1–36; 81–108* (Hermeneia; Minneapolis: Fortress, 2001), 434–50; Loren T. Stuckenbruck, *1 Enoch 91–108* (Commentaries on Early Jewish Literature; Berlin: de Gruyter, 2007), 49–152.

author thinks of the last three weeks as part of a seventh age. If this interpretation is correct, we would have in *1 Enoch* the earliest trace of a seven-age scheme.
Even if this is correct, we are still compelled to note that the scheme is not here
explicitly based on the seven days of creation, nor on Ps 90:4, nor on named biblical heroes. What is in play is the explicit use of the term *week*, itself derived from
the seven days of creation in biblical revelation (Gen 1:1–2:4a).

We come closer to our goal when we turn to the *Second Book of Enoch* (also
known as *Slavonic Enoch*). This work also bristles with difficulties—linguistic,
textual, and chronological. Though the existing manuscripts are medieval,
the priestly concerns evident in the text lead some scholars to date the original composition to the time when the temple was still standing in Jerusalem,
that is, sometime before Matthew's Gospel was written. The book exists in two
forms or recensions. In one of these we find at the beginning of chapter 33:
"God shows Enoch the epoch [age] of this world, the existence of 7000 years,
and the eighth thousand is the end..." (opening of *2 Enoch* 33).[35] This seems
like a chapter heading, perhaps added by a scribe to clarify and to introduce
what follows: "On the 8th day I likewise appointed, so that the 8th day might be
the 1st, the first-created of my week, and that it should revolve in the revolution
of 7000, so that the 8000 might be in the beginning of a time not reckoned and
unending" (*2 Enoch* 33:1–2).

If this text is part of the original work, composed before 70 CE, it would be a
valuable predecessor of Matthew's scheme, because it contains the world week
of seven millennia, seven historical periods, followed by an eighth day of eternal rest. It implies the influence of Genesis 1 and Ps 90:4, but it still does not
link the seven ages with biblical figures or events like the Babylonian exile.

Early Christian Use of the Seven-Age Scheme

Outside of the New Testament, the earliest Christian attestation of the seven-
age scheme occurs in a curious work of the mid-second century, the letter
attributed to St. Barnabas (*Let. Barn.* 15:4).[36]

Pay attention, children, to what he says: "He finished in six days" (Gen 2:2
LXX). He is saying that in six thousand years the Lord will finish everything.

---

[35] This quotation and the next are from Francis I. Andersen, "2 (Slavonic Apocalypse of)
Enoch," in *Old Testament Pseudepigrapha*, ed. James H. Charlesworth, 2 vols (New York:
Doubleday, 1983–1985), 1.91–213, here 1.156; cf. Andrei Orlov, *From Apocalypticism to
Merkabah Mysticism: Studies in Slavonic Pseudepigrapha* (JSJ Supplement 114; Leiden: Brill,
2007).

[36] Robert M. Grant *et al.*, *The Apostolic Fathers*, 6 vols (New York: Nelson, 1965) 3.128. A similar scheme appears in St. Justin, *Dialogue with Trypho* 81.4; St. Irenaeus, *Adversus Haereses*
5.28.3; St. Hippolytus, *Commentary on Daniel* 4.23; St. Clement of Alexandria, *Stromateis*
6.137–45.

For with him the "day" signifies a thousand years. And he bears me witness
(on this point) saying: "Behold, a day of the Lord shall be as a thousand
years" (cf. Ps 90:4). Therefore, children, "in six days"—in six thousand years—
"everything" will be finished" [i.e., the universe will arrive at its term].

Here once again we see the seven-age scheme, based on the same combination
of biblical texts, but without the labeling of the ages according to biblical figures or events. We almost have the impression that Matthew is original in his
connecting the biblical periods with *named* figures and events.

But at least one major church father, St. Augustine of Hippo (354–430),
understood the full scheme underlying Matthew's genealogy. In the time of
testing after Alaric had sacked Rome (410 CE) and the Empire in the West was
tottering toward its collapse, Augustine wrote his enormous, rambling meditation on ancient history in the light of Christian faith. He tried to make sense
of it all in his nine-hundred-page *City of God*. Augustine refers explicitly to
Matthew's scheme and completed it with the first two stages, from Adam to
Noah and from Noah to Abraham. In Books 19–22 of *The City of God*, Augustine
treats carefully the major eschatological texts of the Bible and tries to work
out a synthesis of the data, from the days of creation to the four kingdoms of
Daniel 7, through the Antichrist and the Millennium, to the beatific vision and
the eighth day of the eternal Sabbath in heaven. This all builds up to a magnificent finale, the last paragraph of the entire work (*De civitate Dei*, 22.33.5).[37]

This Sabbath shall appear still more clearly if we count the ages as days, in
accordance with the periods of time defined in Scripture, for that period will
be found to be the seventh. The first age, as the first day, extends from Adam
to the deluge; the second from the deluge to Abraham, equaling the first, not
in length of time, but in the number of generations, there being ten in each.
From Abraham to the advent of Christ there are, as the evangelist Matthew
calculates, three periods, in each of which are fourteen generations—one
period from Abraham to David, a second from David to the captivity, a third
from the captivity to the birth of Christ in the flesh. There are thus five ages
in all. The sixth is now passing, and cannot be measured by any number of
generations, as it has said, "It is not for you to know the times, which
the Father hath put in His own power" (Acts 1:7). After the period God shall
rest as on the seventh day, when He shall give us (who shall be the seventh
day) rest in Himself. But there is not now space to treat of these ages; suffice

[37] St. Augustine, *The City of God*, transl. Marcus Dods (New York: Modern Library, 1955), 867.
Cf. *Oeuvres de St Augustin*, tome 37, *La cité de Dieu*, livres 19–22, ed. Gustave Bardy (Paris:
Desclée de Brouwer, 1960); R.A. Markus, *Saeculum: History and Society in the Theology of St.
Augustine* (Cambridge: Cambridge University Press, 1970); W.G. Most, *Saint Augustine's De
Civitate Dei* (Washington, D.C.: Catholic University of America Press, 1949).

it to say that the seventh shall be our Sabbath, which shall be brought to a close, not by an evening, but by the Lord's day, as an eighth and eternal day, consecrated by the resurrection of Christ, and *prefiguring* the eternal repose not only of the spirit, but also of the body. There we shall rest and see, see and love, love and praise. This is what shall be in the end without end. For what other end do we propose to ourselves than to attain to the kingdom of which there is no end? I think I have now, by God's help, discharged my obligation in writing this large work. Let those who think I have said too little, or those who think I have said too much, forgive me; and let those who think I have said just enough join me in giving thanks to God. Amen.

Augustine, we observe, reckons ten generations in the first two stages, and (following Matthew) fourteen in the next three.[38] We may also note here in passing that the great lifespan of Adam, 930 years according to Gen 5:5, almost amounts to a millennium in itself.

With regard to this concluding passage from Augustine, two main comments are in order, one positive, one negative. We see first that this great Latin church father was able, thanks to his concern, to understand the events of history, including events during which he was living (like the Vandals' siege of his city of Hippo), in the light of faith guided by biblical revelation. Hence he was able to comprehend the full sense of Matthew's genealogical scheme better than any other early Christian known to me. To his credit, he saw that Matthew implied the first two stages even if he did not say so explicitly. On the negative side, due to his neo-Platonic exaggerated spiritualization, and despite his best efforts to overcome his neo-Platonism through faith in the incarnation of the Word, he developed, toward the end of his life, a horror in regard to a millennial kingdom on earth (*De civ. Dei*, 20.7). That is why he blurs so subtly the seventh day in the scheme with the eighth day.

In fairness let it be added that by including the phrase "*prefiguring* the eternal repose" he meant to say that the seventh day on earth, the millennial kingdom, *prefigures* the eternal rest of the eighth day in heaven, thanks to its fulfillment of God's intention for human history—namely, justice, peace, and joy (Rom 14:17). If that is Augustine's meaning, then no criticism is called for. Certainly in his earlier preaching (Sermon 259, PL 38:1197–98), Augustine does hold for a millennial Kingdom on earth. It is usually thought that he dropped this view in *The City of God*.[39] But this may not be correct. If so, then no negative criticism applies.

---

[38] George Foot Moore, "Fourteen Generations: 490 Years: An Explanation of the Genealogy of Jesus," *Harvard Theological Review* 14 (1921) 97–103, here 196. Moore mentions the view of Cornelius Jansen that one goal of the genealogy is to show that the Messiah arrived at the right time, foreseen by biblical prophecy.

[39] Jean Daniélou, *The Bible and the Liturgy* (Notre Dame, IN: University of Notre Dame Press, 1956), 275–86.

To be sure, Augustine was also a genius of human developmental psychology and Christian spirituality. It is not surprising, therefore, that he also applies the seven-age scheme to his own life and thus to the lives of others: infancy, childhood, adolescence, young adulthood, mature adulthood, decline, and old age. This seven-age scheme underlies the thirteen books of Augustine's *Confessions*.[40] It also underlies the structure of Books 15–22 of *The City of God*.[41]

This double use of the seven-age scheme, for personal growth and development as well as for understanding world history, shows its fundamental fruitfulness. In this way Matthew's genealogy becomes meaningful even for our spiritual lives. At least since Denis the Areopagite (sixth century CE), Christian spirituality has presented the life of the graced soul according to a three-age scheme: purgative, illuminative, unitive—or, more biblically, beginners, proficient, perfect. This scheme has influenced both Christian and Jewish believers.[42]

Commentators from 1907 to 2007

My thesis is clear: Matthew in 1:17 is providing an extract from a larger pre-existing world week scheme of seven-thousand-year periods as an outline of a theology of history. Let us now look at some commentaries published in 1907–2007 (mostly German), to see how they understand Matthew's genealogy.

Johannes Weiss, at the beginning of the twentieth century, proposes that Matthew's three sets of fourteen generations can be understood as describing a preparation, a splendor, and a decline. The task of the genealogy is to bring forth the Messiah.[43] Erich Klostermann recognizes a principle of a week (*Hebdomadenprinzip*) or set of sevens. He observes that there are ten generations from Adam to Noah according to Gen 5:1–32 and ten generations from Noah to Abraham according to Gen 11:10–26. This is picked up by the rabbinic text *Mishnah Abot* 5:2–3, and later by Augustine, as we have seen.[44] Paul Billerbeck states that what earlier generations thought and taught about the time of arrival of the Messiah is fulfilled in Jesus.[45]

[40] D. Doncet, "L'ars memoriae dans les Confessions," *Revue des Etudes augustiennes* 33 (1987) 49–69.

[41] Auguste Luneau, *Histoire du salut chez les Pères de l'Eglise: La doctrine des âges du monde* (Théologie Historique 2; Paris: Beauchesne, 1964). The main passages in Augustine are *De civ. Dei* 16:43; 15:1 and 9; 12:12; 20:19 and 23; 22:7.

[42] Benedict T. Viviano, "Synagogues and Spirituality: The Case of Beth Alfa," in *Jesus and Archeology*, ed. James H. Charlesworth (Grand Rapids, MI: Eerdmans, 2006), 223–35.

[43] Johannes Weiss, *Matthäus-Kommentar* (Göttingen: Vandenhoeck & Ruprecht, 1907), 232–34.

[44] Erich Klostermann, *Matthäus-Kommentar* (Tübingen: Mohr, 1927), 1–6.

[45] Strack and Billerbeck, *Kommentar zum Neuen Testament*, 1.43–45.

Adolf Schlatter remarks that the numerical rhythm for Matthew is a sign of the divine government of all events. Such thinking had been encouraged by Daniel who described the time between the Exile and the Promise as seventy weeks (Dan 9:24–27). Schlatter also notes that the rabbis emphasize that major events in salvation history often occur on the same day of the year. For example, in their interpretation of Exod 12:42, the rabbis and Targumists say that on the fourteenth day of the month of Nisan the creation, the binding of Isaac, the exodus from Egypt, and the future arrival of the Messiah all occur. On the ninth of Ab the two destructions of Jerusalem and its temple occur.[46]

Joachim Gnilka also verifies that behind the artificially constructed symmetry lurks a plan of God. The play with numbers means that God guides history to its intended goal. *Christologically*, Jesus born of Mary is the awaited Christ. *Ecclesiologically*, the history of the People of God is to be conceived as a history of promise. Gnilka recognizes the role of Enoch's world week, but adds consideration of the twice fourteen days of the lunar calendar as well as of the Hebrew gematria value of fourteen as the number for David.[47] The characteristic feature of Matthew's genealogy is the penetration of the messianic promise fulfilled in Jesus with the history of the people of Israel: "This penetration validates the universality of the messianic promise, because of its start with Abraham and because of its mention of the four women, but also it points to the traces of God's guidance of history. Despite many oppositions and low points, it reaches its goal."

The historical descent of Jesus from the Jewish people is today largely undisputed. Whereas Nazi-era exegesis tried in vain to prove that Jesus was of "Aryan" descent, today we recognize that Jesus was a Jew, a son of Abraham. For Matthew it is self-evident and theologically necessary that salvation comes from Israel. Jesus' Davidic origins are widely attested in the New Testament (e.g., Rom 1:3; Heb 7:13). These origins are traced legally through Joseph, not biologically through Mary. Joseph was from a lateral branch of the Davidic line, not from the direct royal line. Nevertheless, Gnilka observes that the genealogy had relatively little influence on later Christian life, perhaps because it was not considered very edifying.[48]

The recent commentary on Matthew by Peter Fiedler reflects the interests of the younger generation, with its focus on narrative literary criticism and the role of the reader. For Fiedler Matt 1:17 is the narrator's commentary on the genealogy to help the reader interpret the lists of names in a deeper sense, as a theology of history. The periods are a means to see God's guiding hand at work in the chaos of events. This apocalyptic historical determinism has

---

[46] Adolf Schlatter, *Der Evangelist Matthäus* (Stuttgart: Calwer, 1929), 6–7.

[47] In Hebrew reckoning, the name David (D-V-D) may be understood as a series of numbers: D = 4; V = 6; D = 4; total = 14.

[48] Joachim Gnilka, *Das Matthäusevangelium*, 2 vols (Freiburg: Herder, 1986–1988), 1.11–14.

deeply marked Matthew (cf. Dan 11:36). There is a "providential design" (in the words of Donald Hagner). Matthew 1:17 invites the reader to pause and to reflect before the next phase is told. The next phase is going to be the special time of Jesus and the Church. We should react, not with hopelessness due to the perceived chaos, but with the confidence that comes from seeing the orderly plan of God. From the verse we can derive comfort and stability as we interpret the present.

According to Fiedler, the genealogy is an ideal (i.e., unreal) table of ancestors to legitimize someone formally as Messiah. Jesus is the messianic Son of David because he fulfills the genealogical presuppositions precisely. Israel's whole history flows to him, and he is the selection filter for the genealogical sequence. But the sense of Matt 1:1 (Jesus as son of David, son of Abraham) will only become clear in the course of the whole narrative.[49]

For Ulrich Luz the point is to present Jesus as a human, historical figure. He cites St. Irenaeus: the meek and humble human being was preserved (*Adv. Haer.* 3.11.8).[50] W.D. Davies and Dale Allison note that, besides 1:17, Matthew likes to write summary verses, such as 4:23 and 9:35.[51] Like Luz, Davies and Allison know of but show little interest in the scheme of the seven ages of the world week because they seem not to be very interested in a theology of history or in an apocalyptic kingdom of God coming in the future.

In last place we may note an article by Karl-Heinrich Ostmeyer. He makes two points that are rarely found in the earlier literature. The first point is that the three sections of the genealogy each represent a different aspect of the biblical record. The first section speaks of the patriarchal era, with pagan or foreign wives. The second offers the royal descent. The third is actually *priestly*. Matthew thereby wishes to include the priestly-temple aspect of the biblical tradition as does the Letter to the Hebrews, even though both know that Jesus is of the tribe of Judah, not of Levi. (This is probably a correct perception of Matthew's intention.)

Ostmeyer's second point is that if you add up the three sets of fourteen generations it gives you approximately forty generations. Now forty weeks is about the time of a full pregnancy. So it took forty generations for salvation history to gestate the Promised One. Jesus was born "in the fullness of time," as Paul says (Gal 4:4). Matthew does not explicitly mention the number forty here because it was common knowledge. Ostmeyer's two ideas are interesting and fresh contributions, but it is not self-evident that Matthew had them sharply in view.[52]

---

[49] Peter Fiedler, *Matthäus* (Stuttgart: Kohlhammer, 2005).

[50] Ulrich Luz, *Matthew 1–7* (Hermeneia; Minneapolis: Fortress, 2007), 85–88.

[51] Davies and Allison, *St Matthew*, 1.185–88.

[52] Karl-Heinrich Ostmeyer, "Der Stammbaum des Verheissenen: Theologische Implikationen der Namen und Zahlen in Mt. 1.1–17," *New Testament Studies* 46 (2000), 175–92.

Conclusions

From these gleanings in the works of earlier commentators, we may draw a few main conclusions. The first is christological. The genealogy not only presents Jesus as true king and son of David, but also as priest in some sense (if Ostmeyer is to be trusted). Jesus as prophet is not so clearly emphasized here. Jesus is rather presented as the fulfillment of the prophets' hopes for an anointed savior. To be sure, Jesus as prophet will come later in Matthew (e.g., Matt 12:17–21, 39–41)—and especially in John's envoy Christology and in his development of Jesus as the prophet like Moses (Deut 18:18).

Is Jesus implicitly the Danielic divine Son of Man in the genealogy? This depends upon the missing fourteenth name in the third set of the genealogy. Theoretically this omission could be due to error or carelessness or due to the fact that Mathew only found thirteen names in his source and he was too scrupulous to invent a fourteenth.[53] It is better, however, to respect the intelligence and competence of the author Matthew who elsewhere shows signs of meticulous care in composition. That is why Stendahl's solution is so attractive. His suggestion is that the missing fourteenth name is the future coming Son of Man. It is theologically satisfying because the title may be understood as a divine one and it corresponds to a documentable interest by Matthew in the Son of Man as linked with the Kingdom of God.

Ecclesiologically, the two dominant titles Son of David and Son of Abraham (Matt 1:1) can be unpacked in this way. The Son of David title connects Jesus with a historic people, the united kingdom of Judah and Israel, the south and the north. (The quest for the reunion of the two kingdoms is the ecumenical problem specific to the Hebrew Bible.) Jesus comes with a people, the people of God, and at the moment of his arrival he is largely confined to the Jewish people. But the title Son of Abraham suggests an expanding horizon whereby the people of God are widened to include all the nations as they receive Jesus' message and become his disciples. This is the progressive expansion that occurs in the Gospel itself. The restriction of the mission only to the lost sheep of the house of Israel (Matt 10:5–6; 15:24) finally gives way to the great commission to all the nations (Matt 28:18–20).

---

[53] Davies and Allison, *St Matthew*, 1.185–88.

Chapter 8

Matthew's Nativity Stories: Historical and Theological Questions for Today's Readers

Bernard P. Robinson

Matthew's infancy narrative is seldom considered on its own, without reference to Luke's. When, however, it is so read, it poses a number of problems and is in some ways difficult for the modern reader to assimilate. Among its most difficult aspects for today's readers are its male-centered (androcentric) approach and its heavy reliance on quotations from the Old Testament ("formula citations").

I propose first to discuss the relationship, if any, of Matthew's infancy story to Luke's and their genre. Then I shall note the androcentric character of the narrative episodes, and after that I shall examine each of them in turn in order to try to catch their drift. After a few observations on Matthew's "formula citations" and on his use of the Old Testament generally (he "quotes the OT at least twice as often as any other Gospel writer"),[1] also on his use of foreshadowing techniques, I shall proceed to a conclusion. At the outset, though, it may be useful to set out what I take to be the main emphases in Matthew's infancy narrative.

- The life of Jesus, from his conception onward, happened according to the Scriptures;
- Jesus is Davidic and resumes the history of the Jewish people;
- Jesus, not "Herod the king" (2:1, 3, 9), is Israel's true king—the Messiah son of David (2:2, 6);
- Jesus is a sort of new Moses who is set to conduct a greater rescue (or exodus) than Moses (2:15);
- Jesus is God's presence among human beings, Immanuel, the savior of his people;
- His very conception was God's work (1:20–23);
- In his beginning was his end, since the birth stories anticipate later events in his ministry and beyond.

---

[1] John Nolland, *The Gospel of Matthew. A Commentary on the Greek Text* (NIGTC; Grand Rapids: Eerdmans/Bletchley: Paternoster, 2005) 29. In this chapter all biblical translations are my own.

Comparing Matthew and Luke

The differences between the infancy stories found in Matthew and Luke (the only gospels to have such material) are striking. The two evangelists agree in having Jesus born in Bethlehem in the days of Herod the Great (d. 4 BCE); in naming Mary's husband as Joseph and attributing to him Davidic descent (through Solomon according to Matt 1:6, but in Luke 3:31 through Nathan) but in denying Joseph's biological paternity of Jesus; and in treating the nativity as divinely effected.[2] But they seem to agree on little else. Matthew has no census, no shepherds, and no Presentation in the Temple, whereas Luke says nothing about magi, a flight into and return from Egypt, or a massacre of babies. Matthew has Jesus born in a house in Bethlehem, where, he implies, Joseph has his home at the time, while in Luke Joseph is a resident of Nazareth and the Bethlehem manger will presumably be in the public "inn" (a *khan* or caravanserai). In Matthew an unnamed angel visits Joseph after the conception and similarly nameless angels appear to him on two subsequent occasions, whereas in Luke Gabriel visits Mary before the conception.

Verbal agreements exist (e.g., in the use of the words for *holy spirit* [without article; and not personified], *virgin*, *betroth*, and *find*) but they are few in number. It is possible to argue that Luke knew and rewrote Matthew's account (changing magi to shepherds and recasting the account of the flight into Egypt as a story of Joseph and Mary migrating, for the purposes of the census, from Nazareth to Bethlehem),[3] or that Matthew knew and reworked some of the material that ended up in Luke's account,[4] but if so the rehashing of the narratives will have been rather substantial. The opinion favored by most scholars is that the two infancy accounts are independent of each other.

Genre of the Narrative

If Matthew's stories are indeed independent of Luke's, in my judgment it would be rash to place too much credence in the historicity of two accounts that are so very different, except perhaps in respect of the details that they

---

[2] For a list of more than twenty parallels between Matthew's infancy narrative and Luke's, see Patricia McDonald, "Resemblances Between Matthew 1–2 and Luke 1–2," in the appendix of this volume.

[3] So Michael D. Goulder, *Midrash and Lection in Matthew* (London: SPCK, 1974), 452–71; idem, *Luke, A New Paradigm*, 2 vols (JSNT Supplement 20; Sheffield: Sheffield Academic Press, 1989), 1. 22, 246–53; John Drury, *Tradition and Design in Luke's Gospel: A Study in Early Christian Historiography* (London: Darton, Longman & Todd, 1976), 120–73 ("Using Matthew"), esp. 123–28.

[4] So Robert H. Gundry, *Matthew. A Commentary on His Handbook for a Mixed Church Under Persecution*, second edn (Grand Rapids: Eerdmans, 1994), 26, 32, 34.

share. If, on the other hand, a degree of editing of one tradition by the author of the other has been at work, the freedom with which he will have reshaped the material suggests that he will himself have realized that he was generally not dealing in hard historical data. Either way, therefore, readers will be well advised to be cautious about positing a high level of historicity. Attempts are made from time to time to take both the Matthean and the Lukan narratives as substantially historical (the one perhaps preserving Joseph's memories, the other Mary's—as if they are not likely to have compared notes) and to harmonize them, but such attempts are in my view very problematic. If, as we read in Matthew, after a visit from the magi Joseph took the family to Egypt until the death of Herod, the Lukan Presentation in the Temple after forty days, and the touching stories about Simeon and Anna, may begin to look very shaky from a historical perspective. Some have suggested that the magi arrived up to a year after the nativity; others that the family fled to Egypt, then returned to Bethlehem and Jerusalem before finally proceeding to Nazareth. To my mind, there is an air of desperation about such proposals.

If we take Matthew's account on its own, we shall have to say that none of its episodes (discovery of the pregnancy; marriage; visit of the magi; flight into Egypt; massacre; return from Egypt) is in substance impossible, but a number of details are historically very suspect. For example, even if we can accommodate ourselves to the idea that Joseph's actions were on three occasions actuated by a heavenly visitant (many readers today, believers as well as unbelievers, regard the angelophany as a literary device to signal that events are to be interpreted as the effects of divine providence), a Herod who trusts the magi to report back to him, and a star that can pinpoint one particular house will probably strain our credulity. In my analysis, it is likely that Matthew's understanding of the demands of a retelling of Mark's Jesus-story did not preclude the creation of fictitious stories that would attest to deeper truths than those of factual historicity: probable examples (according to many scholars) are his tales of Pilate's washing of his hands (27:24–25), of the role of the Jewish high priests in Jesus' burial (27:62–66; 28:11–15), and of the appearance of Jesus to the Twelve on a mountain in Galilee (28:16–20).[5]

On the other hand, it could also be argued that it strains credulity to suppose Matthew or his source(s) to have simply concocted the stories of the irregular birth, the coming of the magi, the massacre of children, and a journey to and from Egypt. If indeed he had no sources to turn to, as Michael Goulder believes, he will have had to compose the bulk of the material by way of creative reflection on Old Testament and Jewish traditions.[6] Most scholars, however, do assume that there were sources. Some think that Matthew took

---

[5] See Ulrich Luz, *Studies in Matthew*, trans. Rosemary Selle (Grand Rapids: Eerdmans, 2005), 58–60.

[6] Goulder, *Midrash*, 228–42.

over a number of rather disparate oral traditions and wrote them up into a continuous narrative. Others argue that he inherited and edited a continuous narrative, whether oral or written.[7]

The infancy narratives are sometimes called midrash, but although they share many features with that Jewish genre, they differ in an important respect: midrash is an imaginative, creative, form of exegesis of earlier material. Although Matthew draws freely on Old Testament material in the creative way characteristic of midrash, his aim was not to explain what he thought Isaiah or Jeremiah meant. He was concerned rather to give an account of the birth of Jesus Christ. Michael D. Goulder, having originally spoken of the infancy narratives as midrash, latterly, in his 1989 book on Luke, characterized their genre as "embroidery."[8] I shall use the term "creative historiography" myself, since to my ear it sounds less pejorative.

Some scholars have, however, denied that Matthew's infancy narrative employs creative historiography. Charles L. Quarles, for instance, while accepting that the New Testament writers "affirmed and utilized rabbinic methods of scriptural interpretation," says that "this does not imply that they would regard creative historiography as a recognized and acceptable mode of communication."[9] Creative historiography is not, he claims, to be found in the Old Testament, the New Testament, or such Jewish sources as Josephus, Pseudo-Philo, the *Genesis Apocryphon* and *Jubilees*, for when the writers departed from their primary sources it was not because they were resorting to invention but because they were drawing on other sources, written and oral. (This seems very tendentious.) The first occurrence of a whole book with the character of creative historiography, he claims, is to be found in the middle of the second century CE in the *Protevangelium of James* (an apocryphal work). Creative historiography is, he thinks, precisely the sort of material denounced under the designation of "myths" in the later New Testament epistles (1 Tim 4:6–7; Titus 1:14; 2 Pet 1:16). I am not convinced. Quarles is perhaps constrained by his commitment to verbal inerrancy, expressed in his statement: "The essential dismissal of the biblical record of the historical Jesus through applications of midrash criticism demonstrates that ultimately midrash criticism is incompatible with evangelical faith."[10]

By contrast with Quarles, I would suggest that what Matthew is doing is precisely creative historiography. Such ways of writing were not confined in the

---

[7] Oral sources, according to W.D. Davies and Dale C. Allison, *The Gospel According to Saint Matthew*, 3 vols (ICC; Edinburgh: T&T Clark, 1988-97), 1. 192–95. Written sources, according to Raymond E. Brown, *The Birth of the Messiah. A Commentary on the Infancy Narratives in Matthew and Luke*, updated edn (New York: Doubleday, 1993), 96–119.

[8] Goulder, *Midrash*, 3–46; idem, *Luke*, 1.128.

[9] Charles L. Quarles, *Midrash Criticism. Introduction and Appraisal* (Lanham/New York/Oxford: University Press of America, 1998), 54.

[10] Ibid., 145.

ancient world to the Jews. When Virgil came to write the *Aeneid*, his great epic
about the origins of Rome, he began with the traditions that many Romans
were descended from Trojans, and that the ruling Emperor, Augustus, was a
descendant of Aeneas. He decided to use Homer's two great epics to give shape
to his own, and so Books 1–6 were constructed as an *Odyssey* (wanderings) and
7–12 as an *Iliad* (battles). But he faced a problem when he got Aeneas and his
companions to Italy. He brought them to the district called Latium, following
tradition, but tradition (as in Cato the Elder's now-lost *History of Rome*) said
that Latius, the King, was killed by the Trojans.

> That the ancestor and namesake of the Latins should have been killed by
> the Trojans was unacceptable, and Virgil found himself driven to the expe-
> dient of making king Latius an elderly and ineffective ruler, who looks on
> unhappily as younger and more violent men do the fighting. At the end of
> the *Aeneid* he is still alive, to make a union with Aeneas.[11]

What Virgil was doing was very similar to what many biblical writers did in
retelling a story: they made it fit better, on the ground that its meaning, its
message, was more important than the historicity of all its details.

The most obvious case of such creative historiography is the Chronicler. His
source (2 Kgs 21) told, for example, how bad King Manasseh had reigned for
fifty-five years despite the fact that he "shed very much innocent blood, till he
had filled Jerusalem from one end to another" (2 Kgs 21:16). Not a very edifying
story, in the Chronicler's view (he held an old-fashioned belief in "short-range
rewards and punishments").[12] He therefore rewrote the story, making it into a
much more fitting vehicle for theology.[13] Manasseh was a great sinner, and for
this he was punished, being hauled off by the Assyrians into exile in Babylon,
as an object-lesson to the Israelites. As a further example, the Chronicler made
him repent while in Babylon, and had YHWH bring him back to Palestine (2
Chr 33:11–13). Manasseh thus foreshadowed the fate of the people.

A case of creative historiography closer still to the Gospel infancy narratives appears in the treatment of the infancy of Moses by Josephus, Philo, and
Pseudo-Philo.[14] In his *Antiquities of the Jews*, Josephus has an annunciation story,
in which God appears in a dream to Moses' father to foretell his birth and
that of Aaron, and speaks of his future greatness (*A.J.* 2.210–16). Josephus
gives Pharaoh's daughter a name (Thermuthis), and tells us that the boy was

---

[11] Jasper Griffin, *Virgil* (Past Masters; Oxford: Oxford University Press, 1986), 64.

[12] Robert North, "1–2 Chronicles," in *Jerome Biblical Commentary*, ed. Raymond E. Brown *et al.*
      (Englewood Cliffs: Prentice Hall, 1968), 402–26, here 405.

[13] Robert North, "Does Archeology Prove Chronicles Sources?" in *A Light Unto My Path*, ed.
      H.N. Bream *et al.* (FS J. M. Myers; Philadelphia: Temple University Press, 1974), 375–401,
      esp. 383–86.

[14] Brown, *Birth*, 114–16, 599–600.

unusually handsome and precocious (*A.J.* 2.230). He also recounts a story of how when the Pharaoh playfully put his crown on the infant Moses' head, the child—foreshadowing later events—threw it to the ground and trod on it (*A.J.* 2.233). It is interesting to note that, apart from an occasional embellishment, Josephus sticks fairly close to the Pentateuch in his telling of the rest of the Moses-story. We may suspect that the procedure of the Christian evangelists was similar: where they had a traditional account to hand, they followed it, but, where not, they had to a considerable extent to use their imagination, acting on what they thought of as clues from the Old Testament in order to bring out what they saw as the inner meaning of events. They made use of the Old Testament to shape their stories in a similar way to Virgil's use of Homer.

Androcentricity

Matthew's account is, many readers will think, dominated to a distressing extent by male perspectives. He begins his book with a genealogy of Joseph. Mary appears only in parentheses, as it were: "Jacob begot Joseph, the husband of Mary, from whom was born Jesus who is called the Christ" (Matt 1:16). The presence of Tamar, Rahab, Ruth, and the wife of Uriah does not indicate feminist sympathies on the part of the evangelist; they seem to be there only to supply an approximate biblical precedent for the irregular manner of Jesus' conception.[15]

Matthew then announces (1:18) that he is about to speak of Jesus' birth, but in fact he does not narrate the actual nativity, but only its antecedents and its sequel. Mary is again mentioned in an oblique way: "his mother Mary having been betrothed to Joseph..." (1:18a). In 1:18b Mary is actually allowed to be the subject of a verb, but significantly this is in the passive voice: "She was found to be with child, of [the] holy spirit." (What Matthew means by this we will discuss later.) The predicament created by Mary's premature pregnancy is viewed solely from Joseph's angle, and the angelic visitation that ensues, with a view to resolving the problem, is granted not (as in Luke) to Mary, but to Joseph. In 1:25b it is not clear grammatically which parent names the child, but since in 1:21b Joseph has been instructed to do this, we can presume that once again the spotlight is on Joseph. It is by accepting the child and naming him that Joseph gives him legal title to Davidic descent.[16]

In Matthew's second chapter, Mary is again left in the shadows. In the magi narrative, it is true that Joseph does not appear (surprisingly, perhaps), but Mary is mentioned only incidentally: the male magi "found the child with Mary his mother" (2:11). In the story of the flight into Egypt, an angelic message is

---

[15] Ibid., 73–74.
[16] See, e.g., Gundry, *Matthew*, 19.

delivered again to Joseph, whereas Mary's role is entirely passive: "'Take the child and his mother'...He took the child and his mother" (2:13, 14). This pattern is repeated in the narrative of the return from Egypt (2:20, 21). The story (and Matthew's infancy narrative as a whole) ends on the patriarchal note that has prevailed throughout: "He [not *They*] settled in a town called Nazareth" (2:23). Matthew's direct interest in Mary is almost nonexistent. How different from Luke!

That Matthew's Gospel as a whole is more patriarchal in outlook than most other New Testament books is, I think, doubtful. Elaine Wainwright detects within the Matthean communities both a trend toward patriarchy and a "strong tradition of women's discipleship."[17] It may be that in the infancy narrative apologetic considerations have had their part to play. If Matthew, a Jewish Christian, wants to commend Jesus to other Jews, he therefore presents Jesus as the legal, though not the biological, son of Joseph—as such he can claim descent from Abraham. Being also of Davidic stock (1:1), kingship is his by descent, not, as in Herod's case, by favor of the Roman Senate. Stress on the role of Mary would not have advanced Matthew's case.

Leaving aside the genealogy (1:1–17),[18] I proceed immediately to Matthew's account of the preliminaries to Jesus' birth, and its sequel.

Annunciation to Joseph (1:18–25)

Since the Matthean wording is significant for interpretation of this passage, I supply a translation here.

[18]Now the birth of Jesus Christ took place in this way. His mother Mary having been betrothed to Joseph, before they could come together she was found to be with child, of [the] holy spirit; [19]and Joseph, her husband, being a righteous/upright/pious [*dikaios*] man and/but [*kai*] not wishing to expose her to publicity, decided to divorce her privately. [20]But when he had pondered this, lo, an angel of the Lord appeared to him in a dream, saying, "Joseph, son of David, do not fear to take Mary [as] your wife, for that which is conceived in her is of [the] holy spirit; [21]and she will bear a son, and you shall call his name Jesus, for he will save his people from their sins." [22]All this happened so that there might be fulfilled that which had been spoken by the Lord through the prophet, saying: [23]"Behold, the virgin will conceive and bear a son, and they will call his name Immanuel" (which means, God with us). [24]And Joseph, having woken from sleep, did as the angel of the Lord had

---

[17] Elaine M. Wainwright, *Towards a Feminist Critical Reading of the Gospel According to Matthew* (BZNW 60; Berlin, New York, de Gruyter, 1991), passim; here 345.
[18] See Benedict T. Viviano's essay on the Matthean genealogy in the previous chapter.

commanded him; he took his wife, [25]but knew her not up to the time that [*heōs*] she had borne a son; and he called his name Jesus.

In v. 20, we have the first of the five dreams to be found in Matthew 1–2 (cf. 2:12; 2:13–15; 2:19–21; 2:22). The recipient is always Joseph, except in the case of the dream of the magi at 2:12. It is tempting to find in Joseph's dreams some reference here to the dreamer Joseph of the Book of Genesis.[19] The latter's dreams, however, took the form of visual apparitions that portended the future (e.g., Gen 37:5–11). Our Joseph's dreams, on the other hand (the magi's too), are auditory in nature and give directions for action. In this they echo the dreams of other dreamers in Genesis: Abimelech (20:3–8); Jacob (31:10–13; 46:2–4); and Laban (31:24). On the basis of their literary form, too, Matthew's accounts follow the pattern of these dreams rather than of those of the Old Testament Joseph.[20]

Verse 18 perhaps requires some explanation. Betrothal was a legal arrangement (terminated only by divorce or widowhood). The ceremony normally occurred about a year before the marriage, and the girl remained in her parents' house. Sexual relations were not permitted (except, say the Mishnah and the Talmud, in Judea: but this exception may postdate the betrothal in question).[21] The words in v.18, "before they could come together," mean, under the same roof as man and wife. The phrase "of [the] holy spirit" is probably an authorial gloss; Joseph only knows that Mary is pregnant, but the cause is not revealed to him until v. 20.

Verse 19 is more difficult to interpret. According to many texts, Jewish law (also Greek and Roman) *demanded* that a man divorce his wife if she were guilty of adultery.[22] Divorce could be done either in a court of law, or by the husband alone; in the latter case, the husband would perhaps lose the right to keep the dowry. Matthew's exact meaning is in doubt, and there are at least three possibilities: (1) Being a righteous [pious] man, Joseph thought God might be angry if he went ahead with the marriage [because he knew that the conception was miraculous and he feared to interfere with the divine plan]; (2) Suspecting adultery, Joseph as a righteous man decided on divorce, but [being also kindly] determined to do it out of court; (3) Joseph, being a righteous man, and therefore kindly, although he decided on divorce, determined to do it privately. The problem with (1) is that the natural way to take v. 20b is that Joseph only gets to know the cause of the pregnancy at this point (otherwise

---

[19] Brown, *Birth*, 111–12.

[20] Cf. Robert Gnuse, "Dream Genre in the Matthean Infancy Narratives," *Novum Testamentum* 32 (1990) 97–120.

[21] See texts in the Mishnah (*m. Yeb.* 4.10; *m. Ket.* 1.5, 4.12) and the Talmud (*b.Ket.* 9b, 12a).

[22] Divorce by the husband was among the widespread ancient punishments for a wife's adultery; cf. Deut 22:20–21; 24:1; Sir 25:25–26; *m. Git.* 9.10; Demosthenes, *Against Neaera* 87; *Lex Iulia de adulteriis coercendis*; Apuleius, *Met.* 9.27–29; Justinian, *Digest* 48.5.1.

the miraculous conception has to serve as both the cause of Joseph's problem and its solution). Also, if he knew this, would he not, as a righteous man, hesitate before resolving on a divorce that would leave his wife unprotected and economically vulnerable?[23] It is hard to choose between (2) and (3).

In 1:21 we read that Jesus' role will be to save his people from their sins. The word "savior" belongs in the Old Testament to God (Deut 32:15; Pss 24:5; 25:5; Isa 12:2), and the name Jesus (in Hebrew Jehoshua) was understood to mean "YHWH saves." In pagan sources, however, the term "savior" (Greek *sōtēr*) was used with reference not only to the gods but also to Roman emperors such as Augustus and Vespasian.[24] This should warn us not to take the word "sins" here to refer exclusively to the misdeeds of individuals, especially since the text mentions "his people." As the true king of Israel and the representative of God, Jesus (in Matthew's view) will rescue the Jewish people from their collective rejection of YHWH's message and his messengers and will free them from their bondage to the Romans that is one of the consequences of this rejection.[25]

Matthew's Christianity, as Richard Horsley has reminded us,[26] is not simply a matter of theological beliefs and spiritual experience: it is about a just world order, one that is to be established by God rather than through direct human action. The kingdom will come when God's will is done on earth as it already is in heaven (6:10). It will belong to the poor in spirit and the persecuted; it will bring comfort to mourners, food and drink to those who hunger and thirst for righteousness; it will bring mercy for the merciful, the vision of God for the clean of heart, divine paternity for peacemakers, and possession of the land for the humble (5:3–10, the Beatitudes). In 11:4–6 Matthew's Jesus sends word to the imprisoned Baptist (who has asked about Jesus' mission) that it has to do with sight for the blind, mobility for the lame, cleansing for lepers, hearing for the deaf, revival for the dead, and good news for the poor. This is much as Isaiah 35 had envisaged—whether the language was there intended literally or metaphorically—for the time when the Babylonian exile should have finished.

In 1:22–23 ("All this happened so that there might be fulfilled that which had been spoken by the Lord through the prophet") we have the first example of a common Matthean device that is often problematic for the modern

---

[23] Gundry, *Matthew*, 21–22, and Herman Hendrickx, *The Infancy Narratives* (London: Chapman, 1984), 31–32 defend this (now minority) view, but Brown, *Birth*, 126–27 cogently answers it.

[24] For Augustus see the references to the inscriptional evidence in Brown, *Birth*, 415 n. 21. For Vespasian see Josephus, *Jewish War* 7.71.

[25] Cf. Warren Carter, *Matthew and the Margins. A Socio-Political and Religious Reading* (London/ New York: T&T Clark, 2000), 69–70.

[26] Richard A. Horsley, *The Liberation of Christmas: The Infancy Narratives in Social Context* (New York: Continuum, 1989; reprint, Eugene, OR: Wipf & Stock, 2006), passim. See also Carter, *Matthew and the Margins*, passim.

reader, the formula citation—a quotation of the Old Testament introduced by a standard phrase. Formula citations are even commoner in the infancy material (1:23; 2:5, 15, 17, 23) than in the rest of this gospel (3:3; 4:14; 8:17; 12:17; 13:14; 21:4; 26:56; 27:9). In a later section of this essay I shall briefly consider problems raised by the five citations within the infancy narratives.

Matthew's main point in 1:18–25 is that Jesus' origins are the work of the divine spirit. The spirit that brought about the creation of the universe (Gen 1:2) and was predicted to initiate the messianic age (Isa 11:2; 42:1 [cited at Matt 12:18–20]; 44:3; 59:21; 61:1) was in Jesus bringing about an eschatological event.[27] According to the traditional view, Matthew sees this as beginning to happen by means of a virginal conception. Such a miracle shows the unique status of Jesus as Savior. The Old Testament prepared the way for this through Isaiah's prophecy (Isa 7:14: interpreted as predicting a virginal conception) and by narrating the way that God's purposes were advanced by four women whose sex lives were far from normal (Tamar, Rahab, Ruth, and Bathsheba—see Matthew's genealogy).

Some scholars, however (e.g., Jane Schaberg, Robert J. Miller, and Frank Reilly),[28] have recently questioned whether Matthew in fact teaches a virginal conception. Noting that, as remarked by Marie-Joseph Lagrange, "'of [the] *holy spirit*' is not at all a current expression for designating a miraculous conception,"[29] they argue that there was a historical foundation to the Jewish accusation of illegitimacy against Jesus. This accusation is perhaps implied in Mark 6:3 ("the son of Mary") and John 8:41 ("We [Jews] for our part [? as against you, Jesus] are not born of *porneia* [adultery or fornication]"). On this theory, Matthew knew (though he did not wish to highlight this) that Mary had been seduced or raped. This interpretation, it is argued, fits better than the virginal conception idea with the mention of the four women in the genealogy—for one thing, none of these was the beneficiary of a miraculous divine intervention.

In addition, the Isaiah 7 text clearly did not indicate in its original context a virginal conception, and it is not entirely obvious that it needs to be taken so in its Matthean setting. The stress for Matthew will have been less on

---

[27] David E. Garland, *Reading Matthew. A Literary and Theological Commentary on the First Gospel* (London: SPCK, 1993), 23. A similar expectation appears in the Qumran *Messianic Apocalypse* (4Q521 2.ii.6–12).

[28] Jane Schaberg, *The Illegitimacy of Jesus. A Feminist Theological Interpretation of the Infancy Narratives* (expanded twentieth anniversary edition; Sheffield: Sheffield Phoenix, 2006); Robert J. Miller, *Born Divine. The Births of Jesus and Other Sons of God* (Santa Rosa, CA: Polebridge Press, 2003); Frank Reilly, "Jane Schaberg, Raymond E. Brown, and the Problem of the Illegitimacy of Jesus," *Journal of Feminist Studies in Religion* 21 (2005) 56–80 [repr. in 2006 edition of Schaberg, *Illegitimacy*, 258–82].

[29] Marie-Joseph Lagrange, *Évangile selon Saint Matthieu* (EBib; seventh edn; Paris: Lecoffre, 1948), 10, cited by Schaberg, *Illegitimacy*, 66.

the word *parthenos* in the Isaiah text than on the name Immanuel.[30] Matthew may, indeed, have had in mind Deut 22:23–27, which concerns the discovery of the seduction or rape of a betrothed *virgin* (LXX *parthenos*), although the death penalty envisaged by Deuteronomy will, Schaberg argues, not have been enforced in the New Testament period.[31] Schaberg goes on to assert: "The story of this conception... is about a creative act of God that does not replace human paternity. Sexual and divine begetting are integrated... This child's existence is not an unpremeditated accident, and it is not cursed." Just as the fact that, for Paul, Isaac's being "begotten according to spirit" (Gal 4:29) does not imply that he did not have a biological human father, so for Matthew Jesus' being conceived by the holy spirit does not mean that the spirit replaced a human male progenitor.[32] Nevertheless, Galatians uses a different preposition, *kata*, "according to," not *ek*, "of, from."

Schaberg's analysis, though initially perhaps shocking ("very unpleasant" in the words of Raymond Brown),[33] has its attractions in my view. If not consonant with traditional theological orthodoxy, it can be seen as politically correct. Mary can be regarded as embodying the figure of the virgin daughter of Israel, often represented as oppressed and violated (e.g., Isa 37:22; Jer 14:17; Amos 5:2).[34] Elisabeth Schüssler Fiorenza notes too the theological attractiveness today of a Mary who "joins the countless women ravished by soldiers in war and occupation [in] struggling against victimization and for survival and dignity."[35] Robert Miller writes: "If the Son of God could leave this world as the innocent victim of horrifying violence, why is it unacceptable that he could come into this world through an act of violence against an innocent victim?"[36]

Could Matthew, though, have considered that the seduction or rape of Mary was "of/from [the] holy spirit" (1:18)? It is one thing to suppose that he thought that such an outrage had been turned by God to good effect, but Schaberg's analysis seems to require us to suppose that the evangelist saw it as, in her

---

[30] Miller, *Born Divine*, 204–205. He argues (p. 202) that Matthew will not necessarily be taking *parthenos* in the sense of virgin, since in his only other use of the word (the parable of the bridesmaids in 25:1–13) virginity is not at issue.

[31] Schaberg, *Illegitimacy*, 51–64. The following quotation is from p. 67.

[32] Schaberg, "Feminist Interpretations of the Infancy Narrative of Matthew," *Journal of Feminist Studies in Religion* 13 (1997) 35–74 [repr. in 2006 edition of Schaberg, *Illegitimacy*, 231–57], here 51.

[33] Raymond E. Brown, *The Virginal Conception and Bodily Resurrection of Jesus* (New York: Paulist, 1973), 66.

[34] Schaberg, *Illegitimacy*, 108–11.

[35] Elisabeth Schüssler Fiorenza, *Jesus: Miriam's Child, Sophia's Prophet. Critical Issues in Feminist Christology* (New York: Continuum, 1994), 186–87, cited in Reilly, "Jane Schaberg," 80.

[36] Miller, *Born Divine*, 222. He tentatively suggests (p. 220) that perhaps Mary was raped by a soldier when the Romans captured Sepphoris in 4 BCE.

words, "divinely willed,"[37] which is surely very problematical.[38] That Matthew believes in a miraculous virginal conception seems to me more likely than not from the fact that he speaks of Jesus being begotten "of" or "from" [*ek*] Mary (1:16), and also "of" or "from" [*ek*] [the] holy spirit (1:18, 20); he is not begotten "by" (*hypo*) anyone.

Nevertheless, it must be admitted that vv. 18–25 read rather oddly. This may well be the result of less than totally skillful reshaping of an inherited tradition. If we suppose that the story originally had Mary pregnant by another man, and if Matthew balked at this and wished to present the conception as miraculous, he might have produced just such a text as lies before us. As it stands, the passage reflects badly on Mary. If she had known that she was pregnant miraculously, it would have been discourteous of her (to say the least) not to put Joseph in the picture. Her failure to do so, on the other hand, would have made sense in a tradition according to which she had previously had a sexual relationship, voluntary or otherwise, with another man. If he believed in a virginal conception, Matthew might have been better advised to do what Luke was to do after him, namely, have the conception occur after the angelophany.

Whether Matthew wishes to teach a virginal conception must, in my view, remain less than certain. As I have indicated, I am inclined to think that the evangelist does but that he may be using a source that does not. But even if he has no such intention but takes Jesus to be illegitimate (for it is clear that he does not believe that Joseph was the biological father), that does not mean of course that he is necessarily right. What is indisputable is that for Matthew Jesus' existence was, from his conception onward, directed by the holy spirit.

Matt 1:25 asserts: "He knew her not up to the time that [*heōs*] she had borne a son." The way that the Greek word *heōs* is used (unlike the English "until") does not necessarily imply that sexual relations occurred thereafter.[39] Nevertheless, if Matthew had had any clear notion of Mary's perpetual virginity, "he would almost certainly have chosen a less ambiguous expression."[40] His ignorance of it, however, does not of course disprove the doctrine.

Visit of the Magi (2:1–12)

A brief word is necessary first about historicity. Some have thought that the "star" was a comet (Halley's comet appeared in 12 BCE, and hovered over the

---

[37] Schaberg, *Illegitimacy*, 73.

[38] David T. Landry, "Illegitimacy Reconsidered," in the 2006 edition of Schaberg, *Illegitimacy*, 283–99, offers a very judicious appraisal of the evidence for and against the notion of illegitimacy in Matthew.

[39] A similar use of *heōs* ("up to the time that" rather than "until") appears in Matt 10:23; Mark 9:1.

[40] Davies and Allison, *Matthew*, 1. 219.

city of Rome, but that is too early); or a supernova; or a planetary conjunction (as of Mars, Jupiter and Saturn in 7–6 BCE); but how could a comet, or a conjunction of planets, be seen to rest over a particular house (Matt 2:9)? Virgil (*Aen.* 2.693–96) speaks of a star hovering over a house to show Aeneas where Rome would stand, but this too is more credible as fiction than as scientific fact. The idea of a new star or a comet heralding a birth or a death is extremely common in antiquity, which is another reason to question the historicity of Matthew's story here.[41] Again, Matthew's Herod displays extraordinary naiveté, in trusting the magi and not sending an escort.

Many scholars think that Matthew was influenced by a journey to the court of Nero in 66 CE by Tiridates to be formally invested as king of Armenia.[42] According to Suetonius (*Nero* 13.2), Tiridates was made to walk up a ramp and prostrate himself in supplication before Nero. With him, says Pliny (*NH* 30.6.17), he had brought magi. The party returned home by a different route, says Dio Cassius (*Hist.* 62.7).

Further, the incidence of echoes of Old Testament texts in the story of the visit by the magi is considerably greater than in most gospel narratives, for example:

- In Genesis, Isaac blesses Jacob, foretelling that peoples/nations will serve/ bow down to him (Gen 27:40; cf. 25:23). Esau/Edom his brother seeks to kill him (27:41), so Jacob flees the country (28:1–9). Note that King Herod was an Idumean (i.e., an Edomite).
- In Gen 37:9 Joseph (son of Jacob: cf. Matt 1:16) dreams of the sun, the moon, and eleven stars that would bow down before himself. Later his brothers come with gifts of money and myrrh and nuts (Gen 43:11–12) and bow before him (43:26).
- In Num 24:17–18 Balaam, a visionary seer (a *magus* according to Philo, *Mos.* 1.276) from the East (23:7), foresees a star that would rise out of Jacob, a scepter [LXX: a man] from Israel, which would dispossess Edom. This star was taken at Qumran to be the Levitical Messiah (*Damascus Document* 7:20).[43]
- In 1 Kgs 10:1–13 the Queen of Sheba visits Solomon, son of David (cf. Matt 1:1), and offers gifts of gold, spices, and precious stones. She also asks questions (1 Kgs 10:3), as Herod asks the Jewish leaders.
- The treasures of Hezekiah included stores of *incense, myrrh*, silver, and *gold* (LXX Isa 39:2).
- "Nations shall come to your light, and kings to your brightness...All from Sheba shall come bearing *gold and frankincense*" (Isa 60:3, 6).

[41] Brown, *Birth*, 170.
[42] Horsley, *Liberation*, 56–57; Brown, *Birth*, 174.
[43] John J. Collins, *The Scepter and the Star: The Messiahs of the Dead Sea Scrolls and Other Ancient Literature* (New York: Doubleday, 1995), 80–83; cf. Brown, *Birth*, 195 n. 47.

- "The kings of Arabia and Saba shall bring gifts. And all kings shall bow down to him...To him shall be given of the gold of Sheba" (Ps 72:10, 11, 15).
- The bed of Solomon, son of David, is censed with *myrrh and frankincense* (Cant 3:6–7).

There are also some awkward aspects in the construction of the narrative that tend to suggest that it is at least in part fictional. In 2:7 we read that "Herod ascertained from them the exact time of the appearance of the star." Presumably we are to take it that the star had appeared (two years previously),[44] simultaneously with the nativity or later: hence in 2:16 the king's decision to kill boys of two years old and under, "according to the exact time that he had ascertained from the magi." But why should Herod want to know the time when the star had risen before realizing that the magi had deceived him? Is this simply poor plot-construction on Matthew's part? It is unclear from 2:9 whether the star led them from Jerusalem to Bethlehem (rather needlessly, for they had already been directed to go there) or only indicated the right house when they reached Bethlehem. A further question arises regarding 2:12: "Having received a message/response in a dream, they returned to their own country by a different route." Reading this statement, we ask ourselves: How does Matthew know about the dream? Here he acts the part of the "omniscient narrator," seemingly guessing or inventing when he needs to.[45]

We turn now to the meaning that the story will have had for the evangelist. Here the claims of Herod the king (2:1, 3, 9) are held up to ridicule. It is Jesus who will be the true king of the Jews (2:2; 27:37). Matthew's preference for the term "kingdom of heaven" rather than "kingdom of God" should not be taken to mean a kingdom lying beyond death or up in the sky: "heaven" is here simply a pious Jewish periphrasis for "God." Matthew expects Jesus' kingship to be exercised on this earth, just as David's was (or Herod's, for that matter), though it will be nonviolent (26:51–54), for this king will be *praüs*, gentle, humble, patient (5:5; 11:28–30; 21:5).

The sociopolitical outlook of Matthew's infancy story is explored elsewhere in this volume,[46] but deserves to be alluded to, if briefly, here too. The intention to stress Jesus' Davidic descent in the story is quite clear: three times Matthew emphasizes that Bethlehem is in Judea (2:1, 5, 6), as if to counter the Jewish charge that Jesus was a mere Galilean who could not be the Messiah, because

---

[44] Are we to suppose that the journey took the magi two years; or that their departure was delayed? George M. Soares Prabhu, *The Formula Quotations in the Infancy Narratives of Matthew: An Enquiry into the Tradition History of Mt 1–2* (Analecta Biblica 63; Rome: Pontifical Biblical Institute, 1976), 298, argues that the reference to the two years suggests "a reminiscence of some actual event (it is hard to explain it otherwise)"; cf. Richard T. France, "Herod and the Children of Bethlehem," *Novum Testamentum* 21 (1979) 98–120, here 113.

[45] Other examples may be found in Matt 9:3, 36; 12:15; 13:58; 14:9, 14, 30; 21:18, 45–46.

[46] See Warren Carter's essay in the present volume.

the Messiah would be a descendant of David (cf. John 7:41, 42, 52). The angel addresses Joseph as "Joseph, son of David" (1:20). Further, as Robert Gundry observes, the seemingly unnecessary tripling of Herod's designation as the *king* (2:1, 3, 9) "throws into contrast the designation of Jesus as 'the king of the Jews' (v. 2) and sets the stage for a struggle over royal power."[47]

Horsley has written illuminatingly about the political significance of the story of the visit of the magi.[48] Frequently from the time of Augustine onward, this episode has been held to portend the rejection of the gospel by the Jews (supposedly represented by Herod the Great and "all Jerusalem") and its acceptance by the Gentile nations in accordance with Ps 72:10–11 (cf. Matt 28:19, "Go and make disciples of all the nations").[49] In the Western Church, the coming of the magi is commemorated by the separate feast of the Epiphany (January 6), celebrating the manifestation of the Lord to the Gentile world.[50] But the Gentile identity of the magi is not stressed in our text, and nowhere in the gospels does the hated Idumean tyrant Herod the Great, nor "all Jerusalem" (probably meaning the chief priests and their minions, installed by Herod),[51] represent the Jews as a whole: "if anything, they stand over against the people generally."

The magi were, Horsley notes, originally "the highest officers and advisers"[52] of first the Median and then the Persian king—the king who required the profound, semi-divine obeisance that the magi offer to the infant Jesus. They "guided the kings in their relations with the gods" (Strabo 15.1.68), not least through necromancy and astrology. Tertullian said that "the East considers magi almost as kings" (*Adv. Marc.* 3.13.20), so the phrase "star-led chieftains" in the Epiphany verse of the much-loved carol, "O come all ye faithful," may not be too wide of the mark.[53] There is some evidence that the magi protested at and resisted the rise of western imperialism in the shape of the Hellenistic and Roman empires. After the birth of Alexander the Great, the magi are said to have cried out: "Asia's deadly curse was born last night" (Cicero, *Div.* 1.23.47).[54]

Perhaps Matthew's picture is that some magi, longing for the restoration of the power of Persia, directed their steps to Judea. If the narrative has a historical basis and if the "star" was the planetary conjunction of 7–6 BCE, the fact

---

[47] Gundry, *Matthew*, 26.

[48] Horsley, *Liberation*, 53–60.

[49] Brown, *Birth*, 181–82.

[50] In the Byzantine tradition, however, January 6 (the Feast of the Theophany) has more to do with the baptism of the Lord, whereas the coming of the magi is commemorated as part of the feast of December 25.

[51] Horsley, *Liberation*, 51–52. The next quotation is from p. 39.

[52] Ibid., 55.

[53] Ibid., 54. In speaking of the magi as actually kings, the Christian tradition will have been influenced by Isa 60:6 (gold; frankincense), Ps 72:15 (gold), and Cant 3:6 (myrrh; frankincense). Note, however, that the Hebrew word *zāhāb*, usually translated "gold" in Isa 60:6 and Ps 72:15, might have originally denoted gold-colored incense; cf. Brown, *Birth*, 176.

[54] William A. Falconer, *Cicero: De senectute, De amicitia, De divinatione* (LCL; New York: Putnam, 1923), 277.

that "Jupiter is the royal planet and Saturn, as the star of Saturday, was sometimes regarded as the star of the Jews"[55] may have sent them there. Or possibly they knew the prediction mentioned by several sources—admittedly in relation to a somewhat later period, that of the fall of the Jerusalem temple—that a world savior (or saviors) would come from Judea.[56]

In Jerusalem, with some help from Old Testament prophecy, the magi identified the obscure child of Bethlehem as the figure who, they hoped, would lead to the overthrow of western imperialism. Since Isa 44:24–45:25 daringly speaks of the Persian king Cyrus as YHWH's agent, indeed his anointed one (LXX Isa 45:1 uses the Greek term *christos*), who would liberate the Jews from the Babylonian yoke, Matthew may have had this Old Testament text in mind as foreshadowing the obeisance of the magi before the infant Jesus. The star may itself also have sociopolitical resonances, since during the Jewish war against Rome there appeared, according to Josephus, "a star resembling a sword that stood over the city [of Jerusalem] and a comet" (*Jewish War* 6.289), as also "chariots and armed battalions hurtling through the clouds" (6.298).

Does the myrrh, as is sometimes supposed, presage Jesus' death (cf. John 19:39)?[57] Scarcely, since in his passion narrative Matthew actually *changes* "myrrh" to "gall" (Matt 27:34; contrast Mark 15:23). Rather, the gifts for Matthew correspond to offerings brought by foreigners to Jerusalem and to David's son Solomon (see the Old Testament texts listed earlier). "The magi bring the child the most costly gifts possible."[58] Thus the gifts are all (for Matthew) signs of Jesus' kingly status.[59]

Jesus is, though, for Matthew not only king but also Son of God. Gundry notes that in Matthew gifts are only ever offered to God.[60] We should then perhaps see the gifts of the magi as partly attesting the fact that Jesus is Son of God. Again, the worship offered in 2:11 ("Falling down, they did obeisance to him") points in the same direction, so here again Jesus is being portrayed as God's Son.

The turmoil into which Herod and all Jerusalem are cast in 2:3 anticipates later events. It is understandable that Herod should be disturbed to hear talk

---

55 Ulrich Luz, *Matthew 1–7. A Commentary*, trans. James E. Crouch (Hermeneia; Minneapolis: Fortress, 2007), 105, with references.

56 Josephus, *Jewish War* 6.310–25 (savior); Tacitus, *Hist.* 5.13, and Suetonius, *Vesp.* 4 (saviors). All three take the true reference to be to Vespasian (and Titus).

57 Admittedly, the assembling of chief priests and scribes to discuss the "King of the Jews" with the Roman-authorized ruler (Matt 2:2–4) has ominous overtones in light of Matthew's passion narrative (26:3–4; 27:11–12).

58 Luz, *Matthew 1–7*, 115.

59 See Brian M. Nolan, *The Royal Son of God. The Christology of Matthew 1–2 in the Setting of the Gospel* (OBO 23; Göttingen: Vandenhoeck & Ruprecht, 1979), 43–46.

60 Gundry, *Matthew*, 32, with reference to Matt 5:23, 24; 8:4; 15:5; 23:18, 19. Texts describing Jesus as Son of God include Matt 2:15; 3:17; 4:3, 6; 8:29; 14:33; 16:16; 17:5; 26:63–64; 27:54, while texts mentioning obeisance to him include Matt 4:10; 14:33; 17:6; 28:9, 17.

of someone born to be king of the Jews, the title bestowed upon himself by the Roman Senate (Josephus, *A.J.* 16.10.2 #311). But why should the whole of Judea be alarmed? At 21:10 *the whole* city of Jerusalem is shaken (different verb) at Jesus' arrival. Perhaps, therefore, in 2:3 we have an anticipation of later hostility to Jesus by the Jews, and particularly the Jewish leadership. The mention of chief priests and scribes of the people at 2:4 anticipates the trial and ridiculing of Jesus (26:57, 27:1, 41). Whereas King Herod is "mocked" or "duped" (*enepaichthē*) by the magi (2:16), king Jesus will later be "mocked" (27:29, 31, 41: same verb).[61]

I conclude that it is difficult to view Matthew's magi story (as it stands) as history, but it may well contain a historical substratum. Perhaps a group of magi did find their way to Bethlehem and discern in Jesus an omen of the overthrow of western imperialism. For Matthew the principal importance of the story lies in what it says about Jesus' kingship and his divine sonship. Some reference may be intended to the motif of foreign nations flocking to Jerusalem to pay homage and/or present gifts (Isa 2:1–4; Mic 4:1-3; Zech 8:20–23; *1 Enoch* 53:1), but the story has little if anything directly to do with the salvation of Gentiles. If this line of interpretation is correct, the western tradition of celebrating the coming of the magi as the promise of salvation for the Gentile world will not, in Horsley's phrase, be well rooted in the biblical text.[62]

Massacre of the Innocents (2:16–18)

The story of the massacre has been very influential in Christian history: the Innocents have their own feast, in the West on December 28 (in the Middle Ages this was a children's feast, presided over by a boy bishop chosen for the purpose), but in the East on December 29. Matthew is perhaps thinking in terms of quite a small number of martyrs—in light of calculations about the likely size of the population of Bethlehem at this time, Raymond Brown suggests not many more than twenty.[63] However, tradition inflated the number to 14,000 (Byzantine Liturgy), 64,000 (Syrian Liturgy), or even 144,000 (influence of Rev 14:1–5). In the Middle Ages the story probably fanned the flames of Christian hatred of Jews—note the influence on Chaucer's *Prioress' Tale.*[64]

---

[61] A comparison of Jesus with Moses may also be made: just as many innocent babies perished because of Moses' mission (the "plague of the firstborn"), so many guiltless people are likely to suffer as a result of opposition to the Christian cause (as in the Massacre of the Innocents).

[62] Horsley, *Liberation*, 49.

[63] Brown, *Birth*, 204.

[64] In Chaucer's text, an innocent Christian child is murdered by Jews, who are called "cursed folk of Herodes al newe" (line 122), while the later mention of Rachel (line 175) recalls Matt 2:18.

Herod was noted for brutality; he ordered that on his death certain nota-
bles should be killed: "So shall all Judea and every household weep for me,
whether they wish it or no" (Josephus, *Jewish War* 1.659–60; cf. *A.J.* 17.174–79).
Even his family members were not exempt from his cruelty: he killed his wife,
Mariamme, his mother-in-law, and three of his sons. He put to death Pharisees
who predicted that he would lose the throne (Josephus, *A.J.* 17.41–44). The
action here narrated by Matthew would not, therefore, have been out of character, but its historicity is in my view doubtful on several grounds. Matthew
has Jesus escape because his family goes to Egypt but Luke has them go to
Nazareth; having Jesus undertake an Exodus from Egypt is very convenient
for Matthean typology.[65] Further, Josephus dwells at length on Herod's crimes,
but does not mention this story—though it is possible that the killing of a score
or so of children would have seemed to him relatively insignificant.[66] The telling of the story clearly involves authorial creativity. Whether Matthew has created the story (see Michael Goulder) or only embellished it (Donald Hagner;
Richard France) is disputed.[67]

There are various echoes in Matthew's narrative of the Moses traditions in the
Book of Exodus and post-biblical Jewish traditions. Pharaoh tries to put Moses
to death, but Moses makes good his escape and settles in the land of Midian
(Exod 2:15), where YHWH later tells him, "Go back to Egypt, for all those who
wished to kill you are dead" (Exod 4:19): cf. Matt 2:20: "Those [note the plural]
who threatened the child's life are dead." Pharaoh consults wise men/astrolo-
gers (Exod 7:11). In the tenth plague (Exod 12:29), infants were slaughtered.
Apart from biblical texts about Moses, there are echoes too, throughout the
Matthean infancy material, of post-biblical Jewish traditions about Moses, such
as the dream of Moses' father Amram to say that the child to be born will escape
those who watched to destroy him and telling him not to fear on account of his
wife's pregnancy (Josephus, *A.J.* 2.215); of the spirit descending on Miriam; and
of the Pharaoh learning of the coming savior from sacred scribes.[68]

The massacre, for Gundry, anticipates the people's cry at the end of Jesus'
trial: "And answering, all the people said, 'His blood be upon us and upon our
children'" (27:25).[69] I am not certain of this, but I think that the massacre story

---

[65] Brown, *Birth*, 113; Dale C. Allison, *The New Moses: A Matthean Typology* (Minneapolis:
Fortress, 1993), 142–44.

[66] So, e.g., Donald A. Hagner, *Matthew*, 2 vols (WBC 33A,B; Dallas: Word, 1993, 1995), 1.35;
Craig S. Keener, *A Commentary on the Gospel of Matthew* (Grand Rapids: Eerdmans, 1999),
111.

[67] Matthean creation: Goulder, *Midrash*, 239–41. Matthean embellishment: Hagner, *Matthew*,
1.35; France, "Herod," 108–20. Gundry, *Matthew*, 34, implausibly thinks that Matthew has
turned the sacrifice of "two turtledoves or young pigeons" (Luke 2:24) into the massacre
of Jewish babies.

[68] For details, see Davies and Allison, *Matthew*, 1.192–93.

[69] Gundry, *Matthew*, 35. Despite Matt 27:25, the Vatican II document *Nostra Aetate* (#4)
teaches that the Jewish people as a whole can in no way be blamed for the death of Jesus.

will at least signify for Matthew that the construction of the kingdom will not be achieved without suffering and bloodshed. Persecution for Jesus' sake bulks large in this Gospel (cf. 5:10, 12, 44; 10:23; 23:34).

The Flight into Egypt and the Return (2:13–15, 19–23)

Most scholars think the journey to Egypt (a traditional "refuge for persecuted persons")[70] implausible historically, though Luz, on the strength of Jewish traditions about a sojourn of Jesus in Egypt, suspects that it may contain "a kernel of truth."[71] The Mosaic overtones are clear enough: like Moses and the Hebrew people of old, Jesus is delivered from Egypt. The savage rule, however, of Herod and his Roman masters will have created, as Horsley notes, many refugees—Josephus specifically relates the flight of many inhabitants of Emmaus in 4 BCE before its destruction, and the crucifixion of two thousand who were captured.[72] Accordingly, a veiled comment on the styles of kingship that Jesus came in order to replace may have been part of the evangelist's intentions. In our age where the problem of refugees bulks so large, the present-day reader will in that case find considerable relevance here. Even if in Matthew the circumstances of Jesus' birth are comfortable, since he is born at home in Joseph's house, not in a manger in a strange town, afterward he becomes uprooted and homeless.

The Old Testament Formula Citations

Daniel Harrington makes four important observations about Matthew's use of this rather off-putting device: the formula quotations often follow the precise wording of neither the Hebrew nor the Greek Bible; Matthew interprets an Old Testament text without much regard for its original context; he may have drawn on a Christian anthology of messianic Old Testament texts (rather like the Qumran text, 4Q174, known as the *Florilegium*); and the importance of the citations lies for the reader in what they reveal about the evangelist's convictions about Jesus.[73] Thus, to pick up the last point, Hos 11:1 is quoted in Matt 2:15 to show that the exodus experience is summed up in Jesus, while

---

[70] Luz, *Matthew 1–7*, 120.
[71] Ibid., 120 n. 21.
[72] Horsley, *Liberation*, 72–73, citing Josephus, *Jewish War*. 2.71, 75 and *A.J.* 17.291, 295. Horsley goes on to quote Josephus on the refugee problems created by the Romans in the wake of the Jewish War of 66 CE.
[73] Daniel J. Harrington, *The Gospel of Matthew* (Sacra Pagina 1; Collegeville: Liturgical Press, 1991), 39.

Matt 2:17 cites Jer 31:15 to connect Jesus with the patriarchal period, through the mention of Rachel, and with the exile and restoration.

Let us take two examples in more detail. In 2:5–6 we read: "They [= "all the chief priests and the scribes of the people"] said, 'In Bethlehem of Judah, for thus was it written through the prophet: *And you, Bethlehem, land of Judah, [are] by no means least among the tribes of Judah; for from you will come a ruler, he who will shepherd my people, Israel.*'" This is rather a loose citation of Mic 5:2, somewhat different from both the Hebrew and the Greek. Note, for example, the omission of "Ephrathah," the insertion of "by no means," and the substitution of "he will shepherd" for "he will rule," drawing on 2 Sam 5:2 (God says to David, "You shall *shepherd*..."), which neatly fits Matthew's picture of Jesus as the shepherd–king (Matt 9:36; 10:6; 15:24). Jesus was appropriately born in Bethlehem, the place where the young David shepherded the family sheep and from where he went on to shepherd Israel. Bethlehem was also the place from where Micah predicted that a new Davidic king would emerge. Some of the differences may be due to textual variants known to Matthew, but the insertion of "by no means" is likely to be Matthew's own doing.[74] Micah says that Bethlehem is a backwater, but it will produce a messianic king. By contrast, Matthew's version says that Bethlehem is not a backwater because it will produce a messianic king. "The result is much the same," says Nolland.[75] True, but the latitude that Matthew allows himself differs starkly from the fidelity that we expect today with citations.

In 2:23, we have Matthew's most intriguing use of the formula citation device: "Going, he [Joseph] settled in a town called Nazareth, so that there might be fulfilled that which had been spoken through the prophets to the effect that he would be called a *Nazōraios*." Here Matthew does not quote a specific text but refers vaguely to "the prophets." The reader has to conjecture what text(s) Matthew has in mind, as well as what he means by *Nazōraios*. Does he mean a "nazirite" (Hebrew: *nāzîr*), a man dedicated to God—as in Judg 13:5, where an angel tells the barren wife of Manoah, "Behold, you shall have a child in your womb and shall bear a son; he [Samson] shall be a nazirite of God and shall begin to save Israel." That is the view of Goulder and Brown.[76] Yet Gundry and Hagner think this unlikely: Matthew does not portray Jesus as an ascetic and in the Septuagint the term nazirite has the spelling *Naziraios*.[77] The language is close to Matthew's, however, so I think Goulder and Brown may be right. Matthew could instead (or in addition) be thinking of the Hebrew word *nēṣer* ("branch"), used of a messianic Davidic king in Isa 11:1. Does he suppose that the name of the town of Nazareth has some connection with one or

74 Brown, *Birth*, 185.
75 Nolland, *Matthew*, 115.
76 Goulder, *Midrash*, 240–41; Brown, *Birth*, 223–25.
77 Gundry, *Matthew*, 40; Hagner, *Matthew* 1.40–41.

other of these words and think it providential that Joseph settled in a village
whose name bore witness to Jesus' being a dedicated man and/or a messianic
"branch"? Since "in the area of Syria, the home of the Matthean community,
one of the names for a Christian was 'Nazorean,' "[78] Matthew may also be seeing Jesus' settling in Nazareth as prefiguring the establishment of a Christian
community in Syria.

The frequency of the formula citations within the infancy material underlines Matthew's view that Jesus fulfils Old Testament prophecy. In his infancy
stories,

> Matthew sets up a "light" for his readers with his rapid succession of ful-
> fillment quotations. The fulfillment quotations scattered throughout the
> rest of the Gospel are then reminders of this light...They point to basic
> themes of the Matthean understanding of Christ...Matthew programmati-
> cally emphasizes the fulfillment of the entire Bible by Jesus' story and behav-
> ior...Matthew, the Jewish Christian, emphasizes the Jesus community's fun-
> damental claim to Israel's Bible.[79]

Given that Matthew tends to choose or create textual versions of Old
Testament texts that fit his purpose and to pay little regard to the original
context of the material, we must surely acknowledge that Matthew's treatment
of the Old Testament, while explicable in its ancient context, strikes the modern reader as very contrived, and to that extent makes it more difficult for
us to hear sympathetically what he wishes to say. Apart from the ten formula
citations in his Gospel, Matthew has many other quotations from and allusions to the Old Testament; his work "is saturated with the Old Testament."[80]
Frequently it is difficult for us to discover quite what Matthew is doing with
the Old Testament text in question: for example, whether he is claiming that
it directly predicts the Jesus event or only exemplifies a pattern that is to be
detected in the life of Jesus.[81] His use of the Old Testament may therefore be
a stumbling-block to those modern readers who are not expert in the Old
Testament and Jewish studies.

The Anticipatory Function of the Infancy Narrative

Matthew's infancy stories establish Jesus' credentials, showing who and what he
is. He is Son of David, King of the Jews, Son of God, Immanuel, the one conceived

[78] Luz, *Matthew 1–7*, 124.
[79] Ibid., 130.
[80] Nolland, *Matthew*, 29.
[81] Ibid., 36.

of [the] holy spirit, a Nazarene and Galilean, the fulfillment of the hope and destiny of the people of Israel. These and other emphases point the way to the future, since Matthew 1–2 (it has been suggested) stands in much the same relationship to the rest of this Gospel as Genesis 1–11 does to the remainder of that book.[82] Jesus' divine sonship will be a theme picked up as early as the baptism narrative (3:17), while his position as King of the Jews will be confirmed by the title over the cross (27:37) and the God-with-us motif will reappear at 28:20. The spirit that effected his conception will descend on him at his baptism (3:16), will lead him into the wilderness (4:1), and will enable him to practice exorcisms. Mention of Galilee will recur at 4:15, "Galilee of the nations," a phrase that prepares the way for Jesus' valedictory commission to his eleven disciples to make disciples of all nations (28:19).[83] The opposition experienced by the infant Jesus foreshadows his passion and the sufferings of his followers. Thus the infancy narrative is indeed, in Brown's graphic phrase, "a gospel in miniature."[84]

Conclusion

It can scarcely be denied that Luke's narrative, with its universalistic tone and its stress on Jesus' mission to the dispossessed, makes a more immediate appeal to the majority of present-day hearers and readers than does Matthew's. Matthew wants to stress that Jesus sums up and fulfills the history of the Jewish people in the manner of latter-day Moses and David figures, bringing the hope of a Jewish kingdom on earth (to which Gentiles will also be admitted), a kingdom that will spell the end of the oppression represented by the Romans and their Jewish associates. This will not be brought about without pain and grief. The sympathy that we have detected in Matthew for the plight of refugees shows that he was not without a social conscience. (No surprise there—he is, after all, the writer who has given us the Sermon on the Mount.) The androcentricity of Matthew's infancy story, and his frequent use of formula citations, which may both partly betray the evangelist's past as a Jewish scribe (cf. 13:52), are rather unattractive to many modern readers. Is perhaps, however, the very Jewishness of Matthew's account, difficult as many Christians may find it, its most salutary feature, reminding us that Christianity is rooted in its Jewish past ("Look to the rock from which you were hewn," Isa 51:1) and that it is Jesus the Jew who is proclaimed as the hope of the world?[85]

---

[82] Benedict T. Viviano, "The Genres of Matthew 1–2: Light from 1 Timothy 1:4," *Revue Biblique* 97 (1990) 31–53, here 52.

[83] Luz, *Studies in Matthew*, 21–22.

[84] Brown, *Birth*, 183.

[85] "More than Mark and Luke, Matthew stresses the Jewish origin of Jesus": so the Pontifical Biblical Commission, *The Jewish People and their Sacred Scriptures in the Christian Bible* (Vatican City: Libreria Editrice Vaticana, 2002), 157.

Chapter 9

The Magi Story through the Eyes of Pasolini: A Bakhtinian Reading

Christopher Fuller

Few figures outside of Jesus have attracted as much attention in the Gospels as the magi who visit first King Herod and then Jesus in Matt 2:1–12. They have inspired popular devotion through the visual arts and song, and they have also been exploited to fortify political power.[1] Within contemporary popular culture they are three wise kings from the exotic east who bring gifts to the baby Jesus at the manger in Bethlehem. The power of their popular portrayal obscures several facts from Matthew's text; their number is not specified, they are not identified as kings, they do not visit Jesus at the manger (the shepherds do in Luke 2:8–20), and there is dispute about their identification as "wise men." Given their status in Christian tradition, it is no surprise that the magi frequently appear in films on Jesus. This essay will examine how Pier Paolo Pasolini's 1964 film *The Gospel according to Saint Matthew* (henceforth referred to as *The Gospel*), provides a carnivalesque reading of the magi in the First Gospel.

The Magi in the Gospel of Matthew

The word "magi" is the plural form of the Latin *magus*, derived from the Greek term *magos* (plural *magoi*). Magi are not exclusive to the First Gospel, appearing in other literature from the Old Testament (Dan 2:1–13) and the New Testament (Acts 13:6–12). The standard *Greek-English Lexicon of the New Testament* defines a *magos* as a "wise man and priest, who was expert in astrology, interpretation of dreams and various other occult arts."[2] Since Matthew explains that the magi arrived from the east, they have commonly been

---

[1] See Richard C. Trexler, *The Journey of the Magi: Meanings in History of a Christian Story* (Princeton, NJ: Princeton University Press, 1997).

[2] W. Bauer, *A Greek-English Lexicon of the New Testament and Other Early Christian Literature*, ed. W.F. Arndt and F.W. Gingrich; third edn rev. F.W. Gingrich and F.W. Danker (Chicago: University of Chicago Press, 2000), 608.

identified as Persian or Median priests or astrologers. Others have speculated that their origins are in Arabia, Babylon, the Syrian desert, or Asia
Minor.[3]

Because there is no reference outside of the Gospel of Matthew to these
particular magi or their visit to Jesus, some question the historicity of the story.
Raymond Brown argues that an understanding of the historical context within
which Matthew wrote his Gospel provides evidence of verisimilitude but not
history.[4] This context includes messianic expectation that a descendant of
David would arise to rule Israel, widespread interest in astronomy and the
relationship between celestial occurrences and human events, documented
astral events during the period, the reputation of magi in general among Jews
and Gentiles as possessors of special powers, and news of eastern rulers bearing gifts as tribute for rulers in Rome and Jerusalem.

Brown and others argue that the likely background for Matthew's narrative is the story of Balaam in Numbers 22–24.[5] In this tale the Moabite King
Balak summons the diviner Balaam to place a curse on the people of Israel
in order to impede their advance through the plains of Moab. Balaam comes
"from the east" (the same phrase in Matt 2:1 describes the origin of the magi),
together with two servants (Num 22:22). Rather than curse Israel, he frustrates
Balak's plans by assuring him of Israel's future greatness (Numbers 23–24).
The Greek translation of Num 24:17 in the Septuagint describes Balaam as
speaking an oracle, proclaiming that a "star will rise from Jacob, and a man
will stand forth from Israel." During the Second Temple period, this verse had
been applied to the Messiah.[6] Finally, when Balaam completes his oracles he
returns to his home. Thus, Brown argues that this story provides the narrative
impetus for Matthew's story of the magi. An evil king seeks to use a foreign
seer to destroy his enemy, only to have the seer honor the greatness of that
enemy. This same seer proclaims that, like the rising of a star, a descendant
of Jacob will come forth to rule Israel. After completing his oracles, the seer

---

[3] For the range of choices, see Ben Witherington III, "Birth of Jesus," in *Dictionary of Jesus and the Gospels*, ed. Joel B. Green, Scot McKnight, and I. Howard Marshall (Downers Grove: InterVarsity, 1992), 72; Daniel J. Harrington, *The Gospel of Matthew* (Sacra Pagina 1; Collegeville: Liturgical Press, 1991), 42; Raymond E. Brown, *The Birth of the Messiah: A Commentary on the Infancy Narratives in the Gospels of Matthew and Luke*, rev. edn (New York: Doubleday, 1993), 168–70.

[4] Brown, *Birth of the Messiah*, 189–90. See also Bernard Robinson's essay in the previous chapter.

[5] Brown, *Birth of the Messiah*, 193–96; Donald A. Hagner, *Matthew* (WBC 33; Dallas: Word Books, 1993), 48–49; Eduard Schweizer, *The Good News according to Matthew*, trans. David E. Green (Atlanta: John Knox, 1975), 37; Robert H. Gundry, *Matthew: A Commentary on His Handbook for a Mixed Church Under Persecution* (Grand Rapids: Eerdmans, 1994), 27.

[6] The *Damascus Document* (CD 7:18–20) applies it to the kingly and priestly messiah of the Dead Sea Scrolls community; so John J. Collins, *The Scepter and the Star: The Messiahs of the Dead Sea Scrolls and Other Ancient Literature* (New York: Doubleday, 1995), 80–82.

returns home.[7] Brown's argument is strengthened by Philo's description of Balaam (*Life of Moses* 1.276) as a *magos*.[8]

It has long been suggested that the non-Jewish magi foreshadow Jesus' command in Matt 28:19 to "make disciples of all nations" and, as such, prefigure the role of Gentiles in the early Christian community. Brown argues that the story derives its Gentile emphasis from implicit allusions to Isaiah and the Psalter.[9] Isaiah prophesies that "the wealth of the nations shall come to you [Jerusalem]. A multitude of camels shall cover you, the young camels of Midian and Ephah; all those from Sheba shall come. They shall bring gold and frankincense, and shall proclaim the praise of the LORD" (Isa 60:5–6). The psalmist exclaims, "May the kings of Tarshish and of the isles render him tribute, may the kings of Sheba and Seba bring gifts. May all kings fall down before him, all nations give him service" (Ps 72:10–11). Brown concludes that the blending of the Balaam story with these scriptural allusions defines Jesus as the "son of Abraham" (Matt 1:1) in whom all the nations of the world will be blessed (Gen 18:18), just as Matt 1:18–25 explains how Jesus is the "son of David" (Matt 1:1).

Brown also surmises that it is later Christian tradition that promotes the magi to kings through reflection on Ps 72:10–11 as a scriptural background for their story. Though early visual representations provide anywhere from two to twelve magi, the overwhelming tradition of three derives from the number of gifts that they bring to Jesus. Subsequent Christian tradition will also provide names for the three magi.[10]

Neither kings nor wise men

That the magi in Matthew's narrative were not kings is acknowledged by scholarly consensus. What has also attained popularity is the translation of *magoi* as "wise men" because as non-Jews they were able to recognize the coming of Israel's redeemer when the nation's own leaders could not do the same.[11]

---

[7] Brown, *Birth of the Messiah*, 194–96.

[8] F.H. Colson, *Philo, vol. 6: On Abraham, On Joseph, On Moses* (LCL; New York: Putnam, 1935), 418.

[9] Brown, *Birth of the Messiah*, 188. See also Ulrich Luz, *Matthew 1–7: A Commentary*, trans. Wilhem C. Linss (Minneapolis: Augsburg, 1989), 139; Craig S. Keener, *A Commentary on the Gospel of Matthew* (Grand Rapids: Eerdmans, 1999), 105; Warren Carter, *Matthew and the Margins: A Sociopolitical and Religious Reading* (The Bible & Liberation Series; Maryknoll, NY: Orbis: Sheffield: Sheffield Academic Press, 2000), 81. Biblical translations in this chapter are generally quoted from the NRSV.

[10] The names differ. The best known names in the Western Christian tradition are Balthasar, Melchior, and Gaspar (or Casper).

[11] Many Bible translations (e.g., KJV, NKJV, JB, NJB, RSV, and NRSV) translate *magoi* as "wise men."

However, through a careful narrative-critical analysis Mark Allan Powell challenges this argument.[12]

Powell addresses the magi by discerning what the text expects the reader to know about them through intertextual knowledge. This reader to whom the text addresses itself is often called the implied reader. As Powell acknowledges, the implied reader would be expected to understand Matthew's direct citations of and allusions to the Old Testament. However, just because a reader is able to recognize the allusions to Isa 60:5–6 and Ps 72:10–11 and understand that the magi come to Jesus in a manner like kings does not make them literally kings. Powell argues that the intertextual relationship between the magi and the Old Testament texts provokes an association between magi and kings, but not in the way that contemporary Christians have come to understand.

After reviewing Greco-Roman and Jewish midrashic literature as well as the reference to magi in the Greek translation of Daniel (Dan 2:2, 10), Powell concludes that magi in the ancient world are portrayed as lowly servants to kings and subject to these kings' political machinations. They are figures without power who heed the whims of the powerful. Furthermore, they are portrayed as Daniel's enemies and would have, therefore, been perceived in a negative light by the implied reader.[13] Powell then discerns the negative portrayal of royalty and power within the Gospel of Matthew. According to Powell, "In Matthew's narrative, exponents of worldly power, be they political or religious, are invariably aligned with Satan, while the powerless are presented as followers with whom Jesus' disciples must identify."[14]

Powell concludes that the behavior of the magi when they meet Jesus falls within the characterization of servants in the First Gospel rather than kings. Therefore, Matthew's narrator uses the allusions to Ps 72:10–11 and Isa 60:5–6 to create a contrast between the behavior of kings and the behavior of the magi. The implied reader's expectations are overturned by having Jesus worshipped by servants rather than kings.[15]

Powell then addresses the more common understanding of the magi as wise persons—with similar results. He first notes that while it is assumed that the magi employed their special understanding of astrology to find Jesus, the narrative nowhere states this. In fact, it has them ask Herod where the king of the Jews was to be born. Thus, they used what would have been common knowledge at the time that unusual astral events signaled the birth of a great person.[16] Again, Powell surveys Greco-Roman and Jewish literature to conclude

---

[12] Mark Allan Powell, *Chasing the Eastern Star: Adventures in Biblical Reader-Response Criticism* (Louisville: Westminster John Knox, 2001).

[13] Keener, *Matthew*, 99.

[14] Powell, *Chasing*, 144.

[15] Ibid., 146–47.

[16] See Roy A. Rosenberg, "The Star of the Messiah Reconsidered," *Biblica* 53 (1972) 105–109.

that the implied reader would probably regard any special learning or powers of the magi as ridiculous.[17] Further, the magi's question to Herod conveys their misunderstanding of Jesus since they attribute to him a political title ("King of the Jews," Matt 2:2)—a title used by others in the narrative who do not understand Jesus or his mission (Matt 27:11, 29, 37). Finally, Powell argues that the role of the star in the narrative is so overtly presented that virtually anyone could follow it. The magi do not know, as does Herod, the messianic significance of the star. They do not know, as do the Jewish leaders, that the king of the Jews is to be born in Bethlehem. They are not aware, as is the reader, of Herod's malignant intentions. Therefore, the magi are "the most ignorant characters in the story."[18] Interestingly, Monty Python picks up on this quality of the magi by having them visit the wrong manger at the beginning of their 1979 film, *Monty Python's Life of Brian.*

From the preceding analyses Powell concludes that Matthew overturns the implied reader's expectations by presenting the magi not as "representatives of the best of pagan lore and religious perception"[19] who seek Israel's Messiah based on their "secret lore,"[20] but as pagan fools who know nothing and are ignorant before Israel's God. Yet to them God reveals the truth about Jesus. This agrees with the remainder of Matthew's narrative that proposes Galilean fishermen as judges of the twelve tribes of Israel (19:28) and a kingdom that requires its inhabitants to be like children (18:13; 19:14).

The strength of Powell's argument lies not only in his reference to intertextual opinions about Magi and their practices but also in his insightful intratextual analysis that demonstrates the manner with which Matthew's narrator fashions a conflict between the high and powerful (who should be wise) and the low and ignorant (who, in fact, have access to the kingdom). This social and theological reversal demonstrates Jesus' admonition that "the first will be last and the last will be first" (19:30; 20:16).

II. The Magi in *The Gospel According to Saint Matthew*

When examining Pasolini's film of *The Gospel*, it is important to address the common misconception that the movie is a faithful visual retelling of the First Gospel. For example, when it awarded the film its highest honor, the *Office Catholique Internationale du Cinéma* (OCIC) declared, "The author—without renouncing his own ideology—has faithfully translated, with a simplicity and

---

[17] See also Carter, *Matthew and the Margins*, 74–75.
[18] Powell, *Chasing*, 155.
[19] David E. Garland, *Reading Matthew: A Literary and Theological Commentary on the First Gospel* (New York: Crossroad, 1993), 25.
[20] W.D. Davies and Dale C. Allison, *The Gospel According to Saint Matthew I–VII* (ICC; Edinburgh: T&T Clark, 1988), 230.

a human density sometimes moving, the social message of the Gospel—in particular the love of the poor and oppressed—sufficiently respecting the divine dimension of Christ."[21] This perception of fidelity was propagated by Pasolini as he worked on the film. In a letter he stated that his idea was to "follow the Gospel of Matthew point by point" and that he would "faithfully translate it in images without an omission or addition to the story."[22] However, five years after the film, Pasolini suggested that his intentions were other than fidelity:

> I did not want to reconstruct the life of Christ as it really was; I wanted to do the story of Christ plus two thousand years of Christian translation, because it is the two thousand years of Christian history which have mythicized this biography, which would otherwise be an almost insignificant biography as such. My film is the life of Christ plus two thousand years of story-telling about the life of Christ.[23]

Pasolini's shift in objectives is one small manifestation of his provocative and obdurate personality.[24] In addition, a careful analysis of the film reveals that Pasolini omits important sections of the First Gospel, rearranges other sections, and employs visuals and music in a manner that foregrounds the film as a work of interpretation rather than as a faithful translation of the story.[25] Therefore, it should be expected that *The Gospel* offers a critical visual commentary on Matthew's nativity story and not a sense that what the viewer "sees is the way it must have been."[26]

By the time the magi visit the baby Jesus in *The Gospel*, the viewer has already encountered several unusual scenes in the film. Omitting Matthew's genealogy in 1:1–17, it begins with no words of introduction and proceeds in silence for twenty-five seconds with a series of extreme close-ups that cut between Mary and Joseph. Except for atmospheric noises, the silence extends for the next two minutes of the film until the angel appears to Joseph. One is also struck by the headwear of the Jewish leaders that, in its excessive size, calls attention to itself.

---

[21] Quoted in Barth David Schwartz, *Pasolini Requiem* (New York: Vintage, 1995), 453.

[22] Pier Paolo Pasolini, *Il Vangelo Secondo Matteo/Edipo Re/Medea* (Turin: Garzanti, 1991), 16. See the English translation in Pier Paolo Pasolini, *Heretical Empiricism*, trans. Ben Lawton and Louise K. Barnett, ed. Louise K. Barnett (Bloomington & Indianapolis: Indiana University Press, 1988), 508–509.

[23] Oswald Stack, *Pasolini on Pasolini: Interviews with Oswald Stack* (Cinema One 11; Bloomington and London: Indiana University Press, 1969), 83.

[24] For biographies of Pasolini, see Enzo Siciliano, *Pasolini*, trans. John Shepley (New York: Random House, 1982); Schwartz, *Pasolini Requiem*.

[25] For more detailed examinations of Pasolini's omissions, rearrangements, and use of visuals and music, see Christopher C. Fuller, "*'Udiste che fu detto..., ma io dico che...'* Pasolini as Interpreter of the Gospel of Matthew," PhD dissertation (Graduate Theological Union, Berkeley, 2002), 15–25; Zygmunt G. Barański, "The Texts of *Il Vangelo secondo Matteo*," in *Pasolini Old & New*, ed. Zygmunt G. Barański (Dublin: Four Courts Press, 1999), 281–320.

[26] "Best of the New Films," *Catholic Film Newsletter*, February 26, 1966, 1.

However, one is not sure why such headwear is necessary; its purpose is left unexplained. When the magi eventually appear in the film, the spectator thus expects an uncommon rendering of their encounter with the newborn king.

The magi first appear with an establishing shot that views them from behind as they enter Jerusalem. Pasolini retains the Christian tradition of three magi. With the next cut the camera does not follow them but surveys the busy marketplace that they traverse on their way to visit Herod. It eventually finds them as they pass through the city gates. The camera tracks the magi from behind, providing no close-ups until over a minute after their arrival in the film. Eventually the camera reveals them with extreme close-ups as they ask the location of the birth of the king of Jews. The camera then cuts to a tight close-up of Herod that is followed by three more extreme close-ups of Jewish leaders. The final close-up includes a slow pan that reveals three more Jewish leaders in extreme close-up. No words are spoken during this sequence. Eventually the Jewish leaders explain where the king of the Jews is to be born and Herod commissions the magi to find him.

The scene then cuts to a hillside. The camera looks up as the magi descend down the hillside to visit Mary, Joseph, and Jesus. A series of shot-reverse-shots cuts between the descending magi and the holy family as it anticipates its visitors. Here Pasolini follows the First Gospel and not tradition by having the family at their home, not a manger. When the magi are midway down the hillside a song begins. A somber voice intones, "Sometimes I feel like a motherless child... alone... alone... alone."[27] The song continues to play until the magi depart. After the visitors kneel in reverence before Jesus, Mary hands the infant to the center magus who holds the child in close-up. After the magus lifts up the child in homage, the camera cuts to a series of close-ups, first Joseph, then Mary, and then the crowd that surrounds the magi. Eventually the magi encounter the angel who leads them home, away from Herod's machinations. The presence of the magi in the film spans approximately eight minutes of screen time.

There are several striking elements to these two sequences. First, they abound in extreme close-ups most often focusing on smiling faces, particularly in the encounter between the magi and the holy family. Second, *The Gospel* is unique among Jesus films by portraying the magi descending down a hillside to visit Mary, Joseph, and Jesus. Finally, the song's focus on a "motherless child" who is "alone" provides an arresting aural juxtaposition to the infant Jesus who is clearly with his mother and not alone. Unlike the cohesion of visuals, sound, and narrative that one finds in the Hollywood cinema, *The Gospel* provides no obvious criteria by which the spectator can cogently assemble these disparate auditory and visual fragments.

[27] An edition of this negro spiritual song was published by William E. Barton, *Old Plantation Hymns: A Collection of Hitherto Unpublished Melodies of the Slave and the Freedman, with Historical and Descriptive Notes* (Boston: Lamson, Wolffe, 1899).

Allusions to biblical paintings

Pasolini's distinctive visual interpretation of Matthew's nativity story is an example of what he called "stylistic contamination." In the screenplay to *The Gospel* he states that it was his intent to evoke the "figurative inspiration" ("l'ispirazione figurativa") of several artists.[28] For Pasolini this entailed the deliberate framings of scenes in ways that visually quote works of art. It also included the use of music in a manner that was often contrapuntal to the visuals and narrative. In so doing he believed that he "contaminated" one work of art with another.

His particular focus, which first manifested itself in his poetry, was to mix both high (painting) and low (cinema) forms of art to produce a new type of expression. He believed that the contaminated work alerted the spectator to the work as a social construct, thus requiring his or her participation in the making of meaning. Pasolini wrote of the necessity for an active spectator, not only in the act of interpretation but in the act of authoring itself. "For the author, the spectator is merely another author."[29] Thus, as Maurizio Viano notes, *The Gospel* invites the spectator "to judge a relationship between an objective reality (Matthew's text) and the subjective rendering of it (Pasolini's images)."[30] This approach stands in contrast to the dominant Hollywood paradigm that seeks to seamlessly weave narrative, visuals, and sound into a coherent narrative that absorbs a passive spectator.[31]

The descending arrival of the magi is where Pasolini employs visual contamination in his interpretation of Matthew's nativity. Through the diagonal movement of the magi Pasolini visually cites Bartolo di Fredi's *Adoration of the Magi* (1380). This allows Pasolini both to contaminate the scene and also visually to display the action of contamination as the movement from high to low. The visual contamination continues with the prostration of the magi before Mary and the baby Jesus, which evokes Masaccio's *Adoration of the Magi* (1426). In both instances the spectator encounters where Pasolini tells the story of Jesus plus two thousand years of story-telling about Jesus.

Visual allusions to biblical art are a common motif in Hollywood films, so as to appeal to the piety of the audience. For example, the Last Supper scene in *The Greatest Story Ever Told* (1965) clearly alludes to Da Vinci's *Last Supper* (1498). Pasolini undermines this appeal by overlaying this visual contamination with his unusual choice of music, "Sometimes I feel like a motherless

---

[28] Pasolini, *Il Vangelo*, 20.
[29] Pasolini, *Heretical Empiricism*, 269.
[30] Maurizio Viano, *A Certain Realism: Making Use of Pasolini's Film Theory and Practice* (Berkeley: University of California Press, 1993), 140.
[31] For a discussion of the classical Hollywood style, see David Bordwell, *The Classical Hollywood Cinema: Film Style & Mode of Production to 1960* (New York: Columbia University Press, 1985).

child." What further contributes to the song's mutinous effect is that it is an English-language recording by the American blues artist Odetta in an Italian film. It introduces not only a conspicuous contrast to the visual imagery but also a juxtaposition of cultures.

Finally, there are the abundant close-ups in these two scenes, as well as throughout the film. Viano helpfully notes that they are motivated by physiognomic rather than psychological reasons.[32] This insight identifies Pasolini's long-standing interest in representations of the body in his cinema. Pasolini's writing and cinema betray an intense interest in the body and its function as the site where cultural discourses intersect with one another.

The significance of the body

For Pasolini, the body plays an integral part in human communication. He arrives at this insight through his theory of cinema as the written language of reality. He attempts to clarify this assertion by arguing that the cinema "does not evoke reality, as literary language does; it does not copy reality, as painting does; it does not mime reality, as drama does. Cinema *reproduces* reality, image and sound! . . . Cinema expresses reality with reality."[33] If this explanation appears unsatisfactory, he confuses it further by arguing that *"reality is, in the final analysis, nothing more than cinema in nature."*[34]

Because the cinema visually records material reality, it is a language "which compels the enlargement of the concept of language."[35] Pasolini argues that the cinema contributes a consciousness of visual signs that differs from the written–spoken element of human language. This consciousness also reveals the inadequacy of an understanding of language that relies solely upon written–spoken signs. While in literature we are accustomed to perceiving the word as written–spoken without audio-visual qualities, cinema exploits this quality (what Pasolini calls the "kineme") as the linguistic sign *par excellence*.[36]

An understanding of human language is incomplete without the body as the tablet upon which material reality is inscribed as a language. Pasolini argues that this nonverbal signifier is nothing more than the verbal expression of the reality that the cinema records and expresses. If editing is the means through which the cinema communicates reality, the body is the principal material

---

[32] Viano, *A Certain Realism*, 139.
[33] Pasolini, *Heretical Empiricism*, 133.
[34] Ibid., 198 (with his own emphases).
[35] Ibid., 133.
[36] This separation of the visual from the oral (phoneme) and written (grapheme) qualities of language establishes the cinematic sign as an "im-sign." It is the im-sign that enlarges our concept of language by focusing on the body, which functions through physiognomy, behavior, and action as a linguistic signifier equal in communicative impact with the spoken and written word.

expression of this reality. Pasolini even asserts that human "action in reality" is the *first* language of humanity and that the written spoken languages "are nothing more than an integration of this first language."[37]

Pasolini's theoretical examinations of the body as a linguistic signifier in the cinema find ample expression in his movies. One of the most consistent visual tropes throughout his films is a visual examination of the body in whole and in parts. Robert Stam notes its obvious presence in the bodily discharges, the voyeurism, and the gentle visual caresses of the three films that constitute the "Trilogy of Life": *The Decameron* (1971), *The Canterbury Tales* (1972), and *Arabian Nights* (1974).[38] However, it is present throughout his cinema, from the extreme close-ups of *Accatone* (1961) to the cannibalism of *Hawks and Sparrows* (1966) and *Pigsty* (1969), to the sexual deliverance of *Teorema* (1968), to the dismemberments of *Medea* (1970), and to the mutilations of *Salò or 120 Nights of Sodom* (1975). Throughout much of Pasolini's cinema, particularly in the "Trilogy of Life," the bodies of lower-ranking people exhibit a joyous disregard for modern western social order, which Pasolini believed had been subsumed by technology. In this manner, the magi emerge in *The Gospel* as bodily signifiers of an alternative order that confronts the spectator through visual and aural stylistic contamination. The task is now to translate Pasolini's filmic elements into interpretive escorts through the text of Matt 2:1–12. Mikhail Bakhtin's theory of the carnivalesque provides the most useful framework to address this task.[39]

Bakhtin and the Carnivalesque

In his 1965 book, *Rabelais and His World*, Bakhtin explores the carnivalesque as literary expression.[40] Carnival is not associated with a specific date as much as it represents a sense about the world. According to Bakhtin, it is "an extraordinarily flexible form of artistic visualization, a peculiar sort of heuristic principle making possible the discovery of new and as yet unseen things."[41] More than an actual representation of a carnival, he argues that the carnivalesque is a literary strategy that has been influential during all periods of literary development. It flourished during the Renaissance as

---

[37] Pasolini, *Heretical Empiricism*, 198–99; see also 204, 234.

[38] Robert Stam, *Subversive Pleasures: Bakhtin, Cultural Criticism and Film* (Parallax Re-Visions of Culture and Society; Baltimore: Johns Hopkins University Press, 1989), 236.

[39] On the theories of the Russian literary critic Mikhail Bakhtin (1895–1975) applied to the Bible, see Barbara Green, *Mikhail Bakhtin and Biblical Scholarship: An Introduction* (SBL Semeia Studies 38; Atlanta: Society of Biblical Literature, 2000).

[40] Mikhail M. Bakhtin, *Rabelais and His World* [1965], trans. Hélène Iswolsky (Bloomington, IN: Indiana University Press, 1984).

[41] Mikhail M. Bakhtin, *Problems of Dostoevsky's Poetics*, ed. and trans. Caryl Emerson (Theory and History of Literature 8; Minneapolis: University of Minnesota Press, 1984), 166.

a force of opposition against the static unchanging worldview of medieval culture. Bakhtin argues that Socratic expression—an exploration of truth that allows for multiple distinct voices to intersect with one another (what Bakhtin calls "dialogism")—forms the basis of the carnivalesque, in opposition to a singular controlling point of view and its ready-made truth (what Bakhtin calls "monologism").

The carnivalesque has its origins in the festive forms of expression of popular culture. As a form of expression it gives voice to languages that are excluded by official (and monologic) discourse. It celebrates the "temporary liberation from the prevailing truth and from established order; the marked suspension of all hierarchical rank, privileges, norms, and prohibitions."[42] Emanating from popular expression, it combines the sacred with the profane, the high with the low, the great with the insignificant, and the wise with the foolish. It takes the shape of plays, feasts, literature, and other popular celebrations populated by rogues, clowns, and fools who embody otherness in relation to official society.

For Bakhtin, the works of François Rabelais (died 1553) represent the summit of carnivalistic literature. In Rabelais' literature and visual works by painters like Hieronymus Bosch and the elder Breughel, the carnivalesque emerges as a penetration of lower genres into the higher levels of literature. Through this mixing of high and low forms, "the exalted and the lowly, the sacred and the profane are leveled and are all drawn into the same dance."[43] The result is a new creation. "Carnival celebrates the destruction of the old and the birth of the new world—the new year, the new spring, the new kingdom."[44]

Parody is the form through which the carnivalesque is most often expressed. According to Caryl Emerson and Gary Saul Morson, parody undermines authority "with pretensions to be timeless and absolute."[45] Bakhtin adds that "the process of parodying forces us to experience those sides of the object that are not otherwise included in a given genre or style."[46] This is achieved through laughter that is as prevalent in culture as seriousness. It does not achieve this by denying seriousness. Rather, it acts as a liberating force that purifies seriousness of its monologic pretensions. More than just a state of mind, laughter serves as an active defense mechanism that describes the way that humans

---

[42] Bakhtin, *Rabelais and His World*, 10, 121. See also Bakhtin, *Problems of Dostoevsky's Poetics*, 123.

[43] Bakhtin, *Rabelais and His World*, 160.

[44] Ibid., 410.

[45] Caryl Emerson and Gary Saul Morson, *Mikhail Bakhtin: Creation of a Prosaics* (Stanford, CA: Stanford University Press, 1990), 435.

[46] Mikhail M. Bakhtin, "From the Prehistory of Novelistic Discourse," in his essay collection, *The Dialogical Imagination*, trans. Caryl Emerson and Michael Holquist, ed. Michael Holquist (Austin: University of Texas Press, 1981), 41–83, here 55.

see the world. Emerson notes that laughter "helps us to accomplish that most difficult task, to see ourselves as very minor players in a multitude of other people's plots."[47]

The carnivalesque also has to do with the permeation of the boundary between the self and world. This boundary is grounded in the body, particularly its orifices or what Bakhtin calls the "lower bodily stratum."[48] The carnivalesque valorizes all of the functions of these strata (eating, drinking, defecating, and sexual activity) to degrade all that is high, spiritual, ideal, and abstract and relocate them in the material world. Bakhtin calls this "grotesque realism."[49] He writes that "all that is sacred and exalted is rethought on the level of the material bodily stratum or else combined and mixed with its images."[50] Thus, the carnivalesque celebrates the body as a site of multiplicity and dispersion and as the organic center of the world.

The bodily strata also function as the site where the self opens out into the material world. As open permeations between the self and the organic, they are always incomplete. Carnival's emphasis on the grotesque body and its orifices celebrates what is open and cannot be finalized. They form the basis of what Bakhtin calls a "laughing truth" that mocks serious closed systems and inverts their hierarchical structures. The stress is on becoming rather than completion. Bakhtin writes that "the inner movement of being itself was expressed in the passing of one form into another, in the ever completed character of being."[51] This stress ignores what is closed about the body and emphasizes those aspects that protrude beyond the body's own boundaries.

The grotesque body not only refers to the individual but also to the body as a social collective instilled with an orientation to social inversion. As a collective it is immortal. According to Bakhtin, the liberation and openness of the carnivalesque forms persons at the lower levels of society into a collective that mocks the higher order through festivals and the arts. This process creates an understanding within the collective grotesque body of its role in history. Bakhtin argues that "in the grotesque concept of the body a new, concrete, and realistic historic awareness was born and took form: not abstract though about the future but the living sense that each man belongs to the immortal people who create history."[52] Thus, the grotesque body is not a passive bystander to events but participates in them.

---

[47] Caryl Emerson, *The First Hundred Years of Mikhail Bakhtin* (Princeton, NJ: Princeton University Press, 1997), 196.

[48] Bakhtin, *Rabelais and His World*, 21.

[49] Ibid., 18.

[50] Ibid., 370–71.

[51] Ibid., 32.

[52] Ibid., 367.

The image of the banquet

One manner through which the carnivalesque celebrates the body is through the image of the banquet. Eating and drinking represent an important manifestation of the grotesque body. Bakhtin notes, "The encounter of man [*sic*] with the world which takes place inside the open, biting, rending, chewing mouth, is one of the most ancient, and important objects of human thought and imagery."[53] He also notes that the popular-festive banquet through which this encounter is expressed is not the same as images of private eating, gluttony, or drunkenness. It must take place within a social context for it to express the carnivalesque.

The banquet represents a joyful triumph over the world as persons devour without being devoured. For Bakhtin it is, by its nature, a celebration of victory over hierarchy and its social constraints. It achieves this by mixing the profane and the sacred, the lower and the higher, and the spiritual and the material with a great deal of freedom. Though Bakhtin rarely writes about the Bible, he does note that the bodily nature of the banquet provides the opportunity to embrace and renew much of the contents of the Bible. While it is beyond the scope of this study, Bakhtin's celebration of the banquet as the location of the grotesque inversion of hierarchy provokes one to reread the gospel narratives that describe Jesus' table fellowship as well as the use of food in the Bible as possible expressions of the carnivalesque.

There is much in Bakhtin's understanding of the carnivalesque that resonates with Pasolini's movie of *The Gospel* as a visual interpretation of the First Gospel. As a concept that describes the mixing of high and low forms, it is evocative of Pasolini's notion of stylistic contamination. It also provides a conceptual framework to describe Pasolini's use of contamination as an encounter with materiality, particularly through its bodily expression.

Carnivalesque Fools in Search of a King

One of Pasolini's significant omissions in *The Gospel* is the eschatological discourse of Matthew 24–25. This discourse begins in 24:3, opening a new section of Matthew's literary narrative.[54] In this section Jesus tells his disciples of the "birth pangs" of the coming end of the age (24:8). Though he cannot tell the disciples the precise time (24:36), he does lay out the signs that signal the end of the age (24:4–44) and his return as the Son of Man to bring final judgment.

---

[53] Ibid., 281.
[54] Fred W. Burnett, "Prolegomenon to Reading Matthew's Eschatological Discourse: Redundancy and the Education of the Reader in Matthew," *Semeia* 31 (1985) 91–109, here 98; Garland, *Reading Matthew*, 234.

Jesus then follows these statements with a series of parables that emphasize the importance of this final judgment. However, Pasolini only includes 24:1–2 in *The Gospel*. The result is that by omitting 24:3–51 and all of chapter 25, the film considerably strips Jesus of his eschatological orientation—his promise of the future—and more firmly grounds him in the present.

With Bakhtin's assistance we can view *The Gospel*'s world as one that awaits the arrival of the carnivalesque, not the *eschaton* (or final moment), as the fulfillment of God's promise. Naomi Greene describes it as one populated by the landscapes and peasant faces of the poor in conflict with the imposing appearance of the Jewish leaders that "suggests the rigidity and power that adhere to any reigning Establishment."[55] Into this world arrives Jesus who becomes the carnivalesque made flesh. The absence of the eschatological essence of Jesus' ministry in *The Gospel* emphasizes this dimension. The film presents him as the rogue Messiah of the material world whose presence overturns the official authority of Herod and the Jewish leaders.

Bakhtin is reported to have declared, "And the Gospels are carnival too!"[56] He also wrote, "The literature, including rhetoric, of certain eras like Hellenism and the Middle Ages is flooded with various reduced forms of laughter, though we have ceased to be aware of some of them."[57] Unfortunately, he never developed these assertions beyond their provocative brevity. Through its presentation of Jesus and those who respond positively to him like the magi, *The Gospel* agrees with Bakhtin and argues that the carnivalesque is present in the First Gospel.[58]

According to Powell, Matthew intends his readers to view the magi as holy fools who are ignorant within the biblical view, not wise.[59] However, his emphasis on the narrative constraints imposed upon the implied reader prevents him from appreciating the carnivalesque potential that resides in the magi as holy fools. In *The Gospel* they embody stylistic contamination that provokes the spectator to active contemplation rather than passive reception. In particular, Pasolini's prolific use of close-ups imparts his affection for the body in his cinema and in so doing calls to mind Bakhtin's emphasis on the bodily nature of the carnivalesque. The surplus of smiling faces in these close-ups also underscores the laughing subtext of carnival. In this manner the spectator encounters the carnivalesque quality of stylistic contamination.

---

[55] Naomi Greene, *Pier Paolo Pasolini: Cinema as Heresy* (Princeton: Princeton University Press, 1990), 76.
[56] Reported by Vladimir N. Turbin, as quoted in Emerson, *The First Hundred Years of Mikhail Bakhtin*, 37.
[57] Bakhtin, *Rabelais and His World*, 135.
[58] We may also note the grotesque humor in the saying about the speck and the log (Matt 7:3–5).
[59] Powell, *Chasing the Eastern Star*, 155.

Curiously, there has been no examination of the profusion of smiling faces throughout *The Gospel*. They are presented to the spectator silent and without explanation as the expression of the peasant people who come into contact with Jesus and his ministry. Within a Bakhtinian conceptual framework, they come into view as those points where the "merry" time of the carnivalesque breaks into the world. This is a time of laughter "which kills and gives birth, which allows nothing old to be perpetuated and never ceases to generate the new and the youthful."[60] As much as the miracles, perhaps even more so, these smiling faces bear Jesus' ministry as bodies that traverse the boundary of a world ruled by hierarchy to one that testifies to the victory of the future over the past.[61]

When we evaluate Powell's and *The Gospel*'s insights through a Bakhtinian lens, the carnivalesque potential of the magi in the Gospel of Matthew comes into view. They illustrate David McCracken's contention that the carnivalesque appears in the Gospels in the manner with which the normal world is turned upside down through Jesus' ministry.[62] Matthew's text provides no physical description of the magi, so the reader is not confronted by the body and its openings into the world. Therefore, the carnivalesque does not manifest itself in Matt 2:1–12 in a grotesque fashion but as potential to be actively sought by the reader in the remainder of the narrative. Bakhtin reminds us that the carnivalesque is "an extraordinarily flexible form of artistic visualization, a peculiar sort of heuristic principle making possible the discovery of new and as yet unseen things."[63] Carnival is as much a strategy as it is an actual representation of the carnivalesque. However, this does not mean that the body is not entirely absent from the Gospel text.

Walter Reed argues that the carnivalesque in Matthew's narrative emerges when Jesus shares table fellowship with sinners and tax collectors (9:11).[64] Matthew 11:19 emphasizes this feature by describing the criticism of Jesus as a glutton and drunkard for his table practices. This analysis reflects Bakhtin's emphasis on the importance of the banquet within carnivalesque literature. It is a concrete manifestation of the comic. Again, this is less about overt laughter than about how one views the world through the comic activity of the carnivalesque. Banquet scenes mix the profane and the sacred, the lower and the higher, and the spiritual and the material to portray victory over hierarchy and authority.

---

[60] Bakhtin, *Rabelais and His World*, 211.
[61] Ibid., 256.
[62] David McCracken, "Character in the Boundary: Bakhtin's Interdividuality in Biblical Narratives," *Semeia* 63 (1993) 29–42, here 38–39.
[63] Bakhtin, *Problems of Dostoevsky's Poetics*, 166.
[64] Walter L. Reed, *Dialogues of the Word: The Bible as Literature according to Bakhtin* (New York: Oxford University Press, 1993), 82.

Reed identifies a covert example of the carnivalesque but does not explore its presence elsewhere in the Gospels. Therefore, he fails to understand the carnivalesque also as potential in the narrative preceding scenes of Jesus' table fellowship. Jesus' scandalous behavior with sinners and tax collectors creates tension within the textual world of the narrative. However, it also attains its capsizing comic force within the world of the reader through the carnivalesque potential of the magi. They not only foreshadow the role of the Gentiles in the future of the Christian community, but also adumbrate the parodic nature of this community by leading the procession of the festival of fools who respond to Jesus' ministry.

Chapter 10

The Nativity in Recent British Poetry

Ann Loades

Both "poetry" and "prose" (as forms of "poiesis") can stretch the resources of human language to their limits when we try to say things of which we can hardly speak or write. This may especially be the case when some understanding of the matter in hand is of the greatest importance to us. In the case of the nativity, we are concerned with one central truth, that God's Son (Jesus of Nazareth) "was incarnate of the Holy Spirit and the Virgin Mary." As Les Murray puts it, God can be regarded as the "poetry caught" (but not trapped) within a religious tradition, and poetry, for Murray, offers the opportunity of "whole thinking."[1]

We can also attend to Elizabeth Jennings' remarks when reviewing a book by a Dominican theologian, Thomas Gilby. There she affirms that he had given poetry "a central and high place in human experience," for its "moments of revelation" involve the whole of a person "transcribing or responding to the most important function of life—knowing by loving and loving by knowing," grasping an experience "not to possess but to be possessed."[2]

The fact that a poet is attending to and expressing a central truth of religion, however, never excuses anything other than one's best work, which will include technical skill and rhythmical dexterity, though even more important are seriousness of purpose and intensity of feeling.[3] Jennings goes on to assert that a specifically Christian poet, writing on a central truth such as that of the Incarnation, must never cease to care, and be prepared to struggle through her task, alert to the experiments and changes of the age in which she finds herself.

Since the seventeenth century, in particular, the poet writes not so much for the public context of worship, but to articulate personal experience of truth. Moreover, not only does the poem indeed spring from the whole person, but a

---

[1] Les Murray, "Poetry and Religion," *Collected Poems* (Manchester: Carcanet, 1998), 267.

[2] Elizabeth Jennings, *Every Changing Shape. Mystical Experience and the Making of Poems* (Manchester: Carcanet, 1996), 213–15.

[3] Elizabeth Jennings, *Christianity and Poetry* (Fact and Faith Books 122; London: Burns & Oates, 1965), 11, 93. On poetic inspiration, see also H.D. [= Hilda Doolittle], "The Walls do not Fall: 20," in H.D., *Trilogy* (Manchester: Carcanet, 1973), 29.

specifically Christian poet readily acknowledges that her "making" is "a small participation in the divine and unceasing act of creation"—whether everyone recognizes this or not.[4] And she assesses what is happening in the making of poetry in the broadest sense—which we may take to be true of the biblical poets too—when she reflects that "the first vivid vision is bound to fade a little when words intervene. On the other hand, how can a man or woman know what they have experienced until they try to speak about it? Poetry would certainly seem to be the most suitable medium for such explanations."

Despite these observations, it does not follow that poets will be free from doubt and difficulties in regard either to their work or to their faith. On the contrary, the more perceptive one is, the more agonized one might feel about the way things in life seem to go and the relationship of God to it all.

Biblical Poetry

When we turn to the biblical poets of the nativity, we need to reflect on more than the first few chapters of the Gospels of Matthew and Luke if we are to begin to be able to grasp their distinctive poetry as they grappled with the astonishing claims made by early Christianity. As the Christian tradition developed, the Roman winter solstice celebrations were displaced by celebrations of Jesus' birth, quite likely in the fourth century of the Christian era. The imperial Sun of Victory was displaced by the celebration of a divine and human Son, whose victory was profoundly different in what it offered to the hopes and longings of human beings.

One major text of great importance for expressing Christian convictions—read out loud, chanted, and learned by heart—was the Book of Isaiah.[5] The prophet who gave the whole book its name was deemed to have foreseen the arrival of the anointed one, the Messiah, the Christ, someone of special importance as the sign of God's presence with and among humankind (Isa 7:14). The original prophet had addressed a message to his king, Ahaz, in the besieged city of Jerusalem, promising that by the time a young woman—probably Ahaz's wife—had conceived and borne a son (Immanuel), the city would be free of its enemies. By the time of the birth of Jesus, these words were known both to Hebrew- and to Greek-speaking hearers and readers of Scripture.[6] Picked up by the writer of the first Gospel (Matt 1:23), they interpreted the meaning of the message given to Joseph by an angel, in a dream about the significance of

---

[4] Jennings, *Christianity and Poetry*, 18. The next quotation is from p. 111.
[5] John F.A. Sawyer, *The Fifth Gospel: Isaiah in the History of Christianity* (Cambridge: Cambridge University Press, 1996), 65–82, on "The Cult of the Virgin Mary."
[6] Whereas the Hebrew text of Isa 7:14 mentions a "young woman" (*'almah*), the Greek translation refers to a "virgin" (*parthenos*).

the child to be born to Mary. The writer was simply continuing what seems likely to have been the tradition of Christians since well before his own time, that of finding in their Scriptures, shared with Jewish friends and neighbors and fellow-worshipers, the language by which he and others could express and interpret what was going on in the nativity. And as early as the second century, a representation of Isaiah was to be found in a wall painting near to an image of Mary with her child on her lap—Christ sprung from the root of Jesse—with Isaiah pointing to them.[7] In this painting Isaiah also points to a star near them, the "star out of Jacob" (Num 24:17), the star of Matthew's second chapter that guides the mysterious magi on their way (Matt 2:2).

So Isaiah the prophet was also seen as Isaiah the evangelist, with some two hundred and fifty quotations from or allusions to the Book of Isaiah in Christian Scriptures, from Matthew to Revelation. It later even became a tradition to write up the whole narrative of Christ's life and its meaning, from Nativity to Last Judgment, in the very language of Isaiah.[8] It was as though, having grasped the significance of Christ in connection with the promise of salvation so characteristic of the Book of Isaiah, Christians could use poetry already familiar in order to retell the meaning of the Incarnation. It may even be the case that the poetry of Isaiah formed both Mary's own understanding of her role in bringing the divine presence among humanity in an unprecedented way, and then formed Jesus' own struggle to understand his relationship to God, his mission and death, and even perhaps God-given resurrection (see Isa 25:7–8).

The Book of Isaiah contains the words of a poet of the most profound insight and the most extraordinary expectations. For he spoke also of a multitude of camels coming from Midian, Ephah, and Sheba, bearing gold and frankincense, proclaiming the praise of the Lord (Isa 60:6). It was like the kings spoken of by the Psalmist, with kings of Tarshish, Sheba, and Seba rendering tribute (Ps 72:10–11). In Isaiah they are, as it were, silenced by what they come to see in Christ: "Kings shall shut their mouths because of him; for that which has not been told them they shall see, and that which they have not heard they shall understand" (Isa 52:15). And there was the exultant praise of God to be found later in Isaiah, where the poet writes of being clothed with "garments of salvation" and "the robe of righteousness," like a groom and bride adorned for their marriage: "For as the earth brings forth its shoots, and as a garden causes what is sown in it to spring up, so the Lord God will cause righteousness and praise to spring forth before all the nations" (Isa 61:10–11).[9]

---

[7] This wall painting, from the Roman catacomb in the Church of St Priscilla, is noted by Sawyer, *The Fifth Gospel*, 65, 76 (depicted in Plate 3).

[8] For instance, much of the text of Handel's 1742 oratorio *Messiah* comes from the Book of Isaiah.

[9] For these themes, see also Isa 45:8 and 1 Sam 2:1–8.

Moreover, Isaiah acknowledged the created context in which human beings are set, not only with his vision of the holy mountain and its restored and paradisal state (Isa 11:6-9), but also remembering and recalling how interdependent human beings remain with their animal companions and work-mates, naming specifically the ox and ass as beasts of burden indeed, but capable of knowing their owner and stable (Isa 1:3). Long after Christian Scriptures had been identified and agreed as authoritative, these animal companions turned up in paintings, dramatic representations, and inevitably, in poetry. In addition, because Luke's Gospel brings shepherds to Jesus' birthplace, there might be lambs too, in all their shivering vulnerability, associated so closely with the infant that they may symbolize him.[10]

Mother, Father, and God

We can keep other biblical texts in mind too before we turn to the poetry concerned with the nativity, poetry that is very much of our own era. Of central importance was something shared with most human beings about the significance of children to families and their networks of kin. Indeed, children have been especially significant when the divine blessing of fertility was jeopardized in poor communities by inadequate food and scarcity of resources, and inevitably untreated and untreatable infections in those of uncertain health. If we attend to the high mortality rate for both women and newborns in all but the most privileged societies, we can refresh our sensitivity not only to the way in which divine creativity was deemed to be present in the "genesis" and growth of the child in her or his mother's womb (e.g., Job 10:10; Ps 139:13–16; Ps 22:9–10—from the Psalm attributed to Christ in his last agony), but also to the point that a child's being brought safely through birth, and being nurtured and reared, yielded insight into God's own compassion (Isa 42:14; 46:3–4).

The relationship between the nascent and born child and mother is surely the primary model of altruism and intra-dependence in human societies. In scriptural texts, it is also the primary model for the cooperation of divine grace and human well-being as expressed in fertility. There were children born blind, deaf, mute, or otherwise disabled, but none of the risks either to mother or to child destroyed this conviction. Being safely born to the one whose heartbeat had been known before birth, able to breathe and suckle, being given to one's mother to feed and nurture, just able to focus eyes to eyes on her loving, smiling, singing, and talking face, learning to sing-along, being

---

[10] See "Agnus Dei" in Denise Levertov, *Selected Poems* (Newcastle upon Tyne: Bloodaxe Books, 1994), from "Mass for the Day of St Thomas Didymus," 175–81, especially p. 181: "is it implied that *we* / must protect this perversely weak / animal, whose muzzle's nudgings / suppose there is milk to be found in us? / Must hold to our icy hearts / a shivering God?"

cleaned up, kept safe enough, seen through being sick, sleepless, runny-nosed, disruptive, demanding, and impossible to please (just like an adult!), eager, curious, enjoying play of all kinds, making things for fun, learning companionship and conviviality in the sharing of food, learning how to let go of hurts and harms so that life could go on—all this might be involved as a child grew into the "image of God," as well as becoming of an age to learn Scripture by heart and sing it to others. Moreover, it is no accident that images of a breast-feeding maternal figure are so central in human art, not least in Christian art and poetry, since if a child's birth-mother could not feed him or her, or if she died, the child's very life depended upon another woman being able and willing to do so. Hence it remains a central image of human and divine charity.

Important too is the father's role. Being a "father"—as even the unnameable but awesomely named "Adonai" could sometimes be addressed (Isa 63:16)— had to do with creativity, intimacy, and hope, and above all with the understanding that Adonai was self-revealed as mercy (Exod 3:14; 34:6). So we need to keep Joseph in mind, and arguably give him far more attention than has been commonly the case, despite the efforts of some from the seventeenth century onward. Whatever may have been taken for granted in biblical or other times and places about a father's presence in his family, it cannot always be so taken for granted today. And it would be easy to break a man's heart if he thought that the one to whom he was betrothed had been unfaithful to him. So if Joseph is to embody in his own distinctive way the divine compassion, both to a vulnerable young woman and to the child she bears, he needs that promise from Isaiah.[11]

As is now widely appreciated, Matthew's Gospel genealogy associates Jesus with some vulnerable, marginal, possibly scandalous, and indeed unconventional women, but Joseph, we may suppose, had never thought himself likely to be involved with one such.[12] So his consent to Mary's well-being and that of her child is crucial for their gift of life to the community in which they will live, every birth bringing with it the promise of new beginnings. It was not just one more mouth to feed. We might well think that there is an untapped vein

---

[11] Gabriel's dealings with Joseph in W.H. Auden's *For the Time Being* have the heading "The Temptation of St. Joseph," with the result that Gabriel simply silences Joseph; see W.H. Auden, *Collected Longer Poems* (London: Faber and Faber, 1968), 149–51. With grim realism, R.S. Thomas depicts Joseph teaching Jesus "the true trade: to go / with the grain. / He left me / For a new master / who put him to the fashioning / of a cross for himself"; see R.S. Thomas, "Covenanters," in his *Collected Poems 1945–1990* (London: Dent, 1993), 404–406, here 405. See also George Mackay Brown, "Stations of the Cross," in his *Collected Poems*, ed. Archie Bevan and Brian Murray (London: Murray, 2005), 178–92; in no. 5 ("Carpenter"), the carpenter on this occasion sends elsewhere the centurion who has come to order a gallows: "Mary stood in the door, curling cold hands like leaves / Round the fruit of her womb. / 'Hurry,' she said, 'Let the saw sing. / Soon it will be time for the cradle to rock my boy' " (p. 184).

[12] On the women named in Matthew's genealogy, see, e.g., Irene Nowell, "Jesus' Great-Grandmothers: Matthew's Four and More," *Catholic Biblical Quarterly* 70 (2008) 1–15.

of reflection here, not least for poets of our own time, and for societies where a "parent" may not be genetically related to a child but a good parent nonetheless, and where all adults care for and respect one another's children.

So far as Joseph himself is concerned, and what Jesus may have learned from him about the divine "fatherhood," one of the most illuminating comments comes not from a poet but from someone concerned precisely with the fate of children in our own societies. As Alice Miller says, even someone who assumes that Jesus owed his capacity to love, his authenticity, and his goodness to the grace of his divine father may well wonder why God entrusted Jesus to these particular parents.[13] It makes more sense, however, generously to think of Joseph's also being graced by God, and so to deepen our appreciation of the role of Joseph in Jesus' life, never calling attention to himself, protecting and loving Mary and the child, encouraging him, assigning him central importance, and serving him, doing his share of making it possible for the child to distinguish what was true and to experience the meaning of love.[14]

The consequences of Joseph's actions were to be of the greatest significance, as indicated in the conclusion to Pamela Vermes' poem, "Think":

> Think that uniquely,
> in all the history of holiness,
> a man lived in the Presence,
> as a son with his father,
> walking hand in hand,
> speaking mouth to mouth.
>
> Think that uniquely,
> in all the history of holiness,
> a man said,
> with his life and death,
> Be a child
> as I am the child
> of our father in heaven.
>
> That the prophecy of Hosea might be fulfilled.
> That whereas it had been said of them,
> You are not my people,
> it might be said of them,
> CHILDREN OF THE LIVING GOD.[15]

---

[13] Alice Miller, *Thou Shalt Not Be Aware: Society's Betrayal of the Child* (London: Pluto, 1991), 98.
[14] Ibid., 96.
[15] Pamela Vermes, *The Riddle of the Sparks* (Oxford: Foxcombe, 1993), 55; cf. Hos 1:10 (2:1).

At the very least we may say that it is not unfitting to attribute Jesus' extraordinary confidence in addressing God and listening for God, responding to God, to his experience of human fathering by Joseph. The child and other children valued by Joseph would be cherished by the community to which they belonged, with its care for one another through the generations. So his support (for as long as it was present) was central to Jesus' earthly life. However, Joseph's support does not seem to have lasted until Jesus reached adult standing, for Joseph—through death, presumably—disappears from the narrative of his son's life (see Mark 6:3).

Poetry, Nativity, and Context

As a result of entirely new studies, we may well have a much better comprehension of the world into which Jesus was born, and the place of his mother within her village society.[16] She would need to be tough enough to survive pregnancy and a safe birth, healthy enough to feed and nurture her child, while living as one of a group of adults of different generations, with a swarm of children, all as soon as they were able likely to be involved in securing food and clothing and shelter as an ever-urgent priority. Their religious life would take place in village assemblies, including the developing synagogue tradition, with oral teaching not only of Torah but of other Scriptures—including the Book of Isaiah, as has been suggested earlier. Daily prayer was part and parcel of life, as was Sabbath respite from back-breaking work, and a round of festivals. No one would readily draw upon themselves and their community the attention of the "authorities," least of all the attention of the occupying power, which had no qualms about destroying opposition, polluting village wells with corpses, wrecking vineyards and fields, razing villages to the ground, crucifying the men, and turning women and children off to fend for themselves if they could—or else to die if they could not.

Whatever we make of Mary's relationship to Jesus while young, some of the personal differences between them of which we have glimpses in the Gospels (e.g., Mark 3:31–35) may well have stemmed from her grasp of the fact that he put his kin at risk by his preaching and behavior. Virtually none of this appears as yet in British poetry of our time, and generally there is little realism about Jesus' birth either.

Just occasionally someone risks the provocation of insisting on that realism—such as Guy Reid's tiny statue of Mary and her child to be found in St Matthew's Anglican Church, Westminster. Not only is Reid's "Mary" no example of great physical beauty such as we associate with some of the greatest

---

[16] See, for instance, Elizabeth A. Johnson, *Truly Our Sister: A Theology of Mary in the Communion of Saints* (London: Continuum, 2003).

paintings of the past; she is also completely naked, and the child—equally naked, as had become familiar in art from the past, though here no advertisement for infant beauty—is perched very uneasily on his mother's knee.[17] So far as I am aware, this is the first representation of a fully naked Mary ever produced by a British artist, and it prompted outrage in some quarters—in a society in which female nudity or near-nudity is hardly unfamiliar in anything from "lap-dancing" to advertising and fashion-wear (all of which may be part of the problem). The outrage nevertheless tells us something about our disquiet at the realism we need if we are to begin to grasp the enormity of the Christian claim about Incarnation. From this perspective, the poem by Alla Renee Bozarth has a powerful message:

> Before his cry,
> her cry.
> Before his sweat
> of blood,
> her bleeding and tears.
> Before his offering, hers.
> . . . .
> And by her body and blood
> alone, his body and blood
> and whole human being.[18]

It seems that we still have not reached the point where we can take such realism for granted, and in any event, it is little to the fore in the poetry discussed here. With or without such realism, the Christian claim about the truth of the Incarnation remains astonishing, as Denise Levertov points up in her poem "On the Mystery of the Incarnation":

> It's when we face for a moment
> the worst our kind can do, and shudder to know
> the taint in our own selves, that awe
> cracks the mind's shell and enters the heart:
> not to a flower, not to a dolphin,

[17] A small photograph of the sculpture, completed in 2000, appears on Guy Reid's website (www.guyreidsculpture.com), which includes an excellent review of the work by Mark Vernon, "Defrocking: Contested Images of Nudity in the Church," *New Statesman*, February 5, 2001. In addition, see "The Virgin Punishing the Infant," after the 1926 painting by Max Ernst, in Carol Ann Duffy, *Selected Poems* (London: Penguin, 1994) 51. Ernst's painting initially had to be removed from the gallery in which it was first exhibited.

[18] Part of the poem "Maria Sacerdota," by Alla Renee Bozarth, from *Life Prayers*, ed. Elizabeth Roberts and Elias Amidon (San Francisco: Harper, 1996), 169, brought to my attention by the Revd Canon Dr Martin Warner, of St. Paul's Cathedral, London.

> to no innocent form
> but to this creature vainly sure
> it and no other is god-like, God
> (out of compassion for our ugly
> failure to evolve) entrusts,
> as guest, as brother,
> the Word.[19]

The Word, however, is not separated from the non-human creatures whose presence in the nativity scene (as it were) derives originally from Isaiah's visions—not forgetting the Greek version of the prophet Habakkuk, finding God's work between two animals.[20] The creatures on whom human beings so depend are represented (in Levertov's words) by "the wondering animals...unused to human company after dark" who witness the birth, hear the first cry "of earthly breath drawn through the newborn lungs of God / and the cord is cut..." Before any other arrivals the ox and the ass are already kneeling, "the Family's oldest friends."[21]

Given our much greater sense of relationship to the non-human creatures with whom we share so much, it is unsurprising that poets of our time extend the friends of the family to include other creatures. Thus Les Murray's "Animal Nativity" is integral to his collection "Translations from the Natural World," and he writes that the great tale of peace started with the agreement of Mary ("this girl"). He then describes the flitting of swallows within the stable, as if another swallow is hatching and turning human. In the poet's vision, cattle are content that "this calf" must come in human form, and spiders recognize someone else able to walk on water. Finally, Murray speaks of dogs witnessing the nativity scene—not the well-fed pets of our modern western culture, but "starving" dogs, "agog" at the presence of the newborn child.[22]

U. A. Fanthorpe indeed writes as it were from a sheepdog's perspective, the dog recalling the very bright light, "the talking bird," the singing. "And the sky filled up wi' wings / And then the silence." The shepherds, "our lads,"

---

[19] Denise Levertov, *A Door in the Hive, with Evening Train* (Newcastle upon Tyne: Bloodaxe Books, 1993), 56.

[20] The Greek of Hab 3:2 adds the phrase (not found in the Hebrew text), "You will be known in the midst of two living creatures."

[21] Denise Levertov, "The Nativity: an Altarpiece," *A Door in the Hive, with Evening Train*, 92. For other poems in response to paintings, see R.S. Thomas, "The Annunciation by Veneziano," *Collected Poems*, 288, and the section "Mary" from his poem "Covenanters," *Collected Poems*, 404–405; David Scott, "A Botticelli Nativity" (with a peacock getting itself settled on a stone wall before the kings arrive), in his *Selected Poems* (Newcastle upon Tyne: Bloodaxe Books, 1998), 137; William Carlos Williams, the fourth section, "The Adoration of the Kings," of "Pictures from Brueghel," in his *Collected Poems Vol. 2*, ed. Christopher MacGowan (London: Paladin, 1991), 367–68.

[22] Les Murray, "Animal Nativity," *Collected Poems*, 389.

use local dialect to tell the dog to stay with the sheep. They return and report back: what they had seen included camels and kings, with presents—"Not the kind you eat"—as well as a baby. "Presents wes for him. / Our lads took him a lamb."

> I had to stay behind wi't' sheep.
> Pity they didn't tek me along too.
> I'm good wi' lambs,
> And the baby might have liked a dog
> After all that myrrh and such.[23]

It does not seem that poems have yet been written from the perspective of the camels and dromedaries, however, perhaps because such animals are foreign to British and American circumstances, though vital in their relationship with the human beings to whose survival they contribute!

The cosmic context is maintained in two ways, we may think. One is by reference to the mystery of angelic presence: the strange, ambivalent creatures who serve as messengers on occasion, as well as overshadowing the throne of God, provide the divine being with a chariot of perplexing beauty and become warriors for justice. They are perhaps best appreciated, not in words, but rather via Olivier Messiaen's great musical meditation on the Nativity (his 1935 organ suite *La Nativité du Seigneur*), whose sixth section deals with the angels. Indeed he finds them as we do in biblical poetry. They matter not least because they remind us of the worship and celebration of God in which we may participate.

Perhaps more intelligible for us than angels is the significance attributed to the star, which as it were is inevitably associated with singing the magi through their travails of "salt, snow, skulls."[24] Most movingly, George Mackay Brown meditates on the "Desert Rose" of Isa 35:1 (not the "crocus" of modern translations), the rose without thorns traditionally taken as a reference to Mary. The travelers linger, stir the rose's incense, journey on, and the rose is left to suffer "the barren gold of the sun," until a star lifts its head, murmurs to the rose, and "Midnight, the star throng, shed / Dew in my cup like wine."[25] Mackay Brown also imagines himself as a king, one of the magi watching the stars.

---

[23] U. A. Fanthorpe, "The Sheepdog," *Selected Poems* (London: Penguin, 1986), 117. See also poems in George Mackay Brown, *The Wreck of the Archangel* (London: Murray, 1989): "Midnight Words" (p. 102), with a child piping to welcome both kings and shepherds; "Carol: Kings and Shepherds" (p. 103); "Christmas Poem" (p. 104); and "The Twelve Days of Christmas: Tinker Talk" (pp. 95–96), which brings the Nativity within reach of Kirkwall on the Scottish island of Orkney.

[24] George Mackay Brown, "Epiphany Poem," *The Wreck of the Archangel*, 94. See also "Desert Sleepers" (p.54) and "The Last Gate" (pp. 99–100).

[25] George Mackay Brown, "Desert Rose," *The Wreck of the Archangel*, 97.

What wandered about the star streets
Last night, late?
It knocked for shelter at doors of gold, like a lost boy.
My heart was bruised with the image.
I am waiting now at sunset, again, with my charts.
I had perhaps drunk too much midnight wine.

He sits at the window, and the stars identify themselves.

I greet those faithful
Who troop to my dark window.
What should I say
To this one, intruder and stranger?
He has stood there two nights
And is silent still.
I imagine a title,
"Keeper of the Door of Corn."
And a word, "Come."[26]

David Gascoyne has reflected on the genesis of stars discerned by modern astronomy, and finds the star seemingly born of two others:

                              unseen
But shining everywhere
The third star balanced shall henceforward burn
Through all dark still to come, serene,
Ubiquitous, immaculately clear;
A magnet in the middle of the maze, to draw us on
Towards that Bethlehem beyond despair
Where from the womb of Nothing shall be born
A Son.[27]

The star becomes not just the star of the magi, but a star for us, however mysterious the "Nothing" of divine being. Like the writers of the Gospels, the poet enables us to make something of the event for ourselves.

---

[26] George Mackay Brown, "The Golden Door: The Three Kings," *Collected Poems*, 149–50, here 150. See also "Yule" (pp. 150–51); "A Poem for Shelter" (p. 152); "Stars: A Christmas Patchwork" (pp. 209–12).

[27] David Gascoyne, "The Three Stars: A Prophecy," *Selected Poems* (London: Enitharmon, 1994), 102–103, here 103.

Mary the Mother of Jesus

The Gospel writers, however, have above all to make something of the kind of person Mary, the mother of Jesus, must have been by the time of Jesus' conception, as well as what she was to become. Yet we know little of her as her own person, so to speak, from the glimpses we have of her in the Gospels, leading to her presence in the midst of Jesus' disciples in Acts 1:14 after his resurrection-recreation by God. It is important to keep in mind the trajectory of Spirit-presence to her at the beginning of Luke's Gospel through to the Spirit-presence to her and Jesus' disciples in the new community being formed in Acts. Grace and Spirit do not leave her, whatever her own struggles, as she too becomes a disciple of her son. The greeting of Gabriel to her acknowledges her as graced indeed, even before the conception of her son.

Yet we need a note of caution here, for some theologians have treated her as so entirely dependent on divine grace, dislodging any hint of human self-assertion from her response to Gabriel, that her personal human dignity is eliminated. Rather, we may regard her as indeed a profoundly graced person, so she can be thought of as bringing everything that she was as a life-giver to her response to Gabriel's challenge. She cannot be described as so subservient as to make unintelligible either her response to that or Jesus' own response to God. It is as though she recovers herself in the presence of the angel, no longer somewhat intimidated as she may well have been at first, for she takes the angel on in conversation. She may have considered the risks of being abandoned by Joseph, socially ostracized, dying in childbirth, or surviving but being vulnerable to threats both to herself and to her child, as indeed proved to be the case. Thus, writing on Botticelli's painting "The Cestello Annunciation," Andrew Hudgins has the angel first crowding her and then responding to her backing away.

> He kneels. He's come in all unearthly innocence
> to tell her of glory—not knowing, not remembering
> how terrible it is. And Botticelli
> gives her eternity to turn,...
> ...But her whole body pulls away.
> Only her head, already haloed, bows,
> Acquiescing. And though she will, she's not yet said:
> *Behold, I am the handmaid of the Lord,*
> As Botticelli, in his great pity,
>
> Lets her refuse, accept, refuse, and think again.[28]

---

[28] Andrew Hudgins, "The Cestello Annunciation," in *Upholding Mystery. An Anthology of Contemporary Christian Poetry*, ed. David Impastato (New York: Oxford University Press, 1997), 106–107, here 107, quoted by kind permission of Oxford University Press.

Beyond her graced response to the awesome mystery into which she is drawn, Elizabeth Jennings pictures Mary sitting in ecstasy, now that the terrifying angel has left her:

> She can
> Take comfort from the things she knows
> Though in her heart new loving burns
> Something she never gave to man
> Or god before, and this god grows
>
> Most like a man. She wonders how
> To pray at all, what thanks to give
> And whom to give them to. "Alone
> To all men's eyes I must now go"
> She thinks, "And by myself must live
> With a strange child that is my own."[29]

As it happens, she is not bereft of Joseph's continuing love for her and his support, but she had to consider the possibility in the first place. It hardly makes sense, therefore, to suppose that her ecstatically embracing God's designs for her is to become subservient in becoming "handmaid." It is surely a state of honor, not of subjection. And although Denise Levertov does not explicitly make the connection between learning to attain freefall "and float / into Creator Spirit's deep embrace, knowing no effort earns / that all-surrounding grace"[30] and what she says of Mary, that connection can indeed be made. Mary in that embrace is a figure not of "obedience"—which has never been understood to be a cardinal (let alone a theological) virtue in Christian tradition—but of great courage. Indeed her "Magnificat" (Luke 1:46–55) insistently reminds us of her courage as she allies herself with the divine defeat of evil. She chooses fertility and life, not humiliation and pain, though that may inescapably follow.

In "Annunciation" Denise Levertov indicates the kind of scene we may find in a painting, the furnishing of the room—including lectern and book, and "always / the tall lily."[31] The angelic ambassador arrives and is acknowledged as a guest.

---

[29] Elizabeth Jennings, "The Annunciation," in her *Collected Poems* (Manchester: Carcanet, 1986), 45–46, here 46; see also "Carol for 1997," in *Praises* (Manchester: Carcanet, 1998), 32. Compare Edwin Muir, "The Annunciation," in his *Collected Poems* (London: Faber and Faber, 1979), 223–24; and his lines about invoking God's Spirit to "breathe and live," from the first stanza of "The Annunciation" in his *Selected Poems* (London: Faber and Faber, 1965), 41–42.

[30] Denise Levertov, "The Avowal," in *Oblique Prayers* (Newcastle upon Tyne: Bloodaxe Books, 1986), 70. See also the spirit within the natural world in her poem, "Passage" (p. 80).

[31] Levertov, *A Door in the Hive, with Evening Train*, 87.

But we are told of meek obedience. No one mentions
Courage.
                        The engendering Spirit
Did not enter her without consent.
                                        God waited.

She was free
to accept or to refuse, choice
integral to humanness.

Levertov goes on to query annunciations of one sort or another in most of our lives. We may respond to these and act unwillingly, in sullen pride, uncomprehending, or turn away from them in dread, weakness, despair, or relief: "Ordinary lives continue. / God does not smite them. / But the gates close, the pathway vanishes." Mary had been much like others, except that she wept only for pity and laughed in joy: "Compassion and intelligence / fused in her, indivisible." She did not quail but attended gravely and courteously to what was being asked of her, in due time to

              push out into air, a Man-child
              needing, like any other,
              milk and love—

              but who was God.

              This was the minute no one speaks of,
              when she could still refuse.
              A breath unbreathed,
                            Spirit,
                                  suspended,
                                        waiting.

However, she neither cried her unworthiness, nor appealed to her lack of strength. She neither submitted with gritted teeth, nor raged at being coerced.

              Bravest of all humans,
                            consent illumined her
              The room filled with its light,
                the lily glowed in it,
                            and the iridescent wings.
              Consent,

courage unparalleled,
opened her utterly.[32]

Furthermore, there is nothing in the biblical poetry of the scene that absolutely separates and distinguishes Mary from all other women in her graced
and courageous consent to child-bearing. Indeed, insofar as what is happening is an anticipation of a restored Eden, Mary needs to be allied with "Eve"
(herself "Mother of all living" in Gen 3:20) and not employed to denigrate
"Eve" and the multiple possibilities of women's lives—though we cannot say
that this has been much addressed in theology of our time, let alone in poetry.[33] A new Eden is being found over again:

The child
holds out both his hands
for the breast's apple. The snake is asleep.[34]

No snake poses a danger for the time being, but that does not protect the child
from possible fears.

This God fears the night,
A child so terrified he asks for us.
God is the cry we thought came from our own
Perpetual sense of loss.
Can God be frightened to be so alone?
Does that child dream the Cross?[35]

In fact, he does not need to be thought of as so dreaming, whatever is to be
made of his future significance. Rather, it might well be that he shares the
familiar fears of childhood, fearing that the light will not return.

---

[32] Ibid., 87–88. And in "Letter to a Friend" she wrote, "Courage knows the price of living. /
Courage itself is a form of innocence, of trust or faith" (pp. 154–55, here 155). See also the
memory of the "intrepid angel" in Elizabeth Jennings' work, "The Visitation," in *Collected
Poems*, 46–47.

[33] Tina Beattie, *God's Mother, Eve's Advocate. A Marian Narrative of Women's Salvation* (London:
Continuum, 2000). Attend also to U2's song "Grace," track 11 of *All That You Can't Leave
Behind* (Universal International Music, 2000).

[34] R.S. Thomas, "Mother and Child," in his *Collected Poems*, 461. See also William Carlos
Williams, "The Gift," in his *Collected Poems*, 430–31, where the wise men whose gifts stood
for all that love can bring see the child fed, and recognize it as a miracle, something much
more valuable—gold become milk. In Elizabeth Jennings' "Meditation on the Nativity"
(*Collected Poems*, 116), "her modesties divest / Our guilt of shame as she hands him her
food / And he smiles on her breast."

[35] Elizabeth Jennings, "1 *The Fear*," from "Christmas Suite in Five Movements," in her *Collected
Poems*, 178–81, here 178.

> The night comes up over you, faceless and forbidden,
> over the hawk sunk in earth and the sun drunk by the sea;
> and who can tell, the child said, no matter what they say—
> who can be sure that the sun will rise on another day?[36]

The light indeed returns, and for those who welcome the child, such as Simeon (commemorated at the Feast of Candlemas, the Feast of the Presentation), that certitude sustains them, however terrible life may become.[37] And the snake awakes in good time with "Queen Herod" protecting her own by urging the slaughter of other children.[38] Mary becomes another Rachel (Jer 31:15), weeping and taken by Joseph fleeing into exile, but like Rachel who has the ear of God, able eventually to return to a future—though of a kind no one could have foreseen.

The poet H.D. [= Hilda Doolittle] reflects on that future beyond the eventual tragedy and horror, linking in a most original fashion the gift of one of the magi with the different narratives of the gift of the woman who anoints Jesus' feet, his head, and finally comes to anoint his body. She buys her alabaster jar of ointment from Kasper, the name traditionally given to one of the three magi-turned-kings. In "The Flowering of the Rod," H.D. reimagines the three magi coming to Jesus' birthplace, the ox-stall, with Balthasar and Melchior taking first and second place in their presentation of gifts to the child and making their appropriate reverence to the child and his mother.[39] Balthasar bows low, Melchior kisses the earth, but Kasper stands somewhat to one side, relatively unimportant, bowing his head slightly to indicate the almost negligible part he felt himself to be playing in the ritual of presentation. When she speaks, he looks toward her and sees her youthful shyness. She detects a "most beautiful fragrance," seemingly from his jar, even though its seal is not yet broken. Kasper realizes that the aroma comes from the "bundle of myrrh" that she is holding.

We observed earlier that we need to keep in mind the whole trajectory from Spirit-presence with Mary at the Annunciation to Spirit-presence after Jesus'

---

[36] Judith Wright, "Night and the Child," in her *Collected Poems 1942–1985* (Manchester: Carcanet, 1994), 61-62, here 61. See also her poem "The World and the Child" (pp. 36–37).

[37] On Simeon, see Denise Levertov, *Breathing the Water* (Newcastle upon Tyne: Bloodaxe Books, 1998), 65; for a brief reflection on Candlemas, see part of Amy Clampitt, "A Procession at Candlemas," in *The Faber Book of 20th Century Women's Poetry*, ed. Fleur Adcock (London: Faber and Faber, 1987), 153–58, here 154, where she speaks of the Virgin Mary carrying "fire as though it were a flower," on the supposition that God "might actually need a mother." Denise Levertov's political activism after her move to the United States took many forms, one of which was her poem "Advent 1966" (*Selected Poems*, 84), in which Robert Southwell's "Burning Babe" as an image of redemption is transposed to an image of horror in the burning bodies of children in Vietnam.

[38] Carol Ann Duffy, *The World's Wife* (London: Picador, 1999), 7–10.

[39] H.D., *Trilogy*, 113–72, here 172.

having been raised by God to a transformed life and a new form of presence in human community. H.D. has already made this point in her inimitable way before she names Mary of Magdala or recounts her meeting with Kasper. Writing from the perspective of envisioning the recovered Paradise of human longing, she describes the resurrection as a "bee-line" that goes directly to plunder the "honeycomb" and bring the aroma of "myrrh and balm."[40] In the meantime, so to speak, we can invoke David Gascoyne for our last word, asking that God grant that we

> Give birth to the world's only Prince, *Puer Aeternus*, He
> Whose swordlike Word comes not to bring us peace but war
> Within forever against falsehood and all fratricidal War.[41]

---

[40] Ibid., 123.

[41] David Gascoyne, "Birth of a Prince," from his *Collected Poems* (Oxford: Oxford University Press, 1965), 170, quoted by kind permission of Oxford University Press.

Chapter 11

The Muslim Mary

John Kaltner

Many non-Muslims are surprised to learn that Mary holds a prominent place in Islam and that Muslims value and respect her as a role model. Her high status is apparent in the texts and traditions of Islam, and it has been outwardly expressed by the community since its founding in the early seventh century CE. The Islamic sources that make reference to Mary are the Qur'an, the hadith (authoritative traditions), and certain extra-canonical texts.

The Qur'an is the sacred book of Islam that was revealed to the Prophet Muhammad (570–632 CE) over the course of the last twenty-two years of his life. Mary is mentioned in 70 of the 6300 verses in the Qur'an, and only the names of Moses, Abraham, and Noah appear more frequently in the text. She is the only woman mentioned by name in the entire Qur'an, where she is referred to as Maryam, the Arabic form of her name.[1] Each of the 114 chapters of the Qur'an has a title, and chapter 19 is identified as "Mary," one of only 9 chapter titles that contain the name of a human being.

Mary is mentioned most commonly in the formula "Jesus, son of Mary," but a number of narratives describe events in her life in some detail. While the Qur'an provides more information about her than the New Testament does, it still does not offer a complete biography of Mary. This is similar to the treatment given to other biblical figures mentioned frequently in the Qur'an such as Noah, Moses, Abraham, and Jesus. The two lengthiest Qur'an passages concerning Mary are found at 3:37–47 and 19:16–33, each of which contains an account of events related to Jesus' conception and birth. In this way the Qur'an is similar to the New Testament, which contains two infancy narratives in the Gospels of Matthew and Luke.

A second Islamic source that refers to Mary is a collection of traditions known as the hadith, an Arabic term meaning "report." After his death the words and actions of the Prophet Muhammad continued to function as an example for the members of his community, who would try to model their own behavior on his. These individual reports circulated independently until

---

[1] This matches the form of her name (*Mariam*) found in Greek manuscripts of Matt 13:55 and Luke 1:27.

they were gathered together into collections in the early centuries of Islam. Eventually several of these compilations of hadith achieved a canonical status that is second only to the Qur'an. Each contains thousands of accounts of Muhammad's words and actions that have exerted enormous influence over the lives of Muslims throughout history. Mary is mentioned by name in approximately sixty hadith, and these have contributed much to the important role she plays in Islam. A couple of them in particular, which will be discussed later, have led some Muslim scholars to proclaim Mary as the most perfect woman who has ever lived.

A number of extra-canonical sources also mention Mary, and these often provide information about her that is not found in the Qur'an or the hadith. The origin of this material and its historical value are matters of debate, but these sources offer us valuable insight into the Islamic view of Mary because they sometimes help shape Muslim perceptions of her. These texts can take a variety of forms, including strictly historical works that recount events and more religiously oriented ones like the "Stories of the Prophets" that present accounts of the lives of venerable holy figures of the past.

Some of the extra-canonical sources give additional details about Mary's early life and the birth of Jesus, both of which are described in the Qur'an. Elsewhere they present new information. For example, some of these authors agree that Mary is of the line of King David, and they provide a genealogy that traces her descent through both him and his son Solomon.[2] They also present the details of her death, which is not recorded in the other sources. Similarly, Joseph, the husband of Mary, is not mentioned in the Qur'an but he sometimes plays a role in the non-canonical material. One story has him ask her how she can be pregnant when he learns that she is with child. Another tradition related to Mary that is often cited concerns the actions of Muhammad when he returned to Mecca, the city of his birth, to remove images of other religions from the Ka`ba, the city's main shrine. Upon seeing an image of Mary with the infant Jesus he ordered that it alone be allowed to remain in the Ka`ba.[3]

Mary in Popular Islamic Piety

The important role Mary plays in these texts is visibly manifested by Muslims in a host of ways as many places, texts, and practices are associated with her throughout the Islamic world. Various sites identified with Mary have become important pilgrimage locations, sometimes for Muslims and Christians alike. According to tradition, a tree and a well in the Cairo suburb of Matariyya is a location where Mary, Joseph, and Jesus found shade and water as they

---

[2] Aliah Schleifer, *Mary the Blessed Virgin of Islam* (Louisville: Fons Vitae, 1997), 23.
[3] The historicity of this tradition is challenged by Schleifer, *Mary*, 101–105.

escaped from King Herod. The presence of a church and a mosque nearby, both erected in honor of Mary, underscores the importance of the location for both faiths. Also in Egypt, the House of the Holy Family is a popular pilgrimage destination where Christians and Muslims celebrate their common respect for Mary at an annual meal. In Jerusalem, near St. Stephen's Gate, is Mary's Bath, where childless Muslim women often come to bathe. There is also a gate honoring Mary at the famous Umayyad mosque in Damascus, Syria.[4]

Amy G. Remensnyder points out that during the medieval period such interreligious mixing at locations celebrating Mary was something that spread far and wide, laying the groundwork for present practices. "Members of both faiths could be found venerating Mary at shrines such as Tentudia in western Castile, Saidnaya in Syria, Trapani in Sicily, on the island of Lampedusa, and all along the route of the flight to Egypt—a mingling of Muslims and Christians that in some cases continues to this day."[5]

India and Asia Minor contain many Islamic sanctuaries dedicated to Mary. During the reign of the Mughal Emperor Akbar (1556–1605) the palace contained images of Jesus and Mary. This is something that one would not find in the Arab homeland of Islam due to the faith's stance against depicting human forms, but it is sometimes found in Muslim communities in other places. From the same time period scenes from Mary's life were occasionally used to illustrate Arabic and Persian manuscripts, one of which presents her sitting beneath a palm tree with the child Jesus on her knee. An interesting aspect of this scene is that it depicts her with a flame halo around her head, which in Muslim Indian art normally indicates the person is a prophet.[6]

Among the textual evidence that cites and celebrates Mary are a number of Muslim prayers, hymns, ballads, and poems coming from such diverse places as Spain, the Ottoman Empire, Egypt, and the United States. Among the most interesting are medieval poems from Spain known as *Cantigas de Santa Maria*, which suggest the high level of interaction between Muslims and Christians occurring at this time and place. "These poems also depict Muslims who, without renouncing their own religion, worship the Virgin Mary in Christian style by praying to her in a Christian church, venerating her statue, and even taking a banner with her image on it with them into battle against other Muslims."[7]

---

[4] For information on some of these locations, see Thomas Michel, S.J., "The Role of Mary in Popular Islamic Devotion in Southeast Asia," in *Maria nell'Ebraismo e nell'Islam Oggi*, ed. Elio Peretto (Rome: Edizioni Marianum, 1987), 167–75, here 169.

[5] Amy G. Remensnyder, "Christian Captives, Muslim Maidens, and Mary," *Speculum* 82 (2007) 642–77, here 671.

[6] Shaikh 'Abd Al Wahid Pallavicini, "Corrispondenze Mariane nella Tradizione Islamica: Elementi per un Dialogo," *Maria nell'Ebraismo* (ed. Peretto), 119–40, here 121.

[7] Amy G. Remensnyder, "The Colonization of Sacred Architecture: The Virgin Mary, Mosques, and Temples in Medieval Spain and Early Sixteenth-Century Mexico," in *Monks and Nuns, Saints and Outcasts: Religious Expression and Social Meaning in the Middle Ages*, ed. Sharon Farmer and Barbara Rosenwein (Ithaca: Cornell University Press, 2000), 189–219,

Aspects of popular religiosity associated with Mary can be seen in a number of practices and activities that Muslims engage in frequently. Pregnant women often appeal to Mary for assistance, and many Muslim girls are given the name Mary (or its equivalent) by their parents. New mothers are sometimes given three dates to eat, the same food a tradition states Mary ate upon giving birth to Jesus. In West Java in Indonesia, the country with the highest number of Muslims in the world, an ancient practice has young pregnant women withdraw from their familiar surroundings to pray and fast in a ritual called the "Fast of Sitti Maryam." This recalls similar actions by Mary mentioned in the Qur'an that will be discussed later. This practice predates the advent of Christianity in Indonesia and therefore must be Islamic in origin. Similar fasts have been noted in Baghdad, Tehran, Lebanon, and Syria. It has also been observed that Iranian women often possess statues of Mary.[8]

Many of these practices are clearly related to pregnancy and childbirth, and it is this particular aspect of Mary's life that is the basis for much of the respect and honor she receives within Islam. The important place her pregnancy holds in the Qur'an is testimony to this, as well as other extra-canonical traditions that reinforce this Qur'anic focus. One tradition reports that Mary was one of four miraculous midwives who assisted Khadijah, Muhammad's wife, when she gave birth to his daughter Fatima. This is an intriguing scene that places Mary in the presence of two of the most beloved women in Islam, within a context that highlights her association with childbearing and motherhood.[9]

Various Islamic sects, especially in the Shi`a branch, have their own Marian cult, and at times some of their beliefs and practices fall outside the parameters of mainstream Islamic faith to such a degree that they are perceived as heretical by other Muslims. Mary is venerated as the mother of God by a Turkish group known as the Kizilbach. The Nosairis of Syria celebrate some feasts of Christian origin, including one in honor of Mary. Similarly, certain Bekthachis in Albania are said to commemorate the Assumption of Mary on August 15, a belief that is not held by Muslims anywhere else in the world.[10]

A practice more commonly found is that of inscribing words uttered by Mary in the Qur'an on one of the central architectural features of a mosque. Muslims everywhere pray facing Mecca five times a day, and the *mihrab* is a niche in the

---

here 205–206. For citations of such texts, see Tim Winter, "Mary in Islam," in *Mary: The Complete Resource*, ed. Sarah Jane Boss (New York: Oxford University Press, 2007), 479–502; Ron Barkai, "Une invocation musulmane au nom de Jésus et de Marie," *Revue de l'Histoire des Religions* (1983) 257–68; Schleifer, *Mary*, 98–99.

[8] These practices are mentioned in Pallavicini, "Corrispondenze," 119–20, and Michel, "Role of Mary," 173, as well as R.J. McCarthy, "Mary in Islam," in *Mary's Place in Christian Dialogue*, ed. Alberic Stacpoole (Slough, UK: St Paul Publications; Wilton, CT: Morehouse-Barlow, 1982), 202–13, here 207.

[9] Barbara Freyer Stowasser, *Women in the Qur'an, Traditions, and Interpretation* (New York: Oxford University Press, 1994), 80.

[10] Pallavicini, "Corrispondenze," 122.

wall of every mosque that helps orient the worshipper toward the holy city. These niches are normally decorated with elaborate geometric designs and inscriptions, the latter often taken from the Qur'an. One of the most popular inscriptions is Qur'an 3:37, which reports Mary's words as a young woman living in the temple under the care of Zachariah, the father of John the Baptist.[11]

> So her Lord accepted her graciously. He caused her to grow up well and gave her into the care of Zachariah. Every time Zachariah came to see her in the chamber he found her with provisions. He said, "Oh Mary, where did you get this?" She answered, "It is from God. Truly God provides for whomever He wishes without measure."

One reason why this is a popular inscription in mosques is that the word translated "chamber" is *mihrab* in the original Arabic. But an equally important reason is that Mary expresses supreme trust in God in this verse. This quality is an essential mark of faith within Islam, and Muslims see Mary as the personification of a true believer. Every day when they are in a mosque praying toward Mecca, countless Muslims around the world face words spoken by Mary as they engage in one of the most important rituals of their faith.

A final example of Mary's popular appeal can be seen in the reported sightings of her on the dome of the Church of St. Mary in the Cairo suburb of al-Zaytoun between 1968 and 1970. Many Christians and Muslims claimed to have seen her, and a number of them reported being healed of various physical and emotional ailments as a result of the experience. This is the best known of a number of similar occurrences in the Islamic world where Muslims and Christians have said that Mary has appeared to them.

Many of the practices and beliefs that have been discussed here involve Christians and Muslims interacting in ways that suggest that Mary might be able to function as a meeting point where members of the two faiths might come together. While this might be the case in some circumstances, it would be a mistake to over-generalize about Mary's potential as a figure around whom Muslims and Christians can unite. As Jane I. Smith and Yvonne Y. Haddad point out, Mary has not always played a conciliatory role between the two groups, and it is important to acknowledge that fact.

> Despite the instances of common appreciation of the Virgin at the level of popular piety, however, Christians and Muslims for many centuries have also used her as a vehicle for the expression of their mutual deep mistrust and misunderstanding. Mary often has been at the center of polemical controversies between Christians and Muslims.[12]

---

[11] All translations of the Qur'an are my own.
[12] Jane I. Smith and Yvonne Y. Haddad, "The Virgin Mary in Islamic Tradition and Commentary," *The Muslim World* 79 (1989) 161–87, here 185.

The Annunciation to Mary in Islam

It has already been mentioned that events related to Jesus' conception and birth are described in Qur'an 3:37–47 and 19:16–33. This material is supplemented by extra-Qur'anic traditions that expand the stories and fill in gaps. Each of the Qur'an passages presents an account of the annunciation to Mary of Jesus' birth, but they are two distinct and separate stories with few details in common. The first passage begins with the scene that has already been discussed describing Zachariah's role taking care of Mary in the temple, where she is miraculously provided with food by God. The rest of the passage (3:38–47) is a double annunciation, with the first directed to Zachariah and the second to Mary.

[38]Then and there, Zachariah called upon his Lord saying, "My Lord, grant me good offspring from Yourself. Truly, You hear all prayers." [39]Then the angels called to him while he stood praying in the chamber, "God gives you the good news of John, who will confirm a word from God. He will be noble, chaste, and a prophet from among the righteous." [40]He said, "Oh Lord, how is it that I might have a son when I am old and my wife is barren?" He [an angel] said, "Thus it is. God does what He wills." [41]He said, "My Lord, make for me a sign." He said, "Your sign is that you will not be able to speak to a person for three days except by gestures. Remember your Lord much, and praise Him in the evening and the morning." [42]The angels said, "Oh Mary, God has truly chosen you and purified you. He has chosen you above all other women. [43]Oh Mary, be obedient to your Lord. Prostrate yourself and be among those who bow down."—[44]This is part of the hidden news We reveal to you. You were not with them when they cast lots to see which of them would take care of Mary, nor were you with them when they disputed among themselves.—[45]The angels said, "Oh Mary, God gives you the good news of a word from Him. His name will be the Messiah Jesus, the son of Mary, who will be eminent in this world and the next, and will be one of those brought near [to God]. [46]He shall speak to people from the cradle and in his later years, and he will be one of the righteous." [47]She said, "My Lord, how can I have a child when no man has touched me?" He said, "Thus it is. God creates what He wills. If He decrees something, He only need say 'Be!' and it is."

The discussion here will be limited to the annunciation to Mary, but that scene is clearly tied to the annunciation to Zachariah.[13] In the New Testament,

---

[13] For more detailed analysis of the Qur'an texts, see John Kaltner, *Ishmael Instructs Isaac: An Introduction to the Qur'an for Bible Readers* (Collegeville: Liturgical Press, 1999), 207–39.

Luke (1:11–20) has a similar announcement to Zachariah, but Mary is not a part of it. That Gospel also identifies a kinship relationship between Mary and Zachariah's wife Elizabeth, but this detail is not present in the Qur'an, where the latter is not named. In some extra-Qur'anic traditions, however, her name is given and she is related to Mary, with some even saying they are sisters.

In their words to Mary the angels highlight those qualities that set her apart and make her special. In particular, she is pure and therefore chosen by God. Based on this Qur'an passage and other traditions about her, purity is one of the dominant characteristics of Mary in Islam. The angels also instruct her about how she should behave—Mary is to be obedient, prostrate herself, and bow down. Bowing and prostrating are essential elements of Islamic prayer, and so Mary is being encouraged to adopt a way of life that will conform to the ideal expressed in the Qur'an. She is not being asked to become a Muslim, because the religion of Islam will not exist for another six centuries. Rather, she is being asked to become a *muslim* in the literal sense of the word: one who submits herself completely to God's will. This is typical of the way the Qur'an sometimes presents biblical characters. It tends to Islamize them in ways that underscore the connections between them and the message the Prophet Muhammad brought to his contemporaries. A fundamental notion at the heart of Islam is that Muhammad did not introduce a new religion, but rather called people to reject polytheism and turn back to the strict monotheism that was already present among people like Mary and other figures of the past.

In v. 45 the angels tell Mary that they are bringing her a "word" from God, and the context suggests that this word is Jesus. This is confirmed elsewhere in the Qur'an when in 4:171 it is stated, "The Messiah Jesus, son of Mary, was God's messenger and His word He sent to Mary." The idea that Jesus is the "word of God" is present in the New Testament (John 1:1–18), but Christians should not assume that the Qur'an and their own sacred text are using the term in the same way. In Christianity, the notion that Jesus is the word is related to belief in the incarnation, God taking on human form. For Muslims, however, this would violate the unity of God that is at the core of Islam, and would be an example of *shirk*, which is the sin of associating something created (in this case the person Jesus) with the uncreated Deity. The Qur'an and Muslims therefore understand Jesus as the word in a way that is quite distinct from that of Christians.

There are some interesting connections between this Qur'an passage and some of the extra-canonical Christian writings such as the *Protevangelium of James*, which dates to the mid-second century. The latter text describes a scene in which the widowers of the area are called together by Zachariah to draw lots in order to see who will take Mary as a wife. This appears to be related to what is stated in v. 44 of the Qur'an text, which is a break in the narrative that is directed to the Prophet Muhammad. Similarly, in the *Protevangelium of James*, Mary is taken to the temple and placed in the care of Zachariah, and she also receives a miraculous provision of food. In extra-Qur'anic Muslim traditions Joseph takes care of his cousin Mary because Zachariah is too old for the task. Some sources have them praying together at the temple as a way of expressing the spiritual, and therefore nonsexual, nature of their relationship.[14]

The other annunciation scene in the Qur'an is found at 19:16–21, in the chapter named after her.

[16]Remember Mary in the book. When she withdrew from her family to a place in the east [17]and took cover from them, We sent to her Our spirit, which appeared to her in the form of a normal person. [18]She said, "I take refuge in the merciful one from you if you fear Him." [19]He said, "I am only a messenger from your Lord, to give you a righteous son." [20]She said, "How can I have a son when no man has touched me and I have not been unchaste?" [21]He said, "Thus it is. Your Lord said, 'It is easy for Me. We will make him a sign for people and mercy from Us.' It is an accomplished fact."[15]

Here there is no reference to Zachariah or the birth of John. The location is also different because the scene does not take place in the *mihrab*. Rather, Mary goes off to a place in the east. This reference has puzzled commentators, who have proposed a number of different interpretations. Some have her going to a private area in the eastern part of the house, while others say she went to the temple in Jerusalem. Still others suggest she simply went off with no precise destination.

Whatever her location, she is soon visited by an angel, which is described as God's spirit in human form. This may be the most distinctive aspect of the passage, particularly in light of the message he brings to Mary. He describes his mission as "to give you a righteous son," which could theoretically mean that, in his now-human form, he will help bring about the pregnancy in the usual way. But Muslim commentators have never considered this to be a correct way of reading the text. The virginal conception of Jesus is a central article of Islamic faith, and this passage has always been interpreted in light of it.

The question of precisely how Mary became pregnant has generated much discussion. The Arabic word for "spirit" (*ruh*) can also mean "breath," and this double meaning has contributed to how many scholars have understood the text. One interpretation says that the angel breathed into Mary's mouth, and when his breath reached her belly she conceived. Others maintain that the angel blew into her sleeve, pocket, or a tear in her dress and she conceived.

---

[14] These traditions are discussed in Smith and Haddad, "The Virgin Mary," 166.
[15] At times in the Qur'an God speaks using the first person plural form. Occasionally, as in verse 21 of this passage, the forms shift between third person singular ("He") and first person plural ("We"). This is commonly understood to be an example of the "divine we," which is a well-attested usage (cf. Gen 1:26), and in no way should it be seen as a challenge to Islam's monotheistic belief.

One interpreter has suggested that Mary removed her garment to bathe, and the angel blew into it while it was on the ground. After finishing the bath, she put the clothing back on and became pregnant. A more unusual interpretation has proposed that the angel blew directly into her vulva and caused her pregnancy. Another aspect of the story that scholars have debated concerns the length of Mary's pregnancy. Because it is a miraculous conception some have argued that its duration was equally unusual, with some suggesting it lasted no longer than an hour.

Both of the annunciation scenes highlight the trust and submission that are the essence of the Islamic view of Mary. In each case, when she objects to the news of her pregnancy she is told that God can do anything. Both times, her objection is greeted with the words "Thus it is," indicating an accomplished fact that has undoubtedly come to pass. She is given no tangible sign, but must simply take on faith that what the messenger says is the truth. This element of trust is powerfully conveyed in an extra-canonical tradition that has Joseph confront Mary when he discovers she is pregnant. According to this tradition, Joseph tells Mary he wants to ask her about something. When she replies, "What is it?" he asks, "Has there ever been a tree without a seed? Has there ever been a plant without a seed? Has there ever been a child without a father?" She responds, "Yes. Regarding the tree and the plant, in the first instance God created them without seeds. Regarding the child and the father, God most high created Adam without either father or mother." The story concludes saying that Joseph believed her and found no blame in her pregnancy.

The Nativity of Jesus in Islam

We have seen that events related to Jesus' conception are described in Qur'an 3:37–47 and 19:16–21, supplemented by extra-Qur'anic traditions. By contrast, the only explicit Qur'anic mention of Jesus' birth appears in 19:22–33, and there are no references to Jesus' birth in the hadith literature. The single Qur'anic reference to Jesus' birth follows immediately after the annunciation scene in chapter 19.

[22]She conceived him and withdrew with him to a distant place. [23]The birth pangs led her to the trunk of a palm tree where she cried, "Oh, if only I had died before this and had been forgotten, unremembered!" [24]Then [a voice] called out to her from below her, "Do not grieve. Your Lord has placed a stream beneath you. [25]Shake the trunk of the palm tree and it will drop fresh ripe dates upon you. [26]Eat, drink, and be consoled. If you should see another person say, 'I have vowed a fast to the merciful one and I will not speak to anyone today.'" [27]She carried him [Jesus] to her people who said, "Oh Mary, you have done something strange! [28]Oh sister of Aaron, your father was not

wicked nor was your mother unchaste." [29]Then she pointed to him. They said, "How can we talk to a child in the cradle?"

The story's beginning is similar to that of the annunciation that precedes it, with Mary distancing herself yet further. Here, too, Muslim commentators have suggested a number of locations, including Jerusalem, Bethlehem, and Egypt. The text indicates it is a remote area because Mary finds herself all alone, thirsty and hungry, wishing she were dead. There has been much discussion among scholars about Mary's words in v. 23, which might perhaps indicate her unwillingness to accept the angel's message and submit herself to God's will. This interpretation has found little support in Islamic exegesis of the verse. Rather than taking her anguish as an expression of her lack of belief or trust, most explanations point beyond herself, suggesting for instance her concern that others might mistakenly call Jesus the Son of God.

There are some unusual elements in this passage. One is the voice that speaks from below Mary in vv. 24–26. Some interpreters have understood this to be the angel's voice, while others maintain it is the voice of Jesus trying to assist and console his mother at a difficult time. The latter option is favored by most scholars, who see this as the first of many miracles Jesus will perform throughout his life. As strange as the notion of a speaking infant might be, this is precisely what Jesus does in the next verses after this passage. When Mary's people ask, "How can we talk to a child in the cradle?" the newborn Jesus responds with a statement about who he is.

[30]"I am the servant of God. He has given me the book and has made me a prophet. [31]He has made me blessed wherever I may be, and has commanded me to observe prayer and almsgiving for as long as I live. [32][He has made me] obedient to my mother and has not made me proud or miserable. [33]Peace upon me the day I was born, the day I will die, and the day I will be raised to life."

Here, too, we can see an example of the Qur'an's tendency to Islamize biblical characters, as noted earlier. Jesus is told to observe prayer and to engage in almsgiving, two of the five pillars of Islam that are required of all Muslims.

Another unusual feature of the story is that Mary's people refer to her as "sister of Aaron." This is a strange title that has been interpreted in different ways. Non-Muslim commentators have sometimes suggested that this is evidence of confusion between Mary, Jesus' mother, and Miriam (the Hebrew equivalent of Mary), the sister of Moses and Aaron (Num 26:59). Alternatively, others have said it could be a reference to someone named Aaron who was related to Mary, perhaps her own brother. A further option is that the title refers to spiritual lineage, not actual kinship. Mary is a person of faith just like her "brother" Aaron, who was Moses' biological brother.

It has already been noted that some of the elements of this story, like its set-ting under a palm tree and Mary's fast, have sometimes been a part of popular Islamic piety related to Mary into the present day. The palm tree tradition may be related to what is found in an apocryphal Christian writing known as the *Gospel of Pseudo-Matthew.* In that work a palm tree obeys the child Jesus' orders to bow down and refresh Mary with its fruit and then to open its roots in order to quench the family's thirst.[16] This text comes from sometime between the sixth and eighth centuries and is probably based on the *Protevangelium of James* and the *Infancy Gospel of Thomas.*[17]

When we compare this Qur'an material with the New Testament traditions surrounding Jesus' conception and birth it is clear that the Qur'an texts put emphasis on Mary being alone at critical moments in her life. In particu-lar, Joseph's absence is striking. He plays a key supporting role in the New Testament, but in the Qur'an it is not even stated that she is engaged to be mar-ried at the time of her pregnancy. She has withdrawn and is all alone when she conceives and gives birth to Jesus. We have seen that Joseph appears in other Islamic traditions, but in the Qur'an Mary is a young woman who goes through this experience by herself.

The absence of Joseph, her solitary status, and the miraculous provision of food on several occasions make apparent Mary's total dependence on God in the Qur'an. What happens to her in the *mihrab*, when she withdraws, and under the palm tree indicates that she does not need human help because God is protecting her and is responsive to her needs. This requires complete submission and trust on her part as she faces difficult circumstances alone, but not without divine help.

Issues and Implications for Muslims and Christians

In two frequently cited passages the Qur'an refers to Mary as a sign. "Remember the one who guarded her chastity. We breathed Our spirit into her and made her and her son a sign to all people" (21:91; cf. 23:50). The evidence from the Qur'an and other Islamic sources indicates that one important way Mary functions as a sign is through her obedience and trust. Because she believed and did not doubt God's message, she gave birth to Jesus, who is revered as a

---

[16] Suleiman A. Mourad, "From Hellenism to Christianity and Islam: The Origin of the Palm Tree Story Concerning Mary and Jesus in the Gospel of Pseudo-Matthew and the Qur'an," *Oriens Christianus* 86 (2002) 206–16. Mourad argues that the Greek myth of Leto's labor and Apollo's birth is the original source of the Christian and Muslim traditions.

[17] For these three apocryphal gospels, see Oscar Cullmann, "Infancy Gospels," in *New Testament Apocrypha*, ed. Wilhelm Schneemelcher, second edn, 2 vols (Louisville: Westminster/John Knox, 1991–1992), 1.414–69; for the palm tree incident in the *Gospel of Pseudo-Matthew* see 1.463.

great prophet in Islam. Muslims also maintain that Mary was born without sin, a belief that is supported by a hadith that states, "Every child that is born is touched by Satan and this touch makes it cry, except Mary and her son." This puts Mary in an exalted position, but Christians should avoid associating it with the Catholic doctrine of the Immaculate Conception. That belief holds that Mary, unlike every other person, was born without original sin. Because Islam does not have a doctrine of original sin Mary's sinlessness functions in a different way, and that distinction must be kept in mind.

Two questions about Mary that have attracted the attention of scholars are related to Mary's sinless nature and her role as a sign: (1) Where does Mary rank among all women? (2) Was Mary a prophetess? In Qur'an 3:42 the angels tell Mary that God has chosen her above all women. This led to a debate over whether she is the best woman of all time or just her time. Prominent scholars throughout history have come down on both sides of the issue, and the matter is complicated by a hadith that lists Mary as one of the four greatest women of all time. The other three are Muhammad's wife Khadijah, his daughter Fatima, and Asiya, the wife of the Pharaoh under whom Moses served. There is also a hadith in which the Prophet Muhammad tells Fatima that Mary will be the greatest woman among those in paradise.

The choice has generally come down to either Mary or Fatima as the preeminent woman of all time. Those who favor Mary single out the unique circumstances of her pregnancy as the determining factor, while those who prefer Fatima argue that her biological relationship to Muhammad places her above Mary. Fatima is even referred to by some as "Mary the greater."[18] Shi`a Muslims, in particular, tend to privilege Fatima because of their belief that authentic leadership of the Muslim community can only come from the Prophet Muhammad's family. Fatima was the only one of his children to have offspring, and therefore she played an essential role in the community's history.[19]

The question of whether or not Mary was a prophetess has been a more contentious issue. The general consensus has been that women cannot be prophets because the Qur'an does not allow it. The two main passages usually cited to support this view are 12:109 and 16:43, which both begin in the same way. The verses are addressed to Muhammad and say, "All those We sent before you were men to whom we gave revelation." Most commentators argue that this means only males can be prophets. But those who challenge this interpretation have several misgivings with this reading. They point out that the word "prophet" does not appear in the verses, and that the Arabic word rendered here "men" is not the usual word for males but can include both

---

[18] Smith and Haddad, "The Virgin Mary," 179–80.
[19] For the opinion that Fatima is the preeminent woman, see Jane Dammen McAuliffe, "Chosen of All Women: Mary and Fatima in Qur'anic Exegesis," *Islamochristiana* 7 (1981) 19–28, here 28. For a view that favors Mary, see Schleifer, *Mary*, 63.

men and women. In addition, even in the unlikely event that the texts are meant to exclude women, it is in reference to those who have been sent before Muhammad, not to those who might come after him.[20]

The Qur'an has also been used to support the idea that Mary was a prophetess. Bearing the heading "The Prophets," chapter 21 mentions eighteen individuals either by name or title (including Mary). Every single one of them but Mary is officially recognized by Islam as a prophet. Those who argue for her prophetic status ask why she would be found among such company if she were not one of them.[21] Elsewhere, scholars have maintained that Mary is a prophet by virtue of similarities between her life story and Muhammad's, or because she exhibits certain aspects that are shared by all prophets.[22]

The simplest argument that can be made for Mary being a prophet is that God delivered a message to her, but some counter that it was only an announcement of the coming prophet Jesus and therefore not truly a prophetic message. Among those who disagree with this latter view are two medieval scholars, Ibn Hazm (eleventh century) and al-Qurtubi (thirteenth century). These Andalusian Muslim exegetes offered an alternative to the dominant and exclusively male view of prophecy by arguing that the signs of Mary's prophethood are well established in the Qur'an. They say that when God sends an angel to a woman with glad tidings it is a sign of prophecy. Al-Qurtubi claims that God's choosing of Mary is a standard way of conferring prophetic status on a person. He states, "Truly Maryam is a prophetess because God inspired her through the angel in the same way He inspired the rest of the male prophets." Ibn Hazm believes she is a prophetess because she is called a woman of truth (5:75), just as the prophet Joseph is called a man of truth (12:46).[23]

Ibn Hazm goes on to broaden the ranks of female prophets by including other women mentioned in the Qur'an who had experiences similar to Mary's. "According to Ibn Hazm, the knowledge the mothers of Isaac, Jesus, and Moses received from God (through word or inspiration) was as true as the knowledge received by male prophets (through revelation)."[24] The school of thought to which Ibn Hazm and al-Qurtubi belonged was a relatively obscure

---

[20] For a strong critique of the usual interpretation, see Schleifer, *Mary,* 75.

[21] A similar point is made by R. Marston Speight, "Mary, Mother of Jesus, in Christian and Islamic Traditions," in *Muslims and Christians, Muslims and Jews,* ed. Marilyn Robinson Waldman (Columbus, OH: Islamic Foundation of Central Ohio, 1992), 25–34, here 29.

[22] For connections with Muhammad's life, see Neal Robinson, "Jesus and Mary in the Qur'an: Some Neglected Affinities," *Religion* 20 (1990) 161–75, here 169–71. For similarities with the prophets, see Loren D. Lybarger, "Gender and Prophetic Authority in the Qur'anic Story of Maryam: A Literary Approach," *Journal of Religion* 80 (2000) 240–70, here 246–47.

[23] Much of this discussion is based on Hosn Abboud, " 'Idhan Maryam Nabiyya' (*'Hence Maryam is a Prophetess'*): Muslim Classical Exegetes and Women's Receptiveness to God's Verbal Inspiration," in *Mariam, the Magdalen, and the Mother,* ed. Deirdre Good (Bloomington: Indiana University Press, 2005), 183–96.

[24] Stowasser, *Women,* 77.

and short-lived one, but their arguments in support of Mary's prophethood show that there was disagreement with the mainstream view that has continued to dominate into the present day. The fact they were living in Andalusia, far from the birthplace and center of the Islamic world, probably played a role in enabling them to formulate and offer an alternative position.

A recent defense of Mary as a prophetess has been put forward by Aliah Schleifer in her 1997 book *Mary the Blessed Virgin of Islam*. She says that the evidence does not allow us to know for certain whether or not Mary was a prophetess, but the strongest and most cohesive arguments are those that accept her prophethood. She bases this on the text of Qur'an 3:42, where God chooses Mary above all other women, and the hadith that says that Mary and her son were spared Satan's touch at birth. Schleifer concludes, "As she had the attributes and experiences of prophets, and there is no satisfactory argument against her having achieved their status, she should be logically classified a prophetess, although this should not be regarded as proven beyond dispute."[25]

One final aspect of Mary's identity to consider is that of mediator. Can she serve as a bridge for dialogue between Muslims and Christians? There are many similarities in the ways the members of both faiths tell her story and celebrate her life, so it appears she has the potential to bring them closer together. For that potential to be realized, each side needs to acknowledge and respect the unique perspective the other side brings to the conversation. Christians must avoid viewing the Muslim Mary as a derivative distortion of their own Mary, and Muslims should not see the New Testament Mary as a theological aberration that the Qur'an needed to correct. Marston Speight describes the middle way to be adopted[26]:

> Such an approach requires that we not think of Islam (coming later than Christianity) as "borrowing" from Christianity in its elaboration of the figure of Mary, but rather that we consider both Islam and Christianity as drawing upon a common store of information and inspiration, a fund of material that goes beyond either what the Bible says or what the Qur'an says about Mary.

On the Christian side it is important to recognize that the opportunities and challenges will vary by denomination. Protestant–Muslim relations have been less complicated by Mary because she does not play as significant a role in the economy of salvation for most Protestants, who also do not generally profess belief in Mary's Immaculate Conception, Assumption, or perpetual virginity.[27] These articles of faith are significant within Catholic doctrine and are not

---

[25] Schleifer, *Mary*, 94.

[26] Speight, "Mary, Mother of Jesus," 26.

[27] This issue is discussed in Tim Winter, "Pulchra ut Luna: Some Reflections on the Marian Theme in Muslim-Catholic Dialogue," *Journal of Ecumenical Studies* 36 (1999), 439–69.

shared by Muslims. Nonetheless, Catholics are reminded by teachings such as the Vatican II document *Nostra Aetate*—the 1965 Declaration on the Relation of the Church to Non-Christian Religions—that Muslims share their respect and love of Mary, and they are urged to work toward improving relations with Muslims whenever possible.[28]

> The church also looks upon Muslims with respect. They worship the one God living and subsistent, merciful and almighty, creator of heaven and earth, who has spoken to humanity and to whose decrees, even the hidden ones, they seek to submit themselves whole-heartedly, just as Abraham, to whom the Islamic faith readily relates itself, submitted to God. They venerate Jesus as a prophet, even though they do not acknowledge him as God, and they honor his virgin mother Mary and even sometimes devoutly call on her. Furthermore they await the day of judgment when God will requite all people brought back to life. Hence they have regard for the moral life and worship God especially in prayer, almsgiving and fasting. Although considerable dissensions and enmities between Christians and Muslims may have arisen in the course of the centuries, this synod urges all parties that, forgetting past things, they train themselves towards sincere mutual understanding and together maintain and promote social justice and moral values as well as peace and freedom for all people. (Paragraph 3)

Maura Hearden outlines the common ground shared by Muslims and Catholics in their understanding of Mary, regarded by each tradition as the unique personal bearer of the Word of God. According to Hearden, "Mary is exalted in both the Muslim and Catholic faiths because of the great things that God has done for her. These 'great things' are linked to doctrines that we have in common—namely, the virgin birth and her preservation from sin—but that are interpreted differently."[29]

Certain aspects of the Muslim–Christian relationship will doubtless always remain problematic, most notably those centered on the figure of Jesus. According to the Qur'an, the Christian concept of the Trinity is an impossibility that violates God's nature. The belief that Jesus is the son of God and savior is one that Christians and Muslims will never agree upon. But his mother is another matter entirely. Both communities can agree on much when it comes to Mary—she is recipient of God's message, model of faith and submission, sinless virgin mother, and a sign for all people.

---

[28] The following quotation is from Norman P. Tanner, ed., *Decrees of the Ecumenical Councils*, 2 vols (Washington, DC: Georgetown University Press, 1990), 2.969–70.

[29] Maura Hearden, "Ambassador for the Word: Mary as a Bridge for Dialogue Between Catholicism and Islam," *Journal of Ecumenical Studies* 41 (2004) 18–38, here 19–20.

Chapter 12

Losing Mystery in History: The Challenge of Recalling the Nativity

Thomas O'Loughlin

"What do we know about the origins of Jesus?" Confronted with this question, most people would offer a similar reply—whether they are Christians asked by someone curious about the origins of Christmas, or scholars working on the quest for the historical Jesus. The usual reply would point to the documentary sources from early Christian times and suggest that the answer is to be found in "the Bible," "the New Testament," "the Gospels," or in the Gospels of Matthew and Luke. So, just as the scholarly efforts to search for the historical Jesus evolve into quests for the historical elements in early texts that still survive, our quests for information about the nativity of Jesus become searches for the "historical basis" of Matthew and Luke,[1] sometimes combined with a study of the theological significance of Jesus' birth within those documents.[2] This procedure has been especially widespread among Catholics during the latter half of the twentieth century in both pastoral and academic circles.[3]

Such an approach has much to commend it, not least because historical explanation is a dominating feature in our cultural landscape,[4] but it runs the risk of silently invoking two major historical assumptions—themselves myths within our culture—inherent in any quest for origins. The first assumption is that if we know "what happened back then" in the past, then we know the significance of the event: the happening equates to the significance. Put crudely, if we know that Jesus was born at a certain time and in a specific set of circumstances, then that is the meaning of Christmas. In other words, if we know about the original event, then we know what the commemoration is about, and, indeed, why there is a commemoration: it is a "simple" recollection of "facts."

---

[1] See the introductory remarks of John P. Meier in *A Marginal Jew: Rethinking the Historical Jesus,* 4 vols (New York: Doubleday, 1991–2009), 1.21–31.

[2] See Raymond E. Brown, *The Birth of the Messiah: A Commentary on the Infancy Narratives in Matthew and Luke,* rev. edn (New York: Doubleday, 1993).

[3] For an example of this approach, see Hubert J. Richards, *The First Christmas: What Really Happened?* (London: Fontana, 1973).

[4] On this aspect of the quest for the historical Jesus, see E.L. Krasevac, "Questing for the Historical Jesus: Need We Continue?" *Doctrine and Life* 51 (2001), 590–604.

Second, there is an assumption about historical change, namely, that what actually happened is best understood and reflected in the earliest accounts that survive. These earliest documents form the primitive, and *therefore* the most genuine core of information, whereas every other element in the memory should be seen as a development from (or accretion to) that primary layer. Put simply: distil Matthew and Luke for whatever history might be "behind" or "contained in" their infancy narratives, then arrange the whole tradition as growing from that core and those narratives. Herein lies the fundamental drive behind so much labor on the biblical texts over the past two centuries: try to peel back the community's imaginative embellishments—"accretions" are always suspect within this philosophical model—and we will be left with "the truth": pure, simple, and factual!

These various quests for the historical Jesus have dominated theological scholarship for the best part of two centuries, but, for the most part, this has had little impact outside the theologians' village: most churchgoing people seem quite happy to believe that Jesus was born in Bethlehem, said many wise things, and died on Calvary.[5] However, this easygoing, widespread acceptance of the early churches' traditions as "simple" history often balks at three points: first, the miracle stories; second, the accounts of the resurrection that we celebrate liturgically at Easter; and third, the wondrous stories about the birth that we celebrate liturgically at Christmas. Leaving aside the question of the miracle stories, we are confronted with a profoundly ironic situation. For most of the gospels, and most of the year when we read them liturgically, the majority of people are not bothered by historical questions. Yet the two occasions in the year, Easter and Christmas, when we most emphasize the Christ-event, by the liturgical memory taking on a historical form, are the very times when people are troubled by those issues that belong to the quest for the historical Jesus.[6] Here, I intend to focus on just one of these moments of memory—that surrounding the nativity—but what follows applies to both festivals and memories *mutatis mutandis*.

"Getting Back to Basics"

The endeavor of getting back to "the basic truth of what Christmas is about" sounds both attractive and sensible, and each year there are umpteen attempts "to get back behind the myths" and "to explain" what Christmas is about. But

---

[5] Curiously, even among those Christians who are several centuries distant from the Vulgate, this particular Latinism survives as a recognizable place-name, despite the fact that it never appears on a map of biblical sites in the area of Jerusalem. This is a simple example of how the community's memory is larger than our reading.

[6] Hence we can understand why Raymond E. Brown made his great study, *The Death of the Messiah*, 2 vols (New York: Doubleday, 1994), as well as *The Birth of the Messiah*.

before proceeding, it is worth noting that even for those Christians who avidly search for "origins" and "basic facts," there are, each year, a few disquieting sounds from the margins.

From one side, often in reply to the message put out by some Christians that "Jesus is the reason for the season," someone points out that this festival in December is a legacy of a "pre-Christian" or "pagan" or "non-Christian" (each adjective is theologically loaded) Roman midwinter festival that was "hijacked" or "adapted" or "Christened" (each verb is theologically loaded) by the Church.[7] This observation provokes a question by way of reaction: so we do not know when Jesus was born? And we have to recognize that for those who operate within the historical assumptions we have just noted, if there is a doubt about when someone, long in the past, was born, that can quickly become a doubt whether he or she was ever born.[8] Such a historical figure can easily become lumped together with others that hover on the edges of "fact" within folklore such as Romulus and Remus, Fionn and the Fianna, Hengest and Horsa, or William Tell and his son.

From another side, again each year, comes some query about the star of Bethlehem (Matt 2:2–10). One year it is perhaps a scientist who has found some "scientific" proof that explains it (a comet, a planetary conjunction, or whatever), and we hear, *sotto voce*, the satisfaction that this "proves" the whole Christmas story. The complementary situation also occurs, where a scientist shows there could have been no such star, and this seems to imply that the whole story is just a fiction. And, by definition, to label something as historically "fictitious" is to declare it a falsehood masquerading as truth.

Like it or not, each year we are thrown into the questionings of historians, and when history is invoked, it seems that our story, our memory, and our celebration can appear to be threadbare! This is a problem that is often dodged by theologians, since scriptural study sometimes contents itself with exposing the beauties of the text rather than asking if it refers to something beyond itself. This problem is also frequently dodged by preachers, using a variety of avoidance tactics, yet it touches the whole credibility of Christian faith—credibility in the sense that its message is both worthy of acceptance and capable of being believed without a disquieting feeling that it is just a fairytale for "the children," whose season it is often claimed that Christmas is.[9]

---

[7] See T.J. Talley, "Liturgical Time in the Ancient Church: The State of Research," *Studia Liturgica* 14 (1980–82) 34–51.

[8] See Robert E. van Voorst, *Jesus Outside the New Testament: An Introduction to the Ancient Evidence* (Grand Rapids, MI: Eerdmans, 2000), 6–16.

[9] A biblical scholar, Prof. Sean Freyne of Trinity College, Dublin, was asked, on a Christmas Eve lunchtime radio news broadcast sometime in the 1980s, to comment on whether we "really knew anything" about Jesus: the interviewer was clearly looking for something startling that would generate some controversy on what was otherwise a news-starved day. Prof. Freyne told me subsequently that he was sternly warned that whatever he said about Jesus, he was to say nothing that could be taken as a denial of the existence of Santa Claus!

In fact, the proclamation is often subverted by these notions and pressed to collude with them. How often are clergy told around Christmas time by their parishioners: "Well, it's really for the children, isn't it?" Indeed, in many Catholic communities in Britain the liturgy on Christmas morning can become, in effect, a "Children's Mass," like a "School Mass" for the younger children. I have even seen a community where a school-organized nativity play replaced the gospel reading, the homily, and the profession of faith. Then the celebration can become about toys that came with the dawn, rather than about the One who visits us like the dawn from on high.

But should we see the problems of celebrating the nativity, and recalling our stories about the nativity, as problems in the quest for the historical Jesus? Perhaps we have become so fixated on the gospels as "history" that we have forgotten that, like our ancient texts, our celebration really belongs to the liturgy?

What Do We Remember Liturgically?

For Christians, liturgical remembering has the fuller sense of *anamnesis*: celebrating a historical reality that is constitutive of our "now" as the church. Hence, before we can reflect on how we remember the nativity, we must look at what we remember liturgically. This memory, as a glance at any "religious" Christmas card shows, is far more complex than a "simple" recollection of "facts." I place these latter words in quotation marks because even the briefest introduction to psychology shows that memory is rarely simple and that "facts" in our past are as elusive as subatomic particles. Nevertheless, we as humans have a very strong attachment to the notion that all memory can be understood by analogy to the report to the police officer after a robbery: "The van outside the house this morning was white."

In the Christian memory of Jesus' birth, four major elements have been united: the date, the place, the manger, and the combination of stories from Matthew and Luke. We will now look at each of these elements in turn.

The Date of Jesus' Birth

For us, the memory probably begins with a date: December 25. On this day Jesus was born, it is the feast of his birthday, and that is why—we are told by countless preachers—Christians celebrate. The preacher's jingle proclaims: "Jesus is the reason for the season." This is not simply a single date within the liturgy—by contrast with the date of death of a saint (e.g., that of St Laurence on August 10), where the feast day is often a most reliable "fact." Rather, this birth date links with a string of other feasts. In the current Roman calendar there are twelve other feasts whose celebration is linked to this day—and there were even more in the past in some churches.

There are seven feasts that can be seen as direct "implications" of celebrating the Nativity of Jesus on December 25. Initially, this date gives us June 24 (the Nativity of John the Baptist, six months earlier), and it also implies March 25 (the Annunciation, nine months before Jesus' Nativity),[10] which leads to May 31 (Mary's Visitation of Elizabeth). As further consequences of December 25, we have December 28 (Holy Innocents), January 1 (Circumcision), January 6 (Epiphany), and February 2 (the Presentation in the Temple), as well as the new Feast of the Baptism of the Lord (the Sunday after Epiphany, regulated by the Christmas cycle). In addition, four more dates, observed in Catholic devotion, have arisen indirectly from details of the nativity story: July 26 (Joachim and Anne, Mary's parents), September 8 (the Nativity of Mary), November 21 (her Presentation in the Temple, as a girl), and December 8 (her Conception).[11]

While few may be actively aware of this web of interrelated dates on Christmas Day, it does demonstrate how the primary date has embedded itself in our memory, and reveals two significant aspects of liturgical remembering. First, there is a fondness for "historicizing" and discovering or extracting from established "facts" as many "new" details as possible.[12] Through this process, each generation takes over all it has inherited, adds more details that seem particularly relevant to it, and then seeks to give them a factual calendar location. Such a date then becomes the "icon" for the fact: so the feast of December 8 generates the interest that leads to the whole growth in Catholic theology we link with the idea of Mary's Immaculate Conception, and the feast day also comes to stand for all that its name implies. In recent years we have a secular parallel to how a date becomes iconic for all that is linked with it, in the way we recall the two planes being crashed into the Twin Towers in New York on September 11, 2001. We see that this has become an iconic date in general

---

[10] Whether March 25 is historically derived from December 25, or vice versa, has been a source of debate since the nineteenth century. Here I am not concerned with liturgical history but with the perception of the feast: in our use of the calendar today we celebrate March 25 with reference to December 25, such that if any actual community were asked on March 25 why they were celebrating the annunciation on that date, they would answer that an ideal gestation is nine months, and it is now nine months before Christmas. The more renowned Feast of the Nativity places the Annunciation in its orbit in the minds of most of us.

[11] The way these feasts relate to one another through a form of "exegetical arithmetic" has been examined in Thomas O'Loughlin, "The cult of Mary within the structures of human time: a reading of some early mediaeval Irish martyrologies," *Maria* 3/2 (2003) 135–69.

[12] On this process, see Bruce M. Metzger, "Names for the Nameless in the New Testament: A Study in the Growth of Christian Tradition," in *Kyriakon: Festschrift Johannes Quasten*, ed. Patrick Granfield and Josef A. Jungmann; 2 vols (Münster: Aschendorff, 1970), 1.79–99.

consciousness in the way we refer to it as "9/11" and we use the term "post 9/11."[13]

Second, liturgical memory has the propensity to link and combine details from very different sources into a dense web and then present them as a single, apparently coherent, image. Thus it is fitting to have a feast of Joachim and Anne because we have feasts of Mary and these feasts (such as the post-biblical notion of her Presentation in the Temple)[14] fit together as relating to a single person, and that person is linked into the nativity story by being a central actor within it. We can imagine this by analogy with a collection of snapshots that have the coherence that they come in the sequence of being taken, and collectively have the coherence of being "our family's holiday snaps" (no matter how diverse the contents)—and in this case "our community's valued and celebrated memories."

The Place of Jesus' Birth

Once we have a date for the birth of Jesus, we need a place. This might appear to be the wrong order, because the tradition that Jesus was born in Bethlehem goes back to the latter half of the first century, while that linking his birth with December 25 dates from the fifth century. Within our recollection, however, it is usually the date that comes first: every December our thoughts are drawn to Bethlehem—this place is the scene and the backdrop of our Christmas cards and our cribs or crèches.

The link with Bethlehem is also a deeply layered image: the couple arrive there from Nazareth for the census (Luke's story), going to the inn—presumably in the town. The imagery frequently also includes a cave, and the "little town" is often over the fields in the distance (Christian tradition). Then they leave there for Egypt and later take up residence for the first time in Nazareth (Matthew's story).

This association with Bethlehem also draws in other elements, including the Davidic connections of Jesus to Israel's history (the emphasis in Luke 2:4) and the links to the prophecies of the Messiah (the emphasis in Matt 2:4–5, 17–18). The story of Jesus' birth, as presented in these texts, cannot be separated from that of the whole history of Israel. This is a theme further expanded in our

---

[13] The very fact that British people refer to the date (pronounced "nine-eleven") using the modern American convention of putting the month's number first shows that the date is not just a historical reference marker but an iconic calendar point.

[14] This tradition already appears in the mid-second-century text, the *Protoevangelium of James* (discussed later). While the spelling *Protevangelium* is often used, I will keep the longer spelling. On the place of Mary's Presentation in the Temple in the calendar, see Thomas O'Loughlin, "The *Protoevangelium of James* and the Liturgical Memory of the Roman Rite: a Case Study of the Marian Feasts," *Maria*, forthcoming.

liturgical memory—although it is not the most popular element today—in the liturgical use of Matthew's genealogy,[15] and the derived imagery of the Jesse Tree.[16]

One further link with Bethlehem is the slaughter of the innocents (Matt 2:17–18), where the text seems to assume that the family have been living there for at least two years. This dark episode plays a complex role in Matthew: it links Jesus to yet another prophecy, it prompts the move to Egypt that fulfils another, and its legacy results in the move to settle in Nazareth. Although it has an annual liturgical recollection, it is somewhat "sidelined" within Christmas story, and certainly it is invisible in most crib (or crèche) scenes.[17]

A quick glance at the two infancy narratives suggests that the birth of Jesus in Bethlehem is a historical "fact," as it is witnessed in two distinct traditions—invoking the assumption that a "fact" has gathered two different encrustations of added detail—and it is remarkable how many commentators opt for this simple solution.[18] However, once we begin comparing the accounts we note that their common element is that they want to connect Jesus *of Nazareth* with the royal Davidic Messiah, within the overall strategy of early preaching (like Rom 1:3) that sought to understand Jesus through the memory of Israel's history—hence the link with the city of David's birth, Bethlehem. Here (in my view) is the theological imagination at work in the latter half of the first century and it is a precious insight into early Christology, precisely because it is a work of the churches' imagination. Yet it is evident that this christological strategy was not uniform, since differences remain in the evangelists' preaching: Luke has the parents living in Nazareth and visiting Bethlehem, whereas Matthew has them living in Bethlehem and moving to Nazareth. Nor is the

---

[15] This text (Matt 1:1–17) is included twice in the current Roman Catholic Eucharistic lectionary: first, on December 17, when 1:1–17 is the gospel reading; and, second, as the first part of the gospel for the Vigil Mass of Christmas (December 24). However, the compilers of the lectionary clearly saw that it was not a favorite text, because the full text given for the Vigil Mass of Christmas (1:1–25) has 1:18–25 as a shorter alternative. The compilers did not foresee that this Vigil Mass would within a few years turn into a major celebration in many communities when it became in the late 1970s an "anticipation" of the obligation for Christmas Day. With this development, the choice of gospel passage became even more problematic because congregations often wanted a "short" celebration and also wished to hear the Christmas story. The result is that there are very few congregations that ever hear the genealogy text. On these pastoral problems, see Thomas O'Loughlin, *Liturgical Resources for Advent and Christmastide* (Dublin: Columba, 2006), 174–86. The Lukan genealogy (3:23–38) does not appear in the Roman Catholic lectionary, except as an alternative gospel for January 6 if the Feast of the Epiphany is celebrated on the following Sunday.

[16] On the derivation of the Jesse Tree from Isaiah 11, see John F.A. Sawyer, *The Fifth Gospel: Isaiah in the History of Christianity* (Cambridge, UK: Cambridge University Press, 1996), 74–80.

[17] See O'Loughlin, *Liturgical Resources for Advent and Christmastide*, 156–67.

[18] According to R.D. Cole, "Bethlehem," in *Eerdmans' Dictionary of the Bible*, ed. David Noel Freedman (Grand Rapids, MI: Eerdmans, 2000), 172–73, "Jesus was born in Bethlehem ca. 6 B.C.E." The care over the date, and its form, gives the impression that here is a careful scholarly judgment of the historical questions involved.

christological strategy universal, in that Mark did not preach it and its existence is doubtful in places where John preached.[19]

However, severing a historical link with Bethlehem—and openly recognizing that such a link belongs to the world of theological imagination—is a step that many scholars find difficult and most preachers (if they have recognized the problems posed by the stories) are unwilling to address, usually on the un-evidenced ground that "it would disturb simple faith." We can see these difficulties in a developmental sequence over a period of a decade in the multivolume series *A Marginal Jew* by John P. Meier. In volume 1 (1991) he concludes, after a thorough statement of the evidence,[20] that Jesus was born "perhaps in Bethlehem of Judea but more likely in Nazareth of Galilee." In volume 2 (1994) the probabilities are described in an altered way: he now states that Jesus was born "most likely in Nazareth of Galilee, though possibly in Bethlehem of Judea."[21] Finally in volume 3 (2001) he has settled to follow the historical evidence without reserve: Jesus "was born in the hillside town of Nazareth," and the Bethlehem traditions are presented as "probably later Christian theological dramatizations of the belief that Jesus was the royal Davidic Messiah."[22]

But this gradual path to identifying the Bethlehem stories for what they are—sacramental narratives—is one that many others fear, and they cloak their hesitation with hypothetical doubt presented as scholarly reserve: "there is much we do not know." In my view, the price of this hesitation to face up to the imaginative nature of the Bethlehem stories should not be underestimated. At the level of apologetics it means that anyone wishing to debunk Christianity has simply to point out that the stories "do not add up," and then Christian preaching is perceived as a cover-up.[23] So the best argument (as I see it) is not to hang onto the historical bits and pieces but openly declare these stories to be part of our human imagination's attempts to present the fundamental "fact" about Jesus for those who greet him as Lord: as Matt 16:17 notes, he is more than meets the eye. At the level of Christology, this failure is even more damaging: in our desire to historicize all the details, we fail to appreciate a whole approach to the mystery of Jesus, and the structures of the early preaching that gave rise to the stories in the first place.

When we come to the cave imagery, which is never presented in an urban landscape, or the stable/barn imagery, which is often presented outside an urban landscape (i.e., the stable/barn transposed into the landscape original

---

[19] John 7:41–42 knows the Messiah–Bethlehem link, but shows no awareness of the Jesus–Bethlehem link.

[20] Meier, *A Marginal Jew*, 1.211–29. The quotation is from 1.229

[21] Ibid., 2.1039.

[22] Ibid., 3.615, 3.616.

[23] This form of attack on Christianity can be traced back to the work of Porphyry in the third century, and much of the work by Christians at gospel harmonization (such as that of Eusebius) can be seen largely as a reaction to such attacks.

to the cave), we encounter another level of theological evolution. The cave-outside-the-town-of-Bethlehem imagery is first evidenced in the second century. The cave is, for example, mentioned in section 78 of Justin Martyr's *Dialogue with Trypho*,[24] but the whole scene appears for the first time in the *Protoevangelium of James*.[25] The latter text, which effectively canonizes Christian memory of the nativity from both east and west until modern times,[26] is itself a remarkable example of how remembering, theology, and history are always in a dynamic interplay. It was written to give further "historical" detail to communities all too desirous of such information—it is from this source that we get such stories as that of Joachim and Anne along with that of Mary's Presentation in the Temple—but it also answered three important theological needs. First, it is the earliest conscious attempt to reconcile the conflicting infancy narratives of Matthew and Luke. Second, it develops the theme of the uniqueness of Jesus by stressing not only his virginal conception but also the uniqueness of the conception, birth, and upbringing of Mary—it is with this text we see the growth of links between the nativity story and the churches' memory of Mary. And, third, it demonstrates the need to explain away the historical memory of the brothers and sisters of Jesus so that Mary can be seen as *ever* virgin—and it is as part of this agenda that the birth has to be located outside the city of Bethlehem, and a cave seemed an appropriate covering in such a desert setting.

In sharp contrast to the reticence shown by modern scholars and preachers toward abandoning the "historical" bits of the infancy narratives of Matthew and Luke, the "historical" bits in the infancy narrative of the *Protoevangelium* have been jettisoned with aplomb in modern times! The glossing over of at least 1,850 years of our liturgical remembering is often justified by simply giving the stories the pejorative label of "apocryphal," with the unspoken but horrendous implication that if the stories appeared within the canonical works, then they would be "true"!

Yet, at least for Roman Catholics, our memory will not be dismissed so simply as might be wished by those who would like to reduce it to the canonical (and implicitly much less problematic) "genuine" texts. While in the case of Matthew and Luke we are often so caught by the "historical" bits that we fail to see the theology that produced the stories, in the case of texts such as

---

[24] Thomas P. Halton and Michael Slusser, eds, *St Justin Martyr: Dialogue with Trypho* (Washington, DC: Catholic University of America Press, 2003), 121.

[25] See my article, "The *Protoevangelium of James* and the Liturgical Memory of the Roman Rite" (forthcoming in *Maria*). For a translation of this second-century text, see Oscar Cullmann, "Infancy Gospels," in *New Testament Apocrypha*, ed. Wilhelm Schneemelcher, second edn, 2 vols (Louisville: Westminster/John Knox, 1991–1992), 1.426–37.

[26] See Thomas O'Loughlin, *Adomnán and the Holy Places: The Perceptions of an Insular Monk on the Location of the Biblical Drama* (London: T&T Clark, 2007), 229–32. The cave of Jesus' birth appears as recently as 2007 in the film *The Nativity Story*, directed by Catherine Hardwicke.

the *Protoevangelium* we have almost the reverse situation: its "historical" bits are being gradually forgotten,[27] but the theological implications of those stories stand before us like bare propositions demanding defense but without any adequate ground within our canonical texts. Thus, many places in the Catholic liturgy still refer to Mary as "ever virgin," yet we hear of her many children in the gospels (e.g., Mark 6:3), read in that liturgy. In addition, Catholic piety still celebrates her unique conception and upbringing, despite knowing that there is no early reference to these concerns apart from these "apocryphal" texts and also knowing that the later evolution of this tradition as Mary's Immaculate Conception raises considerable theological questions. We may think that the "historical" details from such texts as the *Protoevangelium* can be easily dropped, but would we be willing to drop the theological positions that were formed by abstraction from those now-forgotten incidents?

The Manger

The core image of the nativity in popular memory is that of Joseph and Mary with an infant lying in a little cot of straw. Representing the Greek term *phatné* (Luke 2:7, 12, 16), the "manger" has a quasi-sacral status, presumably as it is fixed in the memory by such carols as "Away in a manger." But many people today, when asked what is a "manger," only know that it was where the infant Jesus was laid: a manger is a feeding trough for livestock. If the date and the locale are both non-historical, then, at least, *this* must be historical, because Jesus *was born* and at his birth the parents would have looked on with joy, admiration, and, indeed, relief. Surely this is a scene that is common to all human births, if the mother and father can both be present at the time of the birth.

There are, however, several reasons why we should be careful. First, that which is common to all humanity cannot be viewed as falling within human history, in so far as recorded history remembers that which is contingent and distinctive within situations. That human beings cry is a fact of biology and

[27] When I went first went to school in the early-1960s in Dublin (and it was *not* a school run by the Presentation Sisters), I saw a sequence of pictures along the corridor with scenes from the life of Jesus as presented in the gospels (e.g., a picture of Jesus meeting the centurion), but this sequence also included scenes from the life of his mother. Therefore, there was a picture of the Presentation of Mary in the Temple. I have no recollection of when the scene was "explained" to me—it was just part of my absorbed iconographical memory, and so I never thought about it when I later saw similar pictures in the parlors of many Presentation Convents. However, when I showed that image recently to a class of Catholic seminarians, not one of them could identify it—the best attempt was "some scene from the Old Testament." My point is this: these extra-canonical details relating to the life of Jesus (as well as Mary) are not as well-known today as they were only a generation ago among many western Christians. The stories from the *Protoevangelium* are, however, still part of the memory of eastern Christians, since they are depicted in commonly found icons.

psychology, rather than a fact of history.[28] Second, we have no distinctive detail about the birth (e.g., the manger) that is not (in my view) derived from the theological imagination that led to the story of Jesus being born in Bethlehem. And, third, we tend to embellish that core scene to make links between the historical fact of Jesus' birth and our faith in him as the Savior. The most obvious example of this process is the presence of the ox and the ass that derives from the desire to make a link with another prophecy: "The ox knows its owner, and the ass its master's crib; but Israel does not know, my people does not understand" (Isa 1:3). Less obvious is the attitude of the parents that traditional Christian art has usually presented as one of worship rather than human joy over a birth. Indeed, the otherness of this birth is often further developed in images through the use of haloes or a nimbus of light around the infant. The core image is that of the birth of a human being, but the details of the memory point to it being a birth like no other.

The Combination of Nativity Stories from Matthew and Luke

The fourth element in our liturgical memory is that of the visitors who come to worship the newborn, and here the liturgical memory combines the stories from Matthew and Luke into a single coherent narrative and ignores the disharmonies. We have the shepherds from Luke—it is perfectly reasonable that there were shepherds in that region given the importance of sheep herding in pre-modern agriculture. We also have the astrologers from Matthew, a rather less convincing set of visitors, who can gain access to King Herod without further ado and whose speculations lead to the king giving the entire academic hierarchy a special research project to ascertain the correct place for a Messiah to be born. But the important point to notice is that the memory adds in other elements that cannot be contained within a historical narrative. In Luke we have the angels both singing the praises of the infant and communicating with the shepherds, while in Matthew we have the notion that the cosmos is announcing this unique birth through the "star."

The exuberant richness of Matthew's story (with such details as the list of the three gifts) has meant that it has been used allegorically since the beginning to enrich our Christology. This is a use that is wholly appropriate, as this was the original rationale for mentioning "gold, frankincense, and myrrh" (Matt 2:11): the gold and incense came from a messianic reading of Isa 60:6, while the myrrh pointed to the divine throne and royal scepter of Ps 45:6–8. This

---

[28] However, that Jesus wept at the tomb of Lazarus is presented as a fact of "history" according to John 11:35.

story was further developed within the subsequent liturgical memory in that the magi have mutated into the kings of Ps 72:10–11, and their number has been fixed at three: the three gifts fitted with there being three kings derived from the Psalm.

This regal group has left its mark on western culture in many ways. In some countries the Feast of the Epiphany is known as that of the three kings (*Die Feier der Heiligen drei Könige*) and in others as [the feast of] "the kings" (*Los Reyes*). They have been given names within the tradition (Caspar, Melchior, Balthasar), and they still leave their mark on countless doorways in central Europe.[29] English Bible translations (from KJV as far as NRSV) have sought to transform them yet again: they cannot here maintain their royal status, yet the term *magoi* ("magi") is not rendered as "astrologers" but as the far more reasonable "wise men."[30]

This survey of the content of our liturgical memory should have made one point clear: we are not engaging with historical details when we recall liturgically the birth of the Christ. Our memory has wrapped the birth within a web of historical-style garments, in a continuous effort to capture the uniqueness of who we believe the newborn infant to be. However, a great many people imagine that we are engaging with history in its details, and indeed they are often given every encouragement to believe that they are dealing with history. They are then left confused whenever it becomes apparent that our memory's content is not of one piece with that of a historical reconstruction. Meanwhile, the theological insights that gave rise to the stories are often regrettably hidden from view.

Remembering Liturgically

The fundamental premise of all liturgy is that we encounter the divine reality through the medium of reality that exists within our experience of time and space. Without this assumption, the Eucharist, for example, would be either a pageant that serves to jog the memory or else the ritual whereby we manipulate the divine from within the world around us. With this assumption, however, we can engage in a community meal that not only defines us socially, but can unite us with the original actions of Jesus and also anticipate the heavenly banquet.

In our everyday experience we are constantly being separated from one another by space and time, but in liturgy that process is reversed: here is a

---

[29] In many rural localities in central Europe the practice survives of writing this legend on the door lintel (or the door itself) on January 6 each year: *20+C+M+B+09* (i.e., the year's date and the initials of the three kings).

[30] The rendering can be found as early as the sixteenth century (e.g., the Rheims translation of 1582). In Latin the Greek import *magus* was conventionally understood, following Augustine's exegesis, as identical with *mathematicus* (i.e., an astrologer).

moment in a particular place that has present to it the ever-present now of the Incarnation and that is also a moment within the gathering of the angels and saints around the heavenly throne.[31] Such is the time-space formula in the Catholic liturgy at the conclusion of every Eucharistic Preface, which sets the scene for the singing of the Sanctus.

This liturgical remembering, embracing past and future in the activity of the present, is dramatic in its structures but is more than a dramatization of a set of ideas. It invites us, for instance at the Feast of the Epiphany, to enter into the activity of the magi, rather than simply to decode the story as indicating a belief in the Christian claim that this revelation is universal in scope. A dramatization might be no more than a communication device for a system of intellectual propositions, but a liturgical drama enables us to join in the fulfillment of the scriptural text that all kings fall down before the Lord, and all nations serve him (Ps 72:11). Our memory—and the evangelist's intention—is not that we admire an ancient event, but take part in it ourselves.

Decades after this understanding of liturgy was put forward by the great liturgists of the twentieth century (such as Odo Casel), we are now beginning to see how it can affect many aspects of Christian activity. It is frequently invoked in how we present individual sacramental events such as Baptism and the Eucharist, and we are also beginning to see how this understanding is the key to events such as the Great Week (Holy Week), the Paschal Triduum, or the Easter Vigil. By way of contrast, the narrative of the Nativity *seems* more a tale of events than a moment or episode within the Christ-event, and so we do not often think of it in this liturgical way. But the church's keeping of the memory of the Nativity is a liturgical event through and through—and we English-speakers are even reminded of this linguistically in that we call it "Christ – Mass" (= Christmas).

Our annual liturgical celebration of Christmas is not simply an anniversary of an event, but it is the celebration of the event within an annual cycle of liturgy. Most of our commemorations belong to the anniversary type of celebrations: for instance, France remembers the iconic event of the 1789 Revolution on Bastille Day (July 14), but this is not tantamount to saying that today's

---

[31] We cannot understand why liturgy is important to us if we seek to explain its content using a merely historical model of explanation. In fact, at the Sunday Eucharist we celebrate the day of resurrection, and are sacramentally as present to the risen One as those who encountered him on the first Easter Sunday. For us and those earliest Christians, this encounter is "historical" in that it is an encounter that can be dated and the person who encounters the risen One can be located within a time-space grid. But this encounter is also beyond history in that it is greater than that which time and space can contain. Liturgical remembering is, therefore, not just "thinking back" to a time that can then be a point of departure for a narrative of a sequence of changes, but rather it is thinking that is focused on this present moment. Indeed, liturgical remembering draws the whole past into the present moment, and is also mindful of the future, so that both past and present only make sense in that promise as they anticipate a future.

Parisians are also assaulting that long-disappeared fortress. Only our liturgical celebrations belong to the other sort, which we call *anamnesis*. In our Christmas celebrations we are rejoicing with the good news of great joy as we celebrate like the shepherds, and we are joining the magi in acknowledging the Christ as the center of all life.

Because we are pondering in our hearts all that the Christ-event means, the liturgy's great antiphons are framed in the time of the present moment. Hence the entrance antiphon for the Christmas Vigil Mass and the short responsory at First Vespers (drawing on Exod 16:6–7) both state: *Hodie scietis quia veniet Dominus, et mane videbitis gloriam eius* ("Today you will know that the Lord will come, and in the morning you will see his glory"). So too, the antiphon for the Invitatory Psalm on Christmas morning declares: *Christus natus est nobis: venite, adoremus* ("Christ has been born for us: come, let us adore him").

When we seek to recall the nativity within this liturgical mode of understanding, we need to take our time frame from the liturgy itself: it is an event occurring "today" (*hodie*), in liturgical time. Thus, it is an event that is unfolding now, rather than in the past.[32] In popular consciousness, however, the nativity is a wholly past event: it occurs in the mythic or romantic past of "White Christmases" long ago, or in a distant historical past as expressed in the carol "Long time ago in Bethlehem." Indeed, even in formal theological discourse it is often hard to distinguish the present tense proper to our faith in the Incarnation from the past tense inherent in the notion that we have sacred texts that tell of ancient events of ongoing significance.

Regarding this present tense perspective with which we are to approach all that is within our memory about the nativity, it is worth looking at the three Prefaces supplied in the Roman Missal for the feast. In the first Preface of Christmas (P3) the "wonder of the incarnation" is brought to the believers' eyes and engages them now in that they are "caught up in love of the God [they] cannot see." In the second Preface (P4) the memory fills their hearts "today" and the event takes place in the present: "now he is seen as one like us…now he is born in time," and his work is ongoing in fulfilling the nativity's purpose. In the third Preface (P5) it is also "today" that "a new light has dawned," while the effect of the Incarnation, coming to share in the divine nature, is a present and ongoing event.[33]

---

[32] While as a rule of thumb most Christmas hymns or carols do not stand up well to theological critique, we may note just how closely integrated into the nature of liturgical recollection is John Francis Wade's eighteenth-century hymn *Adeste, fideles* ("O come, all ye faithful"). In this hymn, the Christians (*fideles*), rather than all and sundry, are bidden to enter Bethlehem (*venite…in Bethlehem*) this very day (*die hodierna*) on which the singing is taking place, so as to see the birth of the One who is God from God, yet born of the Virgin Mary. The hymn shows how the outcome of the celebration is the group's encounter with the living God, rather than simply their renewal of a memory from the past.

[33] The same time-frame also appears in the Preface of the Epiphany (P6).

Building a Sense of Liturgical Recollection

To bring out some of the implications of the way we can best view the nativity within the church, an analogy may help. Any ancient object that conveys to us a memory of the past can be viewed in two ways. Let us suppose that we have on the one hand an ancient codex (handwritten book) of the gospels and on the another a painted icon. We might view the codex as a kind of icon, an object that may perhaps conjure up for us all the worries and conflicts of the time when it was written (perhaps the fourth or fifth century), and then just marvel at it in reverie. However, our modern scientific instinct is to approach it as a historical artifact, and so the skills of various experts—the codicologist, the paleographer, and the textual critic—are deployed in turn, so that the object can yield up to our understanding as much of its latent information as possible. The aim is to know where and when it was produced, if possible by whom and why, its relationships with other manuscripts and with other gospel texts, and then to see how it can help us understand the transmission of the text, the social culture of the church that commissioned it, and, perhaps, how it may throw light on other theological texts or even help us improve the edition of the New Testament.

Now consider the painted icon. We can study it within the same framework as the codex with all the skills of the art historian, and we can "decode" it as a kind of text by noting, for example, in an icon of the nativity how its imagery may be derived from the *Protoevangelium of James.* However, we can also relate to it as a visual object. Viewing it as an icon, we may be presented with a whole range of images that could never come together in historical time, and all are located in a landscape that is simultaneously familiar and otherworldly. Indeed, the icon does not claim to be history, but a celebration of faith. Moreover, the form of its imagery does not allow us to think of it as primarily a source of historical information in the way that a codex encourages us to view it chiefly as historical evidence (after all, most historical research is based on the study of old books and documents).

Following from this analogy, our task is to view the celebration of Christmas primarily as an icon to be contemplated rather than as a codex to be studied. However, we are hampered in this by two factors. First, the obsession with "the book" as history within western Christianity in recent centuries means that any event narrated in "the book" is doomed to be viewed as history first and foremost, and escaping from this trap is very difficult. For many Christians the only reason to celebrate Christmas is because it is in "the book." The idea that it was a community's celebration of the event of the nativity that gave rise to the stories in "the book" is far too revolutionary a notion for many people to grasp. But while we may think of such Christians who imagine that Christianity is a function of "the Bible" as a defined group, the attitude is far more widely diffused, and is a view that is fostered in countless nativity plays, carol services, and Christmas homilies.

Second, we still have not got over the attitudes that were appropriate in those centuries when Christianity was the sole major religion in western society—the time when (apart from some Jews and a few others) we could take it for granted that people were Christians in some way or other. In such a society the annual festivities could serve the aim of recalling people to "what it means to be a Christian." Today much Christian communication is still based on that assumption, and so a British cleric will go on the BBC radio program "Thought for the Day" in late December and remind people "what it is all about." But for most of the British audience this is simply the same as someone going on the radio on October 21 and reminding people of the debt that Britain owes to Horatio Nelson for his 1805 naval victory at Trafalgar—a victory that explains why a prominent London square is named after an Iberian coastal feature. By continuing to speak to everyone in a liturgical language that only makes sense to those who are celebrating the liturgy, we often betray that language and invite the whole celebration to be viewed simply as an anniversary. In both cases, where our strategies invite our liturgical dramatizations to be regarded as historical records, they are found wanting, and the very message preached is undermined.

Liturgical Recollection and Historical Reconstruction

There is an important difference between liturgical recollection and historical reconstruction. Liturgical recollection is concerned with what is brought to mind for believers within the community's memory,[34] whereas historical study aims to find out what actually happened in the past. Moreover, liturgical memory uses stories from the past to lead into a present encounter of faith, whereas historical research aims to discover from the past merely what can be asserted with the reasonable certitude of historical evidence.[35] We could say that liturgical memory preserves the past in an inclusive way,[36] whereas historical research excludes anything that does not meet the demands of its methodology. Accordingly, we can summarize the differences between

---

[34] This is more than the notion of "what does it mean for us," which could be simply some notion of "relevance" as if that were a theological category. Rather, it brings to mind successive attempts to explicate the mystery through sacramental images, and this assemblage is preserved and its content entered in our act of recollection.

[35] For a useful summary of the nature of this criterion, see Meier, *A Marginal Jew*, 1.21–40.

[36] This aspect of the liturgical memory became one of "the notes" of a "true" development of doctrine within John Henry Newman's scheme for doctrinal development in his *The Development of Christian Doctrine*, part 2, chapter 5, section 6.

viewing Christmas as history (by analogy: the codex) and viewing it as liturgical recollection (by analogy: the painted icon) as given in Table 12.1.

Like all such schematic presentations, and particularly binary contrasts, this is an oversimplification. We cannot avoid engaging with history. In fact, over recent centuries, historical investigations have greatly enriched our understanding of Christian origins. Likewise, the person celebrating cannot just flick a switch that changes him or her from "historical reconstruction" to "liturgical recollection" mode! Equally, we must be careful to assert that the birth, life, and death of Jesus took place within human history and that our faith's appreciation of that life is anchored in history (without being fully contained within it). However, the schematic presentation aims to bring out that there is a genuine difference in what we are doing in recalling the nativity—we are not just seeking to understand a moment in the past. When we study that recollection in early Christian texts such as Matthew and Luke, we might describe it as

Table 12.1   The differences between viewing Christmas as history and as liturgical recollection

Liturgical recollection	Historical reconstruction
Focus:	
(1) Who *is* Jesus, our Lord?	(1) Who *was* Jesus of Nazareth?
(2) What are the ramifications of that event?	(2) What happened in Palestine then?
(3) What does it bring to mind for us within our community's memory?	(3) How did it happen?
Criterion of evidence:	
Those stories that have been found valuable within the community, and also preserved, are asserted as they may provide the basis for an insight into the encounter of faith. The criterion is preservative of the past, and as such is inclusive.	To find what can be asserted with the certitude of historical evidence, and no more than this. The criterion functions to exclude anything that does not meet its strict demands.
Assumption about evidence:	
It will not be consistent within a time-place framework, since it seeks to speak about both the divine and the earthly.	The evidence must be consistent within a coherent time-place framework.
Assumption about the discourse:	
The manifestation of God can never be contained in human words or images, since God is always greater than our understanding.	Contradictions are excluded.
Time focus of the enquiry:	
Today.	The past.
Desired outcome:	
Liturgical celebration leading to a sacramental encounter with the Word made flesh.	Information leading to a greater understanding of the origins and structures of a major world religion.

a "dramatization" or as the "dramatic genre" rather than "history," and when we actually engage in that recollection of ourselves we can call it liturgy.

Consequences for Christian Practice

Recognizing the nature of what we are doing as the church when we celebrate the nativity implies certain ways of acting outside the liturgy, precisely because a memory of our celebrations is now part of the wider human culture. Hence I conclude this essay with five suggestions for how we can recapture the mystery of the nativity in our annual Christmas celebrations.

1. "Winterval"

It is pointless to try to present the whole cultural festival as hanging on our Christian celebration. It was an action of Christians to hook up their celebration of the nativity to an existing party that answered the human need in the northern temperate zone for a celebration during the dullest time in the year.[37] When people want to call this party by other names, we can let them do so. If all were Christians, there would be no need for such a renaming, but since not all are Christians, we should not be trying to monopolize this midwinter party as if it is our property. The whole world can have a party, while we Christians have a party and combine it with our celebration of the nativity.[38] Fighting to "keep Christ in Christmas" is based on an outdated assumption (namely, confusion between an anniversary and liturgical recollection), and such a struggle is a waste of energy. Our energy is better directed to improving the understanding and celebration of the nativity within the community of the People of God who hold their celebrations at the time of the midwinter party—whether that party is called the *Dies natalis solis invicti* (Birthday of the unconquered sun) or the Winterval.

2. Yet another comet!

Each year, it seems, someone comes up with yet another "solution" to some puzzle in the infancy narratives of Matthew or Luke. We have to resist the temptation to grasp at these straws and remember that the whole narrative—all the bits that make the memory—will never "add up" logically. Therefore,

---

[37] Here I pass over the fact that the solstices and equinoxes are ritually significant times within many religions; such speculations would be a distraction here.

[38] Around the same time of the year the Jews celebrate the Feast of Hanukkah to commemorate the Maccabean rededication of the Jerusalem temple (1 Macc 4:59).

imagining that we have a solution to some bit of the memory is to forget what the memory is (namely, our earliest liturgical recollection) and to confuse it with a historical account.

Positively, this means that we do well to avoid any hint in our preaching that might give the impression that what we are reading is a collection of contemporary eyewitness evidence. Since we enjoy the form of history writing with its semblance of realism, and we like the focus given by the rhetorical device of historical exactitude (e.g., "With this very pen X signed the Declaration of Y"), we must be careful lest our historical desires come between us and our celebration of the nativity as a sacramental event today.

3. Books and memory

A further consequence of not treating the recollection as if it were a historical account (or merely an anniversary) is that we would do well to avoid the fundamentalism that sees "the book" as primary, and the community as those who are its people. The Christian community is the reality of continuity with Jesus the Messiah, and the living Word of God is the work of the Spirit within that community.[39] The sacred books are a function of the preaching within that community, and so the books are (in a manner of speaking) the community's "property." Far from the book identifying the community, it is a case of the community possessing its memory enlivened by the Spirit, and the community has made notes on papyrus, parchment, and paper down the centuries.[40]

4. Avoiding confusion

Another consequence of not behaving as if the details of our recollection of the nativity are history is that those who have pastoral responsibilities will avoid giving confusing answers to questions on the spurious grounds that telling people that (for instance) the flight into Egypt is not a historical event will disturb their "faith." Equally, saying that it is "possibly true" is to be avoided: such "possibilities" defy the normal rules of historical evidence—the very rules we appeal to in order to dismiss some of the wilder claims that are made for Jesus'

---

[39] The 1981 *General Instruction on the Lectionary* for the Roman Missal expressed this in these words: "That word constantly proclaimed in the liturgy is always a living, active word (see Heb 4:2) through the power of the Holy Spirit. It expresses the Father's love, that never fails in its effectiveness toward us" (n. 4).

[40] In the face of widespread misunderstanding of the nature of Christianity (including misunderstandings of Christianity by many fundamentalist Christians), we recall that there was a church before there were many of the stories that eventually ended up in the documents that (later still) came to be regarded as "the [New Testament] Scriptures." The living Word can never be identified with the legible marks found on an inert object.

hidden years, such as the suggestions that he visited India or Japan! Anything can (in principle) be declared an option, and therefore a possibility,[41] but historical research is founded on probabilities based on the whole extent of the evidence. Using the latter model, within which historical questions are asked, to introduce hypothetical possibilities (e.g., "They just might have gone to Egypt; we cannot say for certain") is to sow confusion among those for whom one is a teacher—and if this is done knowingly, it amounts to dishonesty.

5. Avoiding historicist reductions

Last, in my view, it is a mistake for us to trim the memory of the bits that we think are "later accretions" on the assumption that we can get back to a basic "core" that is the "real memory." The church is always remembering, always forgetting, and always adding new imagery to its memory in its attempt to draw out yet more of the mystery of the Christ-event. We can, for instance, image the crib-scene as two migrants sheltering in cardboard boxes and packing cases beneath a highway overpass—as I saw on a Christmas card some years ago. Such an image is as valid an exploration of part of the Good News for us to reflect on in our liturgy as that of the infant being visited by three, distinctly oriental-looking, kings.

To conclude, the challenge of celebrating our recollection of the nativity—of giving words to the inexpressible—is summed up in this opening verse of the hymn for First Vespers of the feast in the 1971 Liturgy of the Hours (promulgated by Pope Paul VI), a verse that is devoid of Bethlehem, cribs and straw, shepherds and wise men:

> *Christe, redemptor omnium,*
> *ex Patre, Patris Unice,*
> *solus ante principium*
> *natus ineffabiliter.*[42]

---

[41] In philosophical terms, this is no more than the logical rule that every proposition entails another proposition that is the hypothetical disjunction formed by a term and its complement. The statement *hodie pluit* ("today it is raining") logically entails *hodie aut pluit aut non pluit* ("today either it is raining or it is not raining"). I have expressed this in the older language of traditional logic, but a similar notion can be found in modern propositional logic as the "Rule of v-Introduction"; see Edward John Lemmon, *Beginning Logic* (London: Nelson, 1965), 22. To be sure, I am not suggesting that a propositional calculus can be equated with natural language logic.

[42] *Liturgia horarum* , vol. 1 (Rome: Libreria Editrice Vaticana, 1971), 318. In English: "O Christ, redeemer of all, before the beginning of creation, you alone proceed from the Father; now you are born in a manner beyond our speaking."

Appendix

Resemblances between Matthew 1–2 and Luke 1–2

Patricia M. McDonald, S.H.C.J.

This list expands the resemblances noted by Raymond E. Brown in *The Birth of the Messiah* (rev. edn; New York: Doubleday, 1993; 34–35); and by Joseph A. Fitzmyer in *The Gospel According to Luke I–IX* (Anchor Bible 28; New York: Doubleday, 1981; 307).

1. Jesus' birth is related to the reign of Herod the Great (Matt 2:1; Luke 1:5).
2. Mary, a virgin, is engaged to Joseph but not yet living with him (Matt 1:18; Luke 1:27, 34).
3. Joseph belongs to the house of David (Matt 1:1–16; Luke 1:27), and because of him, Jesus belongs to David's line.
4. An angel announces Jesus' coming birth to one of the parents (Matt 1:20, Joseph; Luke 1:26, Mary; cf. annunciation to Zechariah about John in 1:13).
5. Jesus is recognized as son of David (Matt 1:17, 25; Luke 1:27, 33).
6. Jesus is conceived through the Holy Spirit; an angel announces this to Joseph (Matt 1:20) or Mary (Luke 1:35).
7. Jesus' conception does not involve Joseph (Matt 1:18–19; Luke 1:34–35).
8. "Jesus" is the name given by the angel before the birth (Matt 1:21; Luke 1:31).
9. An angel identifies Jesus as savior (Matt 1:21; Luke 2:11).
10. Jesus is born after Mary and Joseph come to live together (Matt 1:25; Luke 2:5–7), though Mary is still engaged (*emnēsteumenē*) to Joseph in Luke 2:5.
11. Jesus is born in Bethlehem (Matt 2:1; Luke 2:5–7).
12. Outsiders see a sign in the night sky (star, angels), come to visit, enter from the open air, see the child, and return whence they came (magi in Matthew; shepherds in Luke).
13. There is external testimony to Jesus (magi in Matt 2:1–12; Simeon and Anna in Luke 2:25–38).
14. Joseph, Mary, and Jesus settle in Nazareth (Matt 2:23; Luke 2:39, cf. 1:26).

15. Jesus is referred to either as king (*basileus*) of the Jews (Matt 2:2) or as one who will inherit David's throne and reign (*basileuein*) eternally over Jacob's house, and have an unending kingdom (*basileia*, Luke 1:32–33).

16. An angel appears to a male figure (Joseph in Matt 1:20; Zechariah in Luke 1:11).

17. Light imagery is used: the star seen at its rising (*en tē anatolē*) in Matthew (2:2, 9; cf. 2:1); in Luke, the shepherds at night see the glory of the Lord (2:8–9), the dawn is from on high (*anatolē*, 1:78), and God's salvation (Jesus?) is a light for revelation to the Gentiles (2:32).

18. Jesus is termed Christ (*Christos*) in Matt 1:1, 16, 17; 2:4 and Luke 2:11 (and, perhaps, implicitly also in 1:32–33).

19. There are strong, but different, links with Judaism in each story (Old Testament formula citations in Matthew; temple and other liturgy in Luke).

20. Herod or Zechariah "is afraid" (*tarassein*, in Matt 2:3; Luke 1:12).

21. Notes about "joy" and "rejoicing" (*chara, chairein*: Matt 2:10 [both]; Luke 1:14 [verb]; 2:10 [noun]; cf. 1:47).

22. Spilling of male children's blood (by death, Matt 2:16–18) or circumcision (Luke 1:59; 2:21).

23. Motif of fulfillment (five Old Testament formula citations in Matthew; reference in Luke 1:70–75 to the keeping of divine promises).

Dictionary of Technical Terms, Significant Persons, and Ancient Texts

Many of these terms are explained more fully in *The Oxford Dictionary of the Christian Church*, ed. Frank L. Cross and Elizabeth A. Livingstone (third edn; Oxford/New York: Oxford University Press, 2005).

Adonai: Hebrew term for "(my) Lord," used as reverent substitute for YHWH

Anamnesis: Liturgical remembering

Androcentrism: Male-centered attitude

Angelophany: Appearance of an angel to a human person

Annunciation: Story of the angel Gabriel's visit to Mary (Luke 1:26–38)

Aorist: Tense of Greek verbs generally used for past narration

Apocalyptic: Supernatural revelation about heavenly realities, often obtained by dreams, ascent to heaven, or angelic visitation

Apologetics: Explanation of Christian faith to nonbelievers to encourage their conversion

Augustine, Saint (354–430): North African bishop and church father

Bakhtin, Mikhail (1895–1975): Russian literary critic

Benedictus: Zechariah's utterance (Luke 1:68–79)

Canon (canonical) criticism: Study of the sacred text in its final form without reliance on supposed earlier documents

Chiastic structure: Literary pattern (e.g., A-B-C-D-C'-B'A') whereby elements in the second half of a passage or episode match the elements in the first half but in reverse order

Damascus Document: Jewish sectarian text found at Qumran (and in the Cairo Genizah) containing community rules

Diptych: In art, a painting with two facing panels; in biblical studies, a story paralleling the lives of two characters

Docetic (Jesus): Seeming to be human without really being so

Enneateuch: The first nine books of the Hebrew Bible, from Genesis to 1–2 Kings

Enoch, First: Five-part Aramaic apocalyptic text (fully preserved in Ethiopic), mostly completed before the destruction of the Jerusalem temple in 70 CE

Enoch, Second: Slavonic apocalyptic text recounting Enoch's heavenly journey

Enoch, Third: Hebrew mystical text attributed to Rabbi Ishmael

Eschatology: Belief about the end of the world

Florilegium: In literature, an anthology; in biblical studies, a Qumran document (4Q174) interpreting scriptural quotations in a messianic sense

Form criticism: Attempt to discover the literary form (genre) and the life-setting of a text

Formula citations: Quotations of the Old Testament introduced by a standard formula

Gematria: System of interpreting the Hebrew letters of words (e.g., names) as numbers

Genesis Apocryphon: Aramaic retelling of Genesis discovered among Qumran scrolls

Ghirlandaio, Domenico (1449–1494): Italian painter famous for his frescoes

Hadith: Authoritative Islamic traditions later than the Qur'an

Hexateuch: The first six books of the Hebrew Bible, from Genesis to Joshua

Historical criticism: Asking questions of historicity about a text

Historicist: Emphasizing the supreme importance of history

Historicity: The amount of historical fact in a story

Historiography: History writing

Infancy gospels (apocryphal): Non-canonical stories, often legendary, about the birth and childhood of Jesus (and sometimes Mary)

Infancy narratives (canonical): The stories of Jesus' birth and childhood in Matthew 1–2 and Luke 1–2

Josephus: First-century Jewish historian active in Rome, author of *Antiquities of the Jews* (outlining Jewish history from the creation till 66 CE) and the *Jewish War* (describing the Jewish Revolt in 66–70 CE)

Jubilees: Book from second century BCE retelling the story of Genesis and Exodus

LXX, see: Septuagint

Magi (plural of magus): Persian or Babylonian astrologers and inter-preters of dreams

Magnificat: Mary's song of praise (Luke 1:46–55)

Midrash: Retelling of biblical story with explanatory expansions, often legendary

Mishnah Abot: Collection of "Sayings of the Fathers" included in the compilation of Jewish law around 200 CE

Modernist: Movement, condemned by Pope Pius X in 1907, that advocated critical historical examination of the origins of Christianity

Narrative criticism: Analysis of a story as a literary work, focusing on elements such as plot, characterization, viewpoint, and style

Nazirite: In Jewish tradition, a person who makes a vow forbidding consumption of alcohol, cutting the hair, and touching a corpse (Num 6:1–21)

Nunc Dimittis: Simeon's praise of God (Luke 2:29–32)

Pasolini, Pier Paolo (1922–1975): Radical Italian filmmaker

Pelagian: Someone seeking salvation by his or her own efforts

Pentateuch: First five books of the Hebrew Bible, from Genesis to Deuteronomy

Pepysian Gospel Harmony: Medieval English gospel harmony once owned by the diarist Samuel Pepys

Philo: Alexandrian Jewish philosopher active in the early first century CE

Protevangelium (or *Protoevangelium*) *of James*: Second-century apocryphal gospel describing the birth and upbringing of Mary, her betrothal to Joseph, and her giving birth to Jesus in a cave

Psalms of Solomon: Jewish hymns from first century BCE with messianic expectation

Pseudo-Philo: Author (perhaps first century CE, formerly identified with Philo of Alexandria) of a *Book of Biblical Antiquities* retelling the scriptural story from Adam to David

Q (sayings source): Tradition of Jesus' teachings preserved in Matthew and Luke but not in Mark

Qumran: Location beside the Dead Sea where many Hebrew and Aramaic texts from before 70 CE (biblical and non-biblical) were discovered from 1947

Qur'an: Sacred book of Islam believed by Muslims to contain divine revelation made to Muhammad (d. 632 CE)

Redaction criticism: Asking how (and why) a text was edited

Septuagint (abbreviated as LXX): Greek translation of the Old Testament

Septuagintalisms: Greek expressions imitating phraseology of the Septuagint

Source criticism: Attempt to discover written literary sources behind a text

Step parallelism: Parallelism of two characters showing that the second is greater than the first (e.g., Jesus greater than John the Baptist in Luke 1–2)

Suetonius: Roman historian active in the early second century CE

Syntax: Arrangement of words so as to create meaning

Tacitus: Roman historian active in the late first century CE

Talmud: Compilation of Jewish legal tradition around the fifth century CE

Targum: Aramaic translation of texts from the Hebrew Bible

Targumist: Translator of Hebrew biblical texts into Aramaic

Testaments of the 12 Patriarchs: Jewish or Jewish-Christian (or perhaps Christian) document presenting ethical advice purporting to be the final discourses of Jacob's sons

Torah: Law of God for the Jews, often identified with the Pentateuch

Typology: Explanation of Old Testament events or characters as prefiguring events or characters in the New Testament

Virgil: Latin poet of first century BCE

Virginal conception: Mary's miraculous conception of Jesus while still a virgin (Luke 1:34–35)

Visitation: Story of Mary's visit to her relative Elizabeth (Luke 1:39–56)

Vulgate: Latin translation of the Bible made, or edited, by Saint Jerome (d. 420 CE)

Bibliography of Studies on
the Nativity, 1990–2009

This bibliography, compiled by Henry Wansbrough and Jeremy Corley, omits many gospel commentaries and focuses mainly on publications in English. An extensive bibliography of works from 1977 to 1993 appears in the 1993 edition of Raymond E. Brown, *The Birth of the Messiah*, 713–32.

Allison, Dale C., *The New Moses: A Matthean Typology*. Minneapolis: Augsburg Fortress; Edinburgh: T&T Clark, 1993.

——"The Magi's Angel," in his *Studies in Matthew: Interpretation Past and Present*, 17–35. Grand Rapids: Baker Academic, 2005.

Anderson, Janice Capel, "Matthew, Gender and Reading," in *A Feminist Companion to Matthew*, ed. Amy-Jill Levine, 25–51. Sheffield: Sheffield Academic Press, 2001.

Aus, Roger David, *Matthew 1–2 and the Virginal Conception*. Lanham, MD: University Press of America, 2004.

Barker, Margaret, *Christmas: The Original Story*. London: SPCK, 2008.

Bauckham, Richard, *Gospel Women: Studies of the Named Women in the Gospels*. London/New York: T&T Clark, 2002.

Bauer, David R., "The Kingship of Jesus in the Matthean Infancy Narrative: A Literary Analysis," *Catholic Biblical Quarterly* 57 (1995) 306–23.

Beattie, Tina, *God's Mother, Eve's Advocate. A Marian Narrative of Women's Salvation*. London: Continuum, 2000.

Binz, Stephen J., *Advent of the Savior: A Commentary on the Infancy Narratives of Jesus*. Collegeville: Liturgical Press, 1996.

Bockmuehl, Markus, *Seeing the Word: Refocusing New Testament Study*. Grand Rapids: Baker Academic, 2006.

Bogaert, Pierre-Maurice, "Luc et les Ecritures dans l'Evangile de l'enfance à la lumière des 'Antiquités bibliques,'" in *The Scriptures in the Gospels*, ed. Christopher M. Tuckett, 243–70. Leuven: Peeters, 1997.

Boismard, Marie-Emile, *L'évangile de l'enfance (Luc 1–2) selon le proto-Luc*. Paris: Gabalda, 1997.

Borg, Marcus, and John Dominic Crossan, *The First Christmas: What the Gospels Really Teach about Jesus's Birth*. New York: Harper One, 2007.

Boss, Sarah Jane, ed., *Mary: The Complete Resource*. New York: Oxford University Press, 2007.

Bovon, François, *A Commentary on the Gospel of Luke 1:1–9:50*. Hermeneia. Minneapolis: Fortress, 2002.

Bovon, François, *Luke the Theologian: Fifty-Five Years of Research, 1950–2005*. Waco: Baylor University Press, 2006.

Brooke, George J., ed., *The Birth of Jesus: Biblical and Theological Reflections*. Edinburgh: T&T Clark, 2000.

Brown, Raymond E., *The Birth of the Messiah*. Second edn New York: Doubleday, 1993.

Bruner, Frederick D., *Matthew, a Commentary*. Grand Rapids: Eerdmans, 2004.

Buckwalter, H. Douglas, *The Character and Purpose of Luke's Christology*. Cambridge: Cambridge University Press, 1996.

Byrne, Brendan, *The Hospitality of God: A Reading of Luke's Gospel*. Collegeville: Liturgical Press, 2000.

—*Lifting the Burden*. Slough, UK: St Paul's, 2004.

Byrne, Matthew, *The Way It Was: The Narrative of the Birth of Jesus*. Dublin: Columba, 2004.

Carter, Warren, *Matthew and the Margins: A Socio-Political and Religious Reading*. Maryknoll: Orbis Books; Sheffield: Sheffield Academic Press, 2000.

—*Matthew and Empire: Initial Explorations*. Harrisburg: Trinity Press International, 2001.

—"Matthean Christology in Roman Imperial Key: Matthew 1:1," in *The Gospel of Matthew in Its Roman Imperial Context*, ed. John Riches and David C. Sim, 143–65. JSNT Supplement 276; London: T&T Clark, 2005.

Chilton, Bruce, *Rabbi Jesus: An Intimate Biography*. New York: Doubleday, 2000.

Coleridge, Mark, *The Birth of the Lukan Narrative*. JSNT Supplement 88; Sheffield: JSOT Press, 1993.

Collins, John J., *The Scepter and the Star: The Messiahs of the Dead Sea Scrolls and Other Ancient Literature*. New York: Doubleday, 1995.

Crossan, John Dominic, "Virgin Mother or Bastard Child?" in *A Feminist Companion to Mariology*, ed. Amy-Jill Levine with Maria Mayo Robbins, 37–55. Cleveland: Pilgrim; Edinburgh: T&T Clark, 2005.

D'Angelo, Mary Rose, "Women in Luke-Acts: A Redactional View," *Journal of Biblical Literature* 109 (1990) 441–61.

Davison, Lisa Wilson, *Preaching the Women of the Bible*. St. Louis: Chalice, 2006.

Dawes, Gregory W., "Why Historicity Still Matters: Raymond Brown and the Infancy Narratives," *Pacifica* 19 (2006) 156–76.

Dillon, Richard J., "The Benedictus in Micro- and Macro-Context," *Catholic Biblical Quarterly* 68 (2006) 457–80.

Drury, John, *Painting the Word: Christian Pictures and Their Meanings*. London: National Gallery, 1999.

Drury, John, and Murphy, P., *Painting the Christmas Story at the National Gallery*. London: National Gallery, 2002.

Duncan, Geoffrey, *Shine On, Star of Bethlehem: A Worship Resource for Advent, Christmas and Epiphany*. Norwich, UK: Canterbury Press, 2004.

Dunn, James D.G., "'Son of God' and 'Son of Man' in the Dead Sea Scrolls," in *The Scrolls and the Scriptures*, ed. Stanley Porter and Craig Evans, 198–210. JSP Supplement 26. Sheffield: Sheffield Academic Press, 1997.

Elliott, J.K., *A Synopsis of the Apocryphal Nativity and Infancy Narratives*. Boston/Leiden: Brill Academic, 2006.

Fanthorpe, U.A., *Christmas Poems*. London: Enitharmon, 2002.

Farris, Stephen, "The Canticles of Luke's Infancy Narratives: The Appropriation of a Biblical Tradition," in *Into God's Presence: Prayer in the New Testament*, ed. Richard N. Longenecker, 91–112. Grand Rapids: Eerdmans, 2001.

Fitzmyer, Joseph A., *The One Who Is to Come*. Grand Rapids: Eerdmans, 2007.

—*The Interpretation of Scripture*. New York: Paulist Press, 2008.

Franklin, Eric, *Luke: Interpreter of Paul, Critic of Matthew*. JSNT Supplement 92; Sheffield: JSOT Press, 1994.

Freed, Edwin D., *The Stories of Jesus' Birth: A Critical Introduction*. Sheffield: Sheffield Academic Press, 2001.

Gnuse, Robert, "Dream Genre in the Matthean Infancy Narratives," *Novum Testamentum* 32 (1990) 97–120.

Grün, Anselm, *Jesus: The Image of Humanity: Luke's Account*. New York: Continuum, 2003.

Hamilton, James M. Jr., " 'The Virgin Will Conceive': Typological Fulfillment in Matthew 1:18–23," in *Built upon the Rock: Studies in the Gospel of Matthew*, ed. Daniel M. Gurtner and John Nolland, 228–47. Grand Rapids: Eerdmans, 2008.

Harmon, Steven R., "Zechariah's Unbelief and Early Jewish-Christian Relations," *Biblical Theology Bulletin* 31 (2001) 10–16.

Harries, Richard, *A Gallery of Reflections: The Nativity of Christ*. Oxford: Lion, 1995.

Hooker, Morna, *Beginnings: Keys that Open the Gospels*. London: SCM, 1997.

Hornik, Heidi J., and Mikeal C. Parsons, *Illuminating Luke: The Infancy Narrative in Italian Renaissance Painting*. Harrisburg: Trinity Press International, 2003.

Horsley, Richard A., *The Liberation of Christmas: The Infancy Narratives in Social Context*. New York: Continuum, 1989; reprint Eugene, OR: Wipf & Stock, 2006.

Hultgren, Arnold J., "Matthew's Infancy Narrative and the Nativity of an Emerging Community," *Horizons in Biblical Theology* 19 (1997) 91–108.

Instone-Brewer, David, "Balaam-Laban as the Key to the Old Testament Quotations in Matthew 2," in *Built upon the Rock: Studies in the Gospel of Matthew*, ed. Daniel M. Gurtner and John Nolland, 207–27. Grand Rapids: Eerdmans, 2008.

Johnson, Elizabeth, *Truly Our Sister: A Theology of Mary in the Communion of Saints*. New York: Continuum, 2003.

Jones, John Mark, "Subverting the Textuality of Davidic Messianism: Matthew's Presentation of the Genealogy and the Davidic Title," *Catholic Biblical Quarterly* 56 (1994) 256–72.

Jung, Chang-Wook, *The Original Language of the Lukan Infancy Narrative*. JSNT Supplement 267; New York: T&T Clark, 2004.

Karris, Robert J., "Mary's Magnificat," *Bible Today* 39 (2001) 145–49.

Kaut, Thomas, *Befreier und befreites Volk: traditions- und redaktionsgeschichtliche Untersuchung zu Magnifikat und Benediktus im Kontext der vorlukanischen Kindheitsgeschichte*. Frankfurt am Main: Hain, 1990.

Kerr, A.J., " 'No Room in the Kataluma,' " *Expository Times* 103 (1991–1992) 15–16.

Kilgallen, J.J., "The Conception of Jesus," *Biblica* 78 (1997) 225–46.

King, Nicholas, *The New Testament, Freshly Translated*. Stowmarket, UK: Mayhew, 2004.

Kingsbury, Jack Dean, "The Birth Narrative of Matthew," in *The Gospel of Matthew in Current Study*, ed. David E. Aune, 154–65. Grand Rapids: Eerdmans, 2001.

Kuhn, Karl A., "The Point of the Step-Parallelism in Luke 1–2," *New Testament Studies* 17 (2001) 38–49.

Landry, David, "Narrative Logic in the Annunciation to Mary (Luke 1:26–38)," *Journal of Biblical Literature* 114 (1995) 65–79.

Levine, Amy-Jill, "Matthew," in *Women's Bible Commentary*, ed. Carol A. Newsom and Sharon H. Ringe, 252–62. Louisville: Westminster John Knox, 1992.

Levine, Amy-Jill, with Maria Mayo Robbins, eds, *A Feminist Companion to Mariology*. Cleveland: Pilgrim; Edinburgh: T&T Clark, 2005.

Lüdemann, Gerd, *Virgin Birth? The Real Story of Mary and her Son Jesus*. Harrisburg: Trinity Press International, 1998.

Luz, Ulrich, *Matthew 1–7*. Hermeneia. Minneapolis: Fortress, 2007.

Luzzaraga, J., "El Benedictus (Lc 1.68–79) a través del arameo," *Biblica* 80 (1999) 305–59.

Maggioni, Bruno, "The Ordinary Made Extraordinary," *Communio* 31 (2004) 8–15.

Malina, Bruce J., and Jerome H. Neyrey, "Honor and Shame in Luke-Acts: Pivotal Values of the Mediterranean World," in *The Social World of Luke-Acts: Models for Interpretation*, ed. Jerome H. Neyrey, 25–65. Peabody, MA: Hendrickson, 1991.

Maluf, Leonard. J., *The Prophecy of Zechariah: A Study of the Benedictus in the Context of Luke-Acts*. Rome: Pontifical Gregorian University, 2000.

Manns, Frédéric, "Une prière juive reprise en Luc 1,68–69," *Ephemerides Liturgicae* 106 (1992) 162–66.

Marston Speight, R., "Mary, Mother of Jesus, in Christian and Islamic Traditions," in *Muslims and Christians, Muslims and Jews*, ed. Marilyn Robinson Waldman, 25–34. Columbus, OH: Islamic Foundation of Central Ohio, 1992.

Mason, Steven, and Jerome Murphy-O'Connor, "Where was Jesus Born? O Little Town of Nazareth or Bethlehem?" *Bible Review* 16 (2000) 31–46.

McBride, Denis, *The Gospel of Luke: A Reflective Commentary*. Dublin: Dominican Publications, 1991.

—*Where Does the Jesus Story Begin? Reflections on the Beginning of the Gospels*. Chawton, UK: Redemptorist Publications, 2006.

Meier, John P., *A Marginal Jew, vol. 1*. New York: Doubleday, 1991.

Menken, Maarten J.J., "The Sources of the Old Testament Quotation in Matthew 2:23," *Journal of Biblical Literature* 120 (2001) 451–68.

Miller, Geoffrey David, "Trying to Fix the Family Trees of Jesus," *Scripture Bulletin* 39 (2009) 17–30.

Miller, Robert J., *Born Divine: The Births of Jesus and Other Sons of God*. Santa Rosa: Polebridge, 2003.

Mittmann-Richert, Ulrike, *Magnifikat und Benediktus*. WUNT 2/90. Tübingen: Mohr Siebeck, 1996.

Newsom, Carol, and Sharon Ringe, eds, *Women's Bible Commentary. Expanded Edition with Apocrypha*. Louisville: Westminster John Knox, 1998.

Nodet, Etienne, *The Historical Jesus?* New York : T&T Clark, 2008.

Nolland, John, "A Text-Critical Discussion of Matthew 1:16," *Catholic Biblical Quarterly* 58 (1996) 665–73.

—"The Sources for Matthew 2:1–12," *Catholic Biblical Quarterly* 60 (1998) 283–300.

—*The Gospel of Matthew: A Commentary on the Greek Text*. NIGTC. Grand Rapids: Eerdmans/Bletchley: Paternoster, 2005.

Nowell, Irene, "Jesus' Great-Grandmothers: Matthew's Four and More," *Catholic Biblical Quarterly* 70 (2008) 1–15.

Ó Fearghail, Fearghus, *The Introduction to Luke-Acts: A Study of the Role of Lk 1,1–4,44 in the Composition of Luke's Two-Volume Work*. Analecta Biblica 126. Rome: Pontifical Biblical Institute, 1991.

Olley, J.W., "God on the Move–A Further Look at *Kataluma* in Luke," *Expository Times* 103 (1991–1992) 300–301.

O'Loughlin, Thomas, *Liturgical Resources for Advent and Christmastide*. Dublin: Columba, 2006.

Ostmeyer, Karl-Heinrich, "Der Stammbaum des Verheissenen: Theologische Implikationen der Namen und Zahlen in Mt. 1.1–17," *New Testament Studies* 46 (2000) 175–92.

O'Toole, Robert F., *Luke's Presentation of Jesus: A Christology*. Subsidia Biblica 25. Rome: Pontifical Biblical Institute, 2004.

Peacocke, Arthur, "DNA of our DNA," in *The Birth of Jesus: Biblical and Theological Reflections*, ed. George J. Brooke, 59–67. Edinburgh: T&T Clark, 2000.

Pearson, Brooke W.R., "The Lukan Censuses Revisited," *Catholic Biblical Quarterly* 61 (1999) 262–82.

Porter, Stanley E., ed., *The Messiah in the Old and New Testaments*. Grand Rapids: Eerdmans, 2007.

Powell, Mark Allan, *Chasing the Eastern Star: Adventures in Reader-Response Criticism*. Louisville: Westminster John Knox, 2001.

Ravens, David, *Luke and the Restoration of Israel*. Sheffield: JSOT Press, 1995.

Reid, Barbara, *Choosing the Better Part? Women in the Gospel of Luke*. Collegeville: Liturgical Press, 1996.

—*Taking Up the Cross. New Testament Interpretations through Latina and Feminist Eyes*. Minneapolis: Fortress, 2007.

Reilly, Frank, "Jane Schaberg, Raymond E. Brown and the Problem of the Illegitimacy of Jesus," *Journal of Feminist Studies in Religion* 21 (2005) 57–80.

Repschinski, Boris, " 'For He Will Save His People from Their Sins' (Matthew 1:21): A Christology for Christian Jews," *Catholic Biblical Quarterly* 68 (2006) 248–67.

Robinson, Neal, "Jesus and Mary in the Qur'an: Some Neglected Affinities," *Religion* 20 (1990) 161–75.

Ryan, Judith M., "Luke's Infancy Narrative," *Bible Today* 35 (1997) 340–45.

Schaberg, Jane, "Luke," in *Women's Bible Commentary*, ed. Carol A. Newsom and Sharon H. Ringe, 275–92. Louisville: Westminster John Knox, 1992.

—"Feminist Interpretations of the Infancy Narrative of Matthew," in *A Feminist Companion to Mariology*, ed. Amy-Jill Levine with Maria Mayo Robbins, 15–26. Cleveland: Pilgrim; Edinburgh: T&T Clark, 2005.

—*The Illegitimacy of Jesus*. San Francisco: Harper & Row, 1987; expanded twentieth anniversary edition, Sheffield: Sheffield Phoenix, 2006.

Schleifer, Aliah, *Mary the Blessed Virgin of Islam*. Louisville: Fons Vitae, 1997.

Schüssler Fiorenza, Elisabeth, *Jesus: Miriam's Child, Sophia's Prophet. Critical Issues in Feminist Christology*. New York: Continuum, 1994.

Schüssler Fiorenza, Elisabeth, ed., *Searching the Scriptures, vol. 2: A Feminist Commentary.* New York: Crossroad, 1994.

Scobie, Charles H.H., "A Canonical Approach to Interpreting Luke: The Journey Motif as a Hermeneutical Key," in *Reading Luke: Interpretation, Reflection, Formation,* ed. Craig G. Bartholomew, Joel B. Green, and Anthony C. Thiselton, 327–49. Grand Rapids: Zondervan; Milton Keynes: Paternoster, 2005.

Seim, Turid Karlsen, "The Virgin Mother: Mary and ascetic discipleship in Luke," in *A Feminist Companion to Luke,* ed. Amy-Jill Levine, 89–105. FCNTEC 3. New York: Sheffield Academic Press, 2002.

Stendahl, Krister, "Quis et Unde? An Analysis of Matthew 1–2," in *The Interpretation of Matthew,* ed. Graham N. Stanton, 69–80. Second edn Edinburgh: T&T Clark, 1995.

Strauss, Mark L., *The Davidic Messiah in Luke-Acts: The Promise and its Fulfillment in Lukan Christology.* JSNT Supplement 110; Sheffield: Sheffield Academic Press, 1995.

Stuhlmacher, Peter, *Die Geburt des Immanuel: die Weihnachtsgeschichten aus dem Lukas- und Matthäusevangelium.* Göttingen: Vandenhoeck & Ruprecht, 2005.

Tait, Michael, "The Fly in the Ointment: What does Myrrh Foreshadow in Mt 2:11?" *Scripture Bulletin* 39 (2009/2) 63–75.

Tracy, James, and Richard Horsley, *Christmas Unwrapped: Consumerism, Christ, and Culture.* Harrisburg: Trinity Press International, 2001.

Trexler, Richard C., *The Journey of the Magi: Meanings in History of a Christian Story.* Princeton: Princeton University Press, 1997.

Tyson, Joseph B., "The Birth Narratives and the Beginning of Luke's Gospel," *Semeia* 52 (1990) 103–20.

van Aarde, Andries, "The Carpenter's Son (Mt 13.55): Joseph and Jesus in the Gospel of Matthew and Other Texts," *Neotestamentica* 34 (2000) 173–90.

—*Fatherless in Galilee: Jesus as Child of God.* Harrisburg: Trinity Press International, 2001.

Vanhoye, Albert, "L'intérêt de Luc pour la prophétie en Lc 1,76; 4,16-30 et 22,60–65," in *The Four Gospels 1992,* ed. Frans Van Segbroeck *et al.*; 3 vols; Festschrift Frans Neirynck; BETL 100. Leuven: Peeters, 1992. Vol. 2, pp. 1529–48.

Vermes, Geza, *The Nativity: History and Legend.* London: Penguin, 2006.

Viviano, Benedict T., "The Genres of Matthew 1–2: Light from 1 Timothy 1:4," *Revue Biblique* 97 (1990) 31–53.

—"The Movement of the Star, Matthew 2:9 and Numbers 9:17," *Revue Biblique* 103 (1996) 58–64.

—"The Adoration of the Magi: Matthew 2:1–23 and Theological Aesthetics," *Revue Biblique* 115 (2008) 546–67.

Wainwright, Elaine M., *Towards a Feminist Critical Reading of the Gospel According to Matthew.* BZNW 60. Berlin/New York: de Gruyter, 1991.

—"The Gospel of Matthew," in *Searching the Scriptures, vol. 2: A Feminist Commentary,* ed. Elisabeth Schüssler Fiorenza, 633–77. New York: Crossroad, 1994.

Welburn, Andrew J., *From a Virgin Womb: The Apocalypse of Adam and the Virgin Birth.* Biblical Interpretation Series 91. Boston/Leiden: Brill Academic, 2007.

Weren, Wim J.C., "The Five Women in Matthew's Genealogy," *Catholic Biblical Quarterly* 59 (1997) 288–305.

Whitters, Mark F., "Jesus in the Footsteps of Jeremiah," *Catholic Biblical Quarterly* 68 (2006) 229–47.

Wilcox, Max, "Luke 2,36–38: Anna Bat Phanuel, of the Tribe of Asher, a Prophetess...: A Study in Midrash in Material Special to Luke," in *The Four Gospels 1992*, ed. Frans Van Segbroeck *et al.*; 3 vols; Festschrift Frans Neirynck; BETL 100. Leuven: Peeters, 1992. Vol. 2, pp. 1571–79.

Wilson, Brittany E., "Pugnacious Precursors and the Bearer of Peace: Jael, Judith, and Mary in Luke 1:42," *Catholic Biblical Quarterly* 68 (2006) 436–56.

Subject Index

This index omits words occurring very frequently, such as names (e.g., Mary and Joseph), places (e.g., Bethlehem, Nazareth), and Gospels (e.g., Matthew, Luke).